MYSTERIES
OF THE
ANCIENT PAST

A GRAHAM HANCOCK READER

EDITED BY GLENN KREISBERG

Bear & Company
Rochester, Vermont • Toronto, Canada

Bear & Company
One Park Street
Rochester, Vermont 05767
www.BearandCompanyBooks.com

Text stock is SFI certified

Bear & Company is a division of Inner Traditions International

Library of Congress Cataloging-in-Publication Data
Mysteries of the ancient past : a Graham Hancock reader / edited by Glenn
Kreisberg.
     p. cm.
  Includes bibliographical references and index.
  Summary: "Cutting-edge thinkers on the origins of civilization, the Giza
pyramids, pre-Columbian and early America, and the power of human
consciousness"—Provided by publisher.
  ISBN 978-1-59143-155-8 (pbk.) — ISBN 978-1-59143-805-2 (e-book)
  1. Civilization, Ancient. 2. Science and civilization. I. Kreisberg, Glenn.
  CB311.M895 2012
  930—dc23
                                                                    2012019623

Printed and bound in the United States by Lake Book Manufacturing, Inc.
The text stock is SFI certified. The Sustainable Forestry Initiative® program
promotes sustainable forest management.

10 9 8 7 6 5 4 3 2 1

Text design by Jack Nichols
Text layout by Brian Boynton
This book was typeset in Garamond Premier Pro and Gill Sans with Stone Serif,
Copperplate, and Gill Sans used as display typefaces

To send correspondence to the author of this book, mail a first-class letter to the author
c/o Inner Traditions • Bear & Company, One Park Street, Rochester, VT 05767, and
we will forward the communication.

*I would like to dedicate this book to
all my wonderful family, including my mom and dad,
who always encouraged reading, education, and open-
minded exploration; my wife, Stephanie, without whose
help and support this project would not have happened;
and my two great kids, Sophie and Jason, for inspiring
and keeping alive my inner child.*

Contents

Acknowledgments

In compiling this anthology of articles, I had the privilege of working and interacting with a group of writers and researchers from across our ever-shrinking globe who have inspired and challenged our minds to consider reasonable alternatives for the path of human knowledge, technology, civilization, and consciousness. For delving deep into the recesses of our ancient past and helping pull back the veil that separates worlds, giving us a glimpse of our true existence and spiritual reality, I wish to offer my profoundest thanks and recognition to all the authors whose work appears in these pages. Their work offers new pieces for a puzzle whose picture is, more and more, turning out to be far from complete.

Additionally I wish to thank all the kind folks at Inner Traditions • Bear & Co. for their support, encouragement, and patience during the course of this project. And lastly I would like to acknowledge author and researcher Graham Hancock, whose approach, insights, and body of work continue to lay the foundation on which so many of us try to build in the pursuits of our particular passions. Without Graham, all these articles, which he commissioned for online discussion, would not exist.

Introduction

GLENN KREISBERG

In bringing together this collection of articles, building on and complementing the previous volume, *Lost Knowledge of the Ancients,* I looked beyond the sensational, beyond the 2012 prophecies and neo–New Age phenomenon that has peaked since the millennium. Instead, we have not a wild journey of unbridled speculation but one of careful study, analysis, and contemplation of evidence, using common sense sometimes combined with uncommon intuition. The researchers presented come from many different walks of life, a wide range of backgrounds, and various regions of the globe, yet all share a common drive and life passion in their fields of endeavor.

According to G. I. Gurdjieff, one of the world's great spiritual teachers, there was, or is, a secret school or brotherhood (or monastery) that existed in Afghanistan for thousands of years called the Sarmoun Darq. The name of the school translates roughly to "beehive" or "collectors of honey." Gurdjieff is said to have searched the world for many years to find the source of esoteric teaching and to have finally found what he was looking for in the Sarmoun Darq. The school existed to gather up and preserve certain kinds of ancient knowledge regarding the human soul, and it is said many other such schools once existed with a similar purpose. In times when such knowledge was known to be dissipating, these schools served a most important purpose, for without the preservation of this knowledge and its continued reintegration into the human spirit, we would cease to evolve.

Stored, sacred knowledge exists around the world today, and those who collect and store these esoteric principles do so in a way not unlike how bees collect nectar; they concentrate and change the nectars so that when the proper time arrives, the receptacles can be reopened and the knowledge accessed. Seekers of truth and those souls who are deeply curious and find the knowledge, hidden therein, will then inform others and thereby be of value to humanity.

In the process, new bodies of work are created by great teachers seeking to revise old rituals and meditation techniques and bring new meaning to these ancient beliefs. Deep understandings of esoteric secrets are reconfigured and revealed in new forms. Traditions and methods are borrowed and exchanged between one another. Truths that were once obvious but are now obscured await rediscovery and are revealed. We are in such a time now.

Our very salvation may depend on rediscovering these truths about our world and ourselves. The irony of this age, going back over six hundred years and coming nearly full circle in the present, is how the faiths of Western civilization have sent out missionaries to save and educate the "savage" tribes and cultures of the world—tribes and cultures that for thousands of years have developed highly sophisticated belief systems based in the shamanic tradition, a tradition of experiential practice of communing with spirit that's anything but "faith based." And now, through the study of these ancient indigenous practices and shamanic belief systems and their assimilation into our modern lives and culture, we may find the path to a secure and sustainable future, if we're to have any future at all.

We must pay attention to the profound messages in the scriptures from every ancient culture that have been handed down through the ages, messages that now offer cures to the curse of modern life. Cures for the disconnection from nature and cures that offer a true path to a higher human consciousness—the path to a new golden age.

While most of the articles are on this topic, a few have nothing to do with seeking a spiritual path and simply deal with mysteries of the ancient past. However, if we consider a wider context for these articles—that they all share at their heart a search for a deeper truth to the meaning and workings of life and our place in the multiverse—then we notice a reality common to the human condition, that of always thirsting and striving for more and more knowledge. This was the psychology of the ancient mind-set, and it is the common thread that weaves its way through all the written works in this book.

ONE

Welcome to the Revolution

THE RESURGENCE OF ELEMENTAL SHAMANISM IN THE TWENTY-FIRST CENTURY

OMAR ROSALES

Across the planet, from the steppes of the Himalayas to the deepest jungles of Guatemala, a renewed emphasis on ecology, cultural preservation, and spirituality has led to an increased awareness of shamanism as a method to address environmental, humanistic, and intrapersonal challenges. With a shift to indigenous healing traditions and a return to old ways of thought, shamans are rapidly becoming the cultural heroes that bridge the gap between the mystical regions of the upper, middle, and lower worlds, as well as the enigmatic and ethereal realms of the collective unconscious, conscious, and superconscious mind of humanity.

The Rise and Fall of the Plastic Shamans

In the latter half of the twentieth century, a renewed interest in spirituality, politics, and the occult led many on explorative intrapersonal journeys. Fueled by the counterculture influence of the 1960s, icons such as Timothy Leary, Carlos Castaneda, Jim Morrison, and Hunter S. Thompson glamorized the quest for immortal truth, as defined by native indigenous healers or shamans. Yet, the truth would come at a great cost, as facts were oftentimes distorted or entire accounts of ethnographies fabricated. In fact, some of the most important field-work in anthropology had been done forty years before by Bronisław Malinowski, Richard Schultes, and other scholars that few would know outside university circles.[1]

Through research, it was determined that entire accounts of indigenous spiritual and healing traditions, popularized during the 1960s, had been fabricated. Although many continue to quote Don Juan's shamanic insight, the Yaqui shaman Don Juan never existed, except in the mind of Carlos Castaneda.[2] Popular literature in the 1990s continued the Western imagining of how shamans think, pray, and work. There was no walkabout in Australia that yielded a mutant message from Down Under, nor is there a sisterhood of the shields that provides shamanic knowledge.[3] The Western fables continue to this day, with interpretations of 2012 in the Mayan calendar written by self-professed international Mayan elders who are Caucasian and born in Michigan.[4]

With regard to December 21, 2012, in the Mayan calendar, the most important question to ask is, "What is the indigenous Mayan population doing to prepare for 2012?" Do we see villages in the Peten Jungle being razed and moved to safer and higher elevations by Mayan elders? Are entire ethnic subgroups of the Maya, such as the Tz'utujil of Lake Atitlán, selling their worldly possessions and moving to isolated islands in Micronesia? Of course not. The most important aspect of the calendar round, which sensationalist books fail to mention, is that the Mayan calendar never ends. Which brings us back to the wolfsbane of the plastic shamans, that there is no substitute for anthropological research and fieldwork.

So, where do we find out about shamans? What is a shaman? What abilities do shamanic practitioners master? Moreover, do any real shamans still exist? The answer is, once again, in the field.

A Return to Scholarship

Through the meticulous fieldwork and studies of Franz Boas, Michael Harner, Martin Prechtel, and Wade Davis, the shared characteristics between shamans of various cultures have been identified.

Shamans are not like you or me. A shaman is a native healer, who uses plants and herbs to effectuate change in patients. Moreover, a shaman has the ability to enter altered states of consciousness at will, interact with beings in nonordinary realms, and create physical changes in waking reality.[5] A shaman can change her or his energy field to interact with the energy fields of other living objects. Perhaps the most important part of a shaman is that the shaman is typically indigenous. That is, they are transmitting centuries-old cultural knowledge through bloodlines and kinship. Without this bloodline, without this legitimacy of *sang real* (the holy blood, the effervescent teacher) and the enhanced genetic traits from this bloodline, a practitioner is not a true shaman.

One of the most significant roles of the shaman is that of psychopomp.[6] A psychopomp is an intermediary between the world of the living and the land of the dead. The psychopomp will transmit messages, share insight, communicate thoughts, and offer warnings from the land of spirit. Communication occurs through dreams, altered states, and rituals, which allow the shaman to enter a receptive state. The shaman will receive the message either as a symbol or an auditory message to be passed on to the intended receiver.[7]

Another shamanic ability is divination. Through the use of tools such as bones, cards, entrails, sticks, or runes, a shaman will augur the future. The ability to communicate through dreams is another shamanic skill, used by shamans to rely messages over great distances. Some of the more esoteric shamanic abilities, demonstrated by shamanic masters of the last two thousand years, include *loco tempestas* (the ability to control the weather), bilocation, levitation, and flight.[8]

Yet, how do we find true shamans in the modern age? How do we discern the theatrical from the real, the plastic from the authentic? And what is the truth to shamanism and the limits of human potential?

It was a search for these truths that led me on a worldwide quest to find the real among the landscape of illusion. It was this search that brought me to the elemental shamans.

Cherokee Spirit Walker: Expert in Soul Retrieval

In the Valley of the Sun, at the bottom of an ancient ocean, I had my first encounter with soul retrieval and a Cherokee spirit walker. The son of a Cherokee medicine man, Gary Gent is a Vietnam veteran with an unassuming nature and an important skill, the ability to transverse worlds.

Soul retrieval is the ability of a shaman to heal the psychological trauma caused by cognitive disassociation.[9] Shamans believe that our soul is made up of individual pieces. During periods of great stress, fear, or difficulty, soul pieces will fragment and become stuck or attached to a particular place or person.[10] The accompanying psychological effects may include memory loss, unexplained nervousness, and a feeling of disconnection or isolation. It's the role of the shaman to travel to the upper, middle, and lower worlds to obtain information about the soul piece and return it to its owner.

Gent follows this traditional method of soul retrieval, but with a twist. Using a drum as a sonic driver, he can enter an altered state within minutes and retrieve a soul piece. Gent travels to the lower world to obtain guidance from animal and plant guides. Having obtained the guidance of spirits from the lower realm, the Cherokee spirit walker will then travel to the middle world to locate the fragmented soul piece. Once found, the reintegration will begin as the soul piece is returned to the owner. Travel to the upper realms is used for revelation and guidance from gods, deities, and beings of legend.

When the soul piece is found and healed, the shaman uses his breath to blow the piece back into the patient. What is unique about Gent is his uncanny ability to describe where the fragmentation occurred and where the soul piece was found. With regard to my own experience, Gent was able to accurately describe a college dorm room, a military barracks, and a grandparent's home, all without prior knowledge of these locations.

So, how exactly does the Cherokee spirit walker break linear time and glimpse into the patient's past? A more enigmatic question remains: What if the upper, middle, and lower worlds do not exist at all, but are just a method for Gent's consciousness to describe his mind's ability to use quantum mechanics and break linear time?

Mysteries in Guatemala: The Cult of the Maximon

For over fifteen hundred years, shamans in Mayan communities along the Central Highlands, coastal areas, and Peten Jungle region of Guatemala and Mexico have predicted eclipses, created calendars, tracked the movements of Venus, and forecast periods of symbolic creation called *baktuns*. The end of the current cycle of creation, the thirteen baktun, falls on December 21, or December 23, of 2012 (depending on the Greenwich mean time correlation interpretation of the Mayan calendar).[11] So, will the end date of the current cycle usher a period of cataclysms, disease, and catastrophe? Or will life remain the same, relatively unchanged from one day to the next? More importantly, what do the Maya think?

If there were ever a city of shamans, it would be Santiago Atitlán, Guatemala. Nestled on the north shores of Lake Atitlán, the grittiness and squalor of the city is hidden by lush volcanoes. Navigating the ferry or *lancha* on the thirty-minute trip from Panajachel to Santiago, the boat master must steer past a cove to uncover the bizarre magnificence of the city. Homes are incoherently stacked one upon another, like matchboxes organized by drunken hands. Fires burning grass, timber, and tires spin their smoke streams into hazy skies. Landing in Santiago, a traveler's first instinct is clear: get out.

Yet secret brotherhoods called *cofradias* maintain a relative peace in the city and the countryside. Old village families have evolved to control the worship and access to the effigy and saint of the region, the Maximon. It is this lord of the lake, this holy boy, the Maximon (pronounced Mosh-ee-moan) that bestows favors, offers protection, seeks vengeance against enemies, and guards the indigenous Tz'utujil Mayan populace.

More than just a bundle of sticks, the Maximon represents triumph over tyranny, success over slaughter. The effigy is the last living Mayan god, the only survivor of the cosmological onslaught of the Catholic Church and the Spanish conquest. Worship of the deity is tolerated due to a tenuous understanding with the local Catholic priests. The Maximon is always displayed next to a glass coffin containing a statue of Christ. And the Maximon is identified as the son of Christ.

But these interpretations are wrong, as the Maximon is an amalgamation of Mayan nature spirits. The Maximon has the flying ability of Kukulkan, the Mayan god of wind. The statue has the ability to bring rain, like the Mayan god Chac. And the effigy can conquer disease, like Cit-Bolon-Tum, the Mayan god of healing. Some legends continue the syncretism fable, saying that Maximon is Saint Simon, a saint petitioned to provide help for clandestine activities, such as trafficking narcotics and avoiding the law. However, this is also incorrect as there is no Saint Simon in Catholic theology.

Crafted by native hands, the Maximon is said to be carved from a *palo de pito,* or coral tree (*Erythrina corallodendron*). Looking for a suitable vessel for the Mayan deity, two brothers began the search for a tree. The brothers, Juan and David Co, were led by dreams and came upon an enigmatic tree in the midst of a jungle clearing. In the flesh of the tree, on the bark amid gnarls and limbs, the brothers began to see the symbols of the Maya: a stalk of corn, a bird, a jaguar, and a two-headed eagle—the symbol of Mayan kings.

Carving long into the night, the brothers infused the now-fallen tree with the nature spirits from the forest and the DNA-infused sweat from their brows. It was the brother's DNA that gave life and character to the effigy. It was shamans' hands that created their supreme ruler and last Mayan lord. Yet, it was the spirit in the brothers' hearts that held a secret. Once finished, one of the brothers would become the effigy's standard-bearer or *telinel*. The telinel would be responsible for the upkeep and care of the statue. The telinel would be the village's first shaman, with the ability to communicate to the statue of the Maximon via dreams.

A series of events would necessitate the first surgery and maiming of the Maximon. The statue was infused with the trickster spirit in nature and in the brothers' hearts, but what's funny for the trickster is not always funny to the recipient of the trick: The Maximon was caught shape-shifting and visiting the beds of the villagers' wives. As a consequence, the telinel hatched a plan. The village elders got the statue drunk with alcohol and prayer, and then performed a ceremony and, more importantly, an amputation. This is why the modern statue has no feet, is restrained by rope, and is missing a finger. Thus the effigy would never again be mistaken for a human male. And now the statue is forever restrained, to carry out the will of the shamans.

The brotherhoods, or cofradias, manage the upkeep of the statue. With over ten cofradias in Santiago Atitlán, the statue is moved from family center to family center every year, to maintain a tenuous balance of power between rival cofradias and families. Whoever has control of the statue has access to the thousands of dollars given in tribute every year to the Maximon. Every shamanic ceremony around Lake Atitlán must first be approved by the telinel. Without the blessing of the Maximon, and the approval of the telinel, the Mayan shamanic rituals are destined to fail. This is the belief of the local populace, a strong enough belief that can sometimes distort the supernatural nature of spellcasting.

The power to perform magic rests with the practitioner—the shaman. And the tool the shaman uses to break linear time and apply quantum physics is the shaman's own mind and consciousness. The power rests with an individual's beliefs, and the additional electrical and quantum energy generated by the human brain and spinal cord. Still, the Maximon is worshipped and revered all over Central America. So, what other secrets do the Tz'utujil Maya of Santiago Atitlán know?

Ghosts in the Air Realm: Footpaths to Himalayan Glory

Another breed of shamanic practitioners not typically discussed are the Vajrayana Buddhist masters of Tibet and Bhutan. Bon shamanism predated Buddhism in these mountainous and isolated regions of India, Bhutan, and Tibet. The introduction of Buddhism supplanted the beliefs and acceptance of Bon. Yet the most evolved and mystical type of Buddhism, known as Vajrayana, returned to the regional Bon roots. Typified by the recognition of adepts with supernatural powers such as loco tempestas, bilocation, and levitation, the Vajrayana masters use esoteric texts, long periods of chanting and meditation, and secret rituals to refine their concepts of consciousness.

The hallmark of a Vajrayana Buddhist master is the ability to achieve transcendence, break the cycle of karma, and become a bodhisattva, or saint, in one lifetime. Legends tell that the most powerful Buddhist magicians of our age were also Vajrayana adepts. Examples of these healer-magicians include Padmasambhava, also known as Guru Rinpoche, who brought Buddhism to Bhutan from Swat; Milarepa who destroyed an entire village with magic, yet after his remorse and upon his realization, changed his life and became a Buddhist teacher and healer; and Pema Lingpa, a magician from Bhutan, who leapt into a deep river gorge and emerged from the water holding lighted lamps and sacred Buddhist treasures called *tertöns*.

Yet the most startling contradiction along a Vajrayana Buddhist master's pathway is the dissolution of self and ego and the ultimate realization that individual souls do not exist, that power comes from the universe, and that the clear light of the Buddha mind forms a conscious connection with the thoughts and feelings of all living beings. The final realization, the ultimate insight for a Vajrayana Buddhist master, is that we are one. The final answer is that there is no self, but the All.[12]

Don't Ignore the Hydra

The major concepts of modern theoretical physics are refined every two decades. Old science is cut down and gives way to a new head or school of thought. Thirty years ago, concepts such as string theory, time travel, and instantaneous movement between points of space hundreds of thousands of light years apart would have been science fiction. But new research into the folding of space-time, movement through a circular universe, and D-branes, has made theoretical science plausible. But haven't shamans been doing this research for millennia?

When we talk about divination and clairvoyance, doesn't a shaman's altered state of consciousness allow his mind to break the linear time of a three-dimensional-plus-time universe? When we examine the fabric and weavings of the Tz'utujil Maya of Santiago Atitlán and determine that they perceive the universe as a geometric pattern that can be folded to an infinitely small point suitable for instantaneous journeys between solar systems, aren't we describing wormholes and faster-than-light travel? When a Buddhist master says the thoughts of all sentient beings are connected by Buddha mind, aren't we describing string theory and the convocation of D-branes, black p-branes, and Neveu-Schwarz five-branes?[13]

The shamanic world is the world of quantum physics. Yet, are we adapting shamanism and indigenous beliefs to explain science? Or is science evolving to the point where it can explain and quantify indigenous shamanic beliefs? With science, the improbable becomes possible. So, what new breakthroughs will we see in the twenty-first century? And how will shamans continue to teach us?

The Elemental Shamans

Indigenous elemental shamans and healers can give us modern and true answers, which counter the fictionalized accounts penned by unreliable authors. By meticulous research, we determine that there is no need for cultural misappropriation or theft of Native insight. There is no necessity to make up accounts. To learn, all we must do is ask. To discover, we must explore. But the essence will always come back to fieldwork.

There is no substitute for spending time in the jungle. There is no facsimile to visiting Buddhist temples and monasteries in the Himalayas. And there is no faux journey that will substitute for the insight and transdimensional knowledge (predicted by string theory) that is gained by the consumption of the vine of the souls, *ayahuasca,* as distilled by the hands of Peruvian shamans.[14]

If we desire arcane knowledge, ask. If we want to learn about native traditions, journey. Travel to these indigenous healers and ask questions. Ultimately, the journey for shamanic knowledge is the quest to understand culture, explore the quantum potential of the human body, and demystify the consciousness of the human machine.

Evolution is within us, the power is within us, to change our world. It's in the palm of our hands. It's found in the beauty of our speech and thought. The evolution of humanity is determined by the neuroplasticity of our brains, perhaps even already preencoded in our DNA.[15] But shamans have already been teaching us these profound and holy truths for thousands and thousands of years.

Notes

1. Jeremy Narby, *The Cosmic Serpent: DNA and the Origins of Knowledge* (New York: Jeremy P. Tarcher/Putnam, 1999).

2. Richard de Mille, *Castañeda's Journey: The Power and the Allegory* (Lincoln, Neb.: iUniverse, 2001).

3. L. Aldred, "Plastic Shamans and Astroturf Sun Dances: New Age

Commercialization of Native American Spirituality," *American Indian Quarterly* 24, no. 3 (2000): 331–33.

4. Barbara Hand Clow, *The Mayan Code* (Rochester, Vt.: Bear and Company, 2007).

5. Mircea Eliade, *Shamanism: Archaic Techniques of Ecstasy* (Princeton, N.J.: Princeton University Press, 2004).

6. Ibid.

7. Ede Frecska, "The Shaman's Journey, Supernatural or Natural? A Neuro-Ontological Interpretation of Spiritual Experiences," chap. 7 in *Inner Paths to Outer Space: Journeys to Alien Worlds through Psychedelics and Other Spiritual Technologies,* by Rick Strassman et al. (Rochester, Vt.: Park Street Press, 2008), 62–206.

8. Omar W. Rosales, *Elemental Shaman: One Man's Journey into the Heart of Humanity, Spirituality & Ecology* (St. Paul, Minn.: Llewellyn Worldwide, 2009).

9. Ibid.

10. Sandra Ingerman, *Soul Retreival: Mending the Fragmented Self* (New York: HarperCollins Press, 1991).

11. Linda Schele and David Freidel, *A Forest of Kings: The Untold Story of the Ancient Maya* (New York: Harper Perennial, 1990).

12. Rosales, *Elemental Shaman.*

13. A. Giveon and D. Kutasov, "Brane Dynamics and Gauge Theory," *Reviews of Modern Physics* 71, no. 983 (1999).

14. Luis Eduardo Luna, "The Varieties of the Ayahuasca Experience," chap. 5 in *Inner Paths to Outer Space,* 114–41.

15. Graham Hancock, *Supernatural: Meetings with the Ancient Teachers of Mankind* (New York: The Disinformation Company, 2007).

TWO

Higher Consciousness Explains Many Mysteries of the Ancient Past

JOSEPH SELBIE AND DAVID STEINMETZ

There are many intriguing examples of anomalous knowledge that existed in the ancient past: verified knowledge of anatomy and physiology and modernlike medical treatments in use as early as 2500 BCE in Egypt, China, and India; the precision construction of the Great Pyramid in 2600 BCE (or perhaps earlier); and accurate knowledge of math and physics, including the size and nature of the atom, embedded in India's Vedas dating back to the sixth millennium BCE—just to name a few.

The field of alternative history has long sought the answer to where this advanced knowledge came from—and why it didn't survive. One theory, familiar to most of us, is that aliens came to Earth in the distant past and gave knowledge to humanity that was beyond the comprehension of human beings. As the theory goes, when the aliens eventually left, the knowledge quickly died out because humanity wasn't yet ready for it.

Another theory, sometimes put forward by apologists for mainstream archaeology, is that advanced knowledge may have existed in the ancient past but it was due only to chance combinations of primitive technology and individual genius—serendipitous discovery. As the theory goes, when that particular genius or serendipitous circumstance was gone, the knowledge quickly died out because humanity wasn't yet ready for it.

There is, however, another explanation for advanced knowledge in the past—one that comes to us from the ancient past itself and does not rely on aliens or serendipity. The explanation is that human beings had more advanced *consciousness* in the past than they now possess and that it was this advanced consciousness, natural to humans, that *enabled* them to develop advanced knowledge on their own without the need for alien intervention or serendipity.

Common to this explanation as it comes to us from the ancient past is the notion that humanity's consciousness goes through a cycle of development; humanity's awareness, perception, and abilities advance and then decline in a recurring cycle. This concept has been a part of the traditional cultural lore of numerous cultures as far back as anyone can determine. Perhaps best known to those of us in the West is the ancient Greek description of descending ages—from the golden age, through silver and bronze, and finally into the iron age. The tradition of descending ages exists throughout the world. In Giorgio de Santillana's *Hamlet's Mill*, he explores scores of such traditions.

In India, the tradition of descending ages is known as the *yugas* or the yuga cycle. (Yuga simply means "age.") The yuga cycle, however, stands apart from the other traditional descriptions of the same phenomenon. Modern exponents of the yuga cycle, such as Sri Yukteswar, whose description of the yuga cycle appears in his book *The Holy Science*, written in 1894, offer both dates and explanations for cycle.

Sri Yukteswar provides specific dates for the beginning and end of each age or yuga. Moreover, unlike most traditions of descending ages, in which humanity is said to still be at the nadir of its development, Sri Yukteswar states that humanity reached its nadir in 500 CE, but since then people have begun to advance once more—as you can see in figure 2.1.

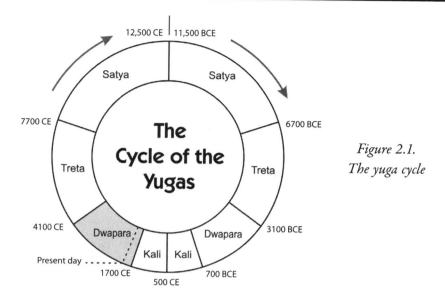

Figure 2.1.
The yuga cycle

Perhaps even more important for explaining the ancient past than the specificity of dates is Sri Yukteswar's description of humanity's consciousness in each yuga. His clear description of ancient humankind's consciousness and abilities may well allow us to finally understand some of the more enduring mysteries of the ancient past.

Case in Point: Treta Yuga and the Vedas

The Rig Veda, a collection of over ten thousand Sanskrit verses, is the oldest known spiritual work in the world and can be dated to as early as 7300 BCE. The Rig Veda is the wellspring of spiritual knowledge for what we know as Hinduism and has remained so for over nine thousand years. It is written in Sanskrit, in all likelihood the oldest language on Earth, and to this day it remains the most precise and internally consistent system of communication in the world. Computer programmers have studied Sanskrit's structure and grammar to help them create programming languages free of ambiguity.

The Vedas were accurately passed down from generation to generation in India by virtue of an extremely methodical system of oral transmission, which involved chanting each verse in ten different ways to cross-check for integrity. It is believed that only *two words* have become corrupted in over nine thousand years.

Such an effective and elaborate system of oral transmission is amazing in itself, but more amazing yet is that there is a large body of astronomical, mathematical, and physical knowledge embedded in the Vedas, knowledge popularly believed not to have been discovered in Europe until the Renaissance and later. Contemporary scientists have found the following facts embedded in the Vedas.

- The sun and planets are spherical.
- Each of the seven colors of the rainbow carries a different amount of energy.
- The sun is the source of all energy for life on Earth.
- Earth rotates around the sun.
- The sun, Earth, and other planets rotate on their own axes.
- Earth's rotation creates night and day.
- Earth's orbital path and axial tilt result in the seasons.
- The poles have six-month-long nights and days.
- The two tropics and the equator are separated by 24 degrees.
- Earth has a slightly elliptical orbit.
- Because of its orbit around the sun, the planet Venus is both the evening star and the morning star.
- The apparent movement of sunspots is due to the rotation of the sun.
- As seen from Earth, the full rotation of the sun takes twenty-seven days.
- Earth's orbit around the sun creates a plane, and on that plane are the twelve divisions of the zodiac.
- The length of a solar year is 365,244 days.
- The moon's light is reflected from the sun.
- The sun's energy is generated by a continuous process at its core.
- The sun is gaseous.
- Seventy percent of Earth's surface is covered by water.
- The clouds consist of heat-produced water vapor, which in turn gives rise to rain.

- The stars are "innumerable."
- The stars exist in collections (*niharikas*), or galaxies, which rotate around their own center points.
- Earth and sun are part of a galaxy that rotates around a center point.
- The physical world is made up of atoms.
- The atoms have an internal structure resembling the solar system.

In addition, the following concepts and calculations are embedded in the Vedas.

- The cause and timing of solar and lunar eclipses
- The precession of the equinoxes
- The symbol and concept for zero
- The decimal system of notation
- The concept of infinity
- The concept of arithmetic progression
- The concept and value of pi
- The formula for calculating the area of a circle
- The concept of a number up to 10^{18}
- The theorem of diagonals (the Pythagorean theorem)
- The means to determine square roots and cube roots
- The concept of negative numbers
- The concept of algebraic equations using letter symbols for unknown quantities
- The conception and expression of quadratic and indeterminate equations
- The geometry of the triangle, parallelogram, rectangle, and circle
- The geometry of the sphere, cone, and pyramid

How does one explain this?

The Vedas are, after all, spiritual tools, sacred writ. The verses of the Vedas are mantras whose purpose is to raise the consciousness of those who chant them. The verses of the Vedas express an intimate relationship of humanity and the Divine. Yet, at the same time, they contain scientific knowledge—knowledge that is currently believed to be attainable only through sequentially developed mathematics, scientific instruments such as the telescope, and a rigorously applied methodology of experimentation.

According to Sri Yukteswar, in the most recent Treta Yuga (6700 to 3100 BCE), during which the Vedas were composed, people were able to directly comprehend that everything is made up of ideas or thoughts. The attunement of Treta Yuga people to thought also made them highly intuitive—able to perceive truths without the need for the cumbersome process of experimentation.

If human beings once possessed such awareness and comprehension in the ancient past then they would have had no need to use the tools of science as we understand them today. They would have perceived these truths directly through intuition. The "scientific" truths of the Vedas were perceived right along with spiritual truths as part of the same indivisible reality.

If such an explanation seems farfetched, let me offer you an interesting example of intuitively derived—and very precise—scientific information that was discovered around the turn of the twentieth century.

Annie Besant and Charles Webster Leadbeater, prominent members of the Theosophical Society, conducted intuitive investigations into the nature of atoms. They compiled a large number of descriptions and drawings of what they observed while in deep trances. Their descriptions and drawings were quite detailed and complex—in fact, more complex than the known facts of the day.

Many years after the deaths of Besant and Leadbeater, physicist Dr. Steven M. Phillips began to study their journals. He published his findings in 1980 in *Extra-Sensory Perception of Quarks*. A thorough examination of their psychic investigations led Phillips to conclude that Besant and Leadbeater had accurately described the number and nature of quarks—subatomic particles that make up the larger structures of the nucleus of the atom, such as protons and neutrons—*years ahead* of their discovery by modern physics.

The yugas, as explained by Sri Yukteswar, require no outside influence to explain the mysteries of the past. The yugas simply say that as humanity's consciousness advances, its knowledge, perception, and abilities advance as well. Humans don't merely know more as the yugas advance, they become more.

My coauthor, David Steinmetz, and I found an amazingly clear archaeological and historical footprint to match the dates and consciousness of each yuga. Nor did we have to rely on the strange, unusual, or controversial to see the footprint. A clear view of the arc of the yugas can be seen in the broad trends and accepted facts of the past and present. We believe that the yuga cycle could serve as a framework for the discoveries and work of many researchers and authors in the field of alternative history.

THREE

The Vedic Literature of Ancient India and Its Many Secrets

DAVID FRAWLEY

Secrets of Ancient Civilizations: The Vedic Connections

Secrets of ancient humanity and lost civilizations can be found all over the world. Yet they are perhaps most common in India, with its characteristic regard for the sacred, where even today the spiritual practices of the ancient world continue. The same types of temples with similar forms of ritual worship that were known in ancient Egypt, Babylonia, or Greece thousands of years ago still occur throughout India today, from Badrinath in the Himalayas to the north to Kanyakumari in the south. Indeed, it seems that the ancient world never ended in India but has continually maintained and, at times, reinvented itself.

Spiritual and occult arts that abounded in the ancient world—including yoga, Vedic astrology, ayurvedic medicine, and the use of rituals (*yajnas*)—to improve all aspects of our lives remain commonly used and are honored by the culture of India as a whole. Indeed, we could say that India is a living museum of the ancient world and its lost civilizations. To understand the ancient world, it may be better to visit the holy places of India where the ancient traditions are still unbroken, rather than try to interpret ancient ruins through bricks and pottery shards, which scholars today usually do according to their own modern mindsets, not recognizing the all-pervasive regard for the sacred that was the basis of ancient life and culture.

Most notably, ancient India presents us with by far the largest surviving literature from the ancient world. The Vedic literature of India, by all accounts dating from well before the time of the Buddha (500 BCE) and by traditional accounts extending back well over five thousand years (3100 BCE), covers several thousand pages. This literature includes the four Vedas (Rig, Yajur, Sama, and Atharva) and their various Brahmanas, Aranyakas, and Upanishads.

The Vedas contain many ancient poems, commentaries, dialogues, and teachings, of which the famous Upanishads and Bhagavad Gita—the bedrock of Indian philosophy and yoga—represent only the last layer or a late summation. There is no comparable ancient literature remaining from any other country, much less an ongoing tradition of its interpretation and application through ritual and meditation.

The Vedas are not directly concerned with history or with the mundane aspects of culture, yet these are mentioned in a peripheral way in the texts. In the Vedas, we can find references to the names of peoples, places, and certain events. In addition to deep spiritual knowledge, there are indications of astronomical, mathematical, and medical knowledge of a profound order. Natural disasters and major geologic events, such as floods, earthquakes, the melting of glaciers, and the shifting of rivers, were also recorded, with a sense of the long history of Earth and how life is based on and has evolved with these changes.

Yet, even by way of understanding their spiritual side, it requires a deeper vision to appreciate the Vedas. The Vedas are composed in a cryptic mantric code that cannot be understood without the proper orientation and right keys. Vedic mantras were said to have been understood by great yogis and seers of the cosmic mind. They reflect a different type of language in which the higher truth is deliberately hidden behind a veil of symbols, sacred sounds, and correspondences. A story that is apparently about seeking cows and horses, for example, can inwardly refer to a development of higher powers of the senses (cows) and *pranas* or vital energies (horses). In fact, Vedic words have many layers of meaning, of which the surface appearance can be misleading, particularly to the modern mind, which is not used to such multidimensional language. This is also a phenomenon that we find throughout the ancient world. The Egyptian Book of the Dead, for example, abounds in similar symbols that, unless we can grasp the spiritual meaning, which few may be willing to look for, can appear quite superstitious.

The Vedas say, "The Gods prefer the cryptic and dislike the obvious." The higher powers speak in symbols, riddles, paradoxes, or conundrums. The Vedas speak of four levels of speech, of which ordinary human beings only know and speak with one (Rig Veda I.164.45). They refer to a divine word or imperishable syllable on which they are based (Rig Veda I.164.39). They reflect a pattern of cosmic sound that underlies all the laws of the universe and has its counterparts on all levels of both individual and cosmic manifestation. For this reason, the Vedas were called the *shruti,* or revelation, behind the Hindu tradition.

The Vedas speak of secret meanings to their mantras that were veiled to protect the teaching from its application by the spiritually immature. To receive the key to the Vedic mantras required years of ascetic practices, such as reciting mantras, practicing yoga, and meditating, along with special initiations and the favor of a teacher who knew the tradition and had deeply realized the teaching in his own consciousness. We cannot expect such cryptic mantras to unlock their secrets to a casual reading, particularly of limited or bad translations in a language and mind-set quite alien to the Vedic or ancient worldview.

Modern scholars, particularly from the West, have not been able decipher this Vedic code. Most have not even recognized that it exists. This is not surprising because scholars have largely failed to understand the deeper meaning of the symbols of ancient Egypt, Sumeria, Mexico, and other ancient cultures. Ancient cultures like India and Egypt were carrying on great traditions of spiritual and occult knowledge, not just the rudiments of technology and trade or empire building.[1] Since modern scholars have little background in that spiritual knowledge, with its recognition of higher states of consciousness extending into the infinite and eternal, naturally they cannot find the symbols in which it is specially encrypted.

Scholars look upon the Vedas in the same way they perceive the religion of the ancient Egyptians—as little more than primitive nature worship. But nature is used to symbolize a vast cosmos. For example, in the Vedas, fire connects to the fire of the breath, the fire of the mind, the fire of consciousness, and the cosmic fire through which the entire universe exists.[2]

This failure to understand the ancient literature is often related to a failure to understand ancient archaeological ruins and their implications. Ancient sites abound in artifacts that reflect the same type of spiritual symbolism of the ancient literature. These are usually dismissed as fetishes rather than looking for any deeper meaning.

Once we have decoded the mantric and symbolic nature of the Vedic language, Vedic literature can help us understand the ancient world and the ancient mind—its symbols, rituals, and aspirations, as well as the legacy and heritage that it has left for us. But it requires that we approach the ancient teachings with an honoring of the sacred, a respect for our elders and gurus, a regard for our ancient human spiritual heritage, and a devotion to the cosmic powers of the greater conscious universe.

The Living Vedic Tradition

The Vedic tradition remains alive, and many great modern yogis have given their comments on the Vedas and have revealed some of the Vedic secrets to the modern world. Sri Aurobindo (1872–1950), perhaps modern India's greatest philosopher, among his voluminous writings wrote several books on the Vedas and translated many Vedic hymns according to an inner yogic meaning.[3] Many of his disciples, such as Kapali Shastri, M. P. Pandit, and R. L. Kashyap, have expanded this work.

Ganapati Muni (1878–1936), the chief disciple of the great Indian guru Ramana Maharshi, left a number of important Sanskrit works on the Vedas, as did his disciple Brahmarshi Daivarata.

Swami Dayananda (1828–1886), founder of the Arya Samaj, the largest modern Hindu sect, based his entire movement on a return to the Vedas and recognition of a deeper spiritual and scientific knowledge in Vedic texts, a task that many of his disciples have expanded in a number of books, teachings, research, and schools.

Maharishi Mahesh Yogi (founder of Transcendental Meditation) based his work on the Vedic mantras and through them promoted a renaissance of all the Vedic sciences including ayurveda, Vedic astrology, and *vaastu shastra.*

Other great modern yogis, like Paramahansa Yogananda, author of *Autobiography of a Yogi,* have written about the greatness of the Vedas, their antiquity, and the Vedic culture as one of the main sources for ancient civilization and world spirituality, though they have not written specifically on the Vedic texts themselves.

The Theosophical Society, particularly the writings of H. P. Blavatsky, similarly affirmed the deeper meaning of the Vedas. She wrote of how the Vedas were composed by the *rishis* mainly when they resided by the Manasarovar Lake by Mount Kailas in Tibet.

Such a view of the Vedas as a spiritual treasure-house of great antiquity remains at odds with dominant academic views, which regard the Vedas as a primitive product of invading nomads into India around 1500 BCE, the so-called Aryan invasion theory. This theory proposed that the Vedic people, called Aryans, were a light-skinned racial group from Central Asia who invaded and destroyed the native cultures of India, bringing in the Vedic literature along with them. Though this theory has never been proved or linked to any conclusive evidence on the ground, it has not been abandoned by textbooks either. This theory, though it has been reduced from an invasion to a migration and now to largely a language change, continues to persist.

The theory that Vedic culture was originally based outside India was first proposed by Western scholarship a few centuries ago to explain connections between the languages of India and Europe, which all belong to the Indo-European family of languages and share many similarities in grammar. An equally valid theory, however—and one that agrees more with both the literary and archaeological data—would have such linguistic influences derive from India and its nearby regions.[4] But during the colonial era, when the Aryan invasion idea was formed, India as a source of Western culture or languages was not such an appealing idea.

The Vedic tradition, we should note, has its own view of history. While the Vedas themselves as religious works do not contain specific or complete historical accounts, the Puranas, another set of ancient Indian literature, have a list of over a hundred kings going back before the time of Buddha and a delineation of many dynasties from throughout greater India going back to Manu, the primal king at the time of a great flood.

More importantly, Vedic and Puranic literature speaks of previous world ages called *yugas* and *kalpas,* extending back many tens of thousands of years and connected to astronomical cycles of various types going back millions of years. They hold that our current civilization is neither the first, nor the highest. In fact, they regard it as a fallen materialistic culture of low spiritual development. The Vedas and Puranas also speak of contact with beings of other worlds, both in subtle realms and other physical planets, regarding true human civilization as linked to the greater universe. Such ideas of human history as determined by cosmic time cycles are shared by many other ancient cultures, such as Egypt, Babylonia, Greece, and Mexico, and are characteristic of ancient thought as a whole.

Sri Yukteswar, guru of Paramahansa Yogananda, in his book *Holy Science,* relates the fifth and last Manu or founder of Indian civilization to a period that ended around 6700 BCE. This information is similar to what the Greeks found in India at the time of Alexander circa 300 BCE. Megasthenes in his Indika, still available in fragments, recorded a tradition of 153 kings in India going back over 6,400 years, to a date around 6700 BCE. The king lists of Egypt are not as long as these.

This Vedic view of the yugas or world ages, particularly the 24,000 great year, such as Yukteswar describes, is important for understanding Vedic thought and its antiquity, as well as its outlook for the future.[5] It tells us that we cannot put the Vedas in a historical time line of three thousand years as scholars would still like to do.*

My Work as a Vedic Scholar and Vedic Practitioner

In my personal work, I have spent more than thirty years studying, translating, and writing on the Vedas and connected Vedic sciences, including yoga, ayurveda, and Vedic astrology. I have written several books on the Vedic view of ancient history, as well as translating over a hundred of the Vedic hymns. This has resulted in more than thirty books and over a hundred articles on these topics.

I learned traditional Vedic Sanskrit and have gone through the Vedic texts repeatedly in the original language, with recourse to Sanskrit commentaries and the works of modern yogis like Ganapati Muni. I approached the Vedas according to an inner vision born of poetry, study of symbolism, and a practice of yoga and meditation. I received a training in the Vedic tradition itself, studying with gurus, pandits, and yogis in India. For this reason, my views of the Vedas can be different than those of scholars writing on the subject, who have not trained in the Vedic tradition and are usually unaware of its views.

_____

*Relative to the Vedic view of the yugas, I would agree with the views of Yukteswar, who places us in the early stages of an ascending Dwapara (bronze) age of 2,400 years, which has given humanity knowledge of and control over subtle forces of electricity and nuclear energy. According to this view, we will not get out of the darker phase of this beginning cycle until around 2100 CE. This may be the topic of another discussion. See "Keys to the Yugas or Cycles of the Ages" by David Frawley. American Institute of Vedic Studies, www.vedanet.com/component/content/article/129-keys-to-the-yugas-or-cycles-of-the-ages.

My views, therefore, are from inside the tradition. These ancient traditions still have their own voices, and hopefully, I can at least provide a good alternative to the nonspiritual approach to Vedic texts, which is what is usually presented in universities today. Early on in my studies, it was obvious to me that what we find in existing historical accounts and translations only touches the surface of the Vedic teachings.

Vedas and Ancient Yogic and Occult Knowledge

The Vedas contain spiritual, occult, and cosmic secrets that we are just beginning to become aware of. The great India-based religions of Hinduism, Buddhism, Jainism, and Sikhism may represent only later aspects of ancient enlightenment traditions that were probably more common during the Vedic era. The Vedas represent the remains of these early traditions, of which there were no doubt many more.

Vedic literature portrays an ancient solar religion of yoga and enlightenment, such as was once common throughout the entire world. The sun is a symbol of the higher self, the *atman* or *purusha* of yogic thought. This Vedic religion of light is a religion of consciousness, which is the supreme form of light.[6]

The Vedic teaching centers a worship of the sacred fire, called *agni*, through which we can connect to the cosmic powers. It details many yajnas, or fire sacrifices, that can help attune us to the blessings of the universe and that remain the foundation of yogic and Hindu rituals to the present day.[7]

The Vedic teaching used special sacred plants called *somas*. These were powerful plants used in preparations to promote longevity, counter disease, aid in rejuvenation, and help us access higher states of consciousness. Vedic doctors are mentioned in Vedic texts along with special herbs, ghees (oils), and soma mixtures of great power.

Yet soma refers not just to the physical plants but to an inner practice. The Vedic science of soma included ways of accessing our own sacred plant or inner set of energies through the spine, brain, and nervous system. Indeed, the original soma was not a single plant but an entire science of inner and outer healing, with soma plants corresponding to inner yogic somas of mantra, *pranayama,* and meditation. Such yogic somas are more important than the plant somas and more crucial for not only accessing but remaining in higher states of awareness.[8]

Outer Vedic ritualistic practices mirror inner yoga practices, balancing the fire and water and the agni and soma within us. Vedic literature contains the secrets of the practice of yoga, including the ascending of the kundalini fire force and the descent of the soma nectar that opens all the chakras. The practice of yoga itself arose from the inner Vedic sacrifice in which speech, mind, and prana were offered to the immortal divine fire present within our own hearts.[9] Vedic deities reflect a profound psychological and spiritual symbolism relative to the practice of yoga and meditation, not just outer ritualistic concerns.

The Vedas may hold in their mantras the keys to the yogic and shamanic secrets of ancient humanity. The Vedic rishis describe in their hymns various higher states of consciousness, including self-realization, like the great sage Vamadeva (Rig Veda IX.26.1), who proclaims "I was Manu and I am the Sun"—a statement quoted in the Upanishads (Brihadaranyaka Upanishad I. 4.10) relative to the realization of Brahman or the absolute.

Vedic mantras have been described as a kind of universal language. Classical Sanskrit, which evolved out of Vedic Sanskrit, remains the most scientific language in the world. The Vedic language is the oldest of all Indo-European languages and the best-preserved language that we have from the ancient world. Since language, itself, is the best repository of culture, the Vedic language is perhaps our best key not only to ancient culture but to the ancient mind, which is very different in its worldview and orientation than the modern mind.

Mathematical secrets of the universe are mentioned in the Vedas, like a time cycle of 4,320,000,000 years and names for numbers from 1 to 10 to 10 followed by twelve zeroes (10,000,000,000,000). The zodiacal number 360 and its divisions and derivatives are common in

Vedic texts. Vedic mantras are said to be inherent in the rays of the sun. Noted Vedic scholar Subhash Kak has found a planetary code in the numbering of the books of the Rig Veda.[10]

Vedic astrology contains an extensive knowledge not only of the planets, signs, and houses but of the twenty-seven *nakshatras* or lunar constellations going back to the Vedas.[11] The Vedas relate the nakshatras to various deities and rishis and state that after death the soul can travel to the star it is most connected to in life. The mythology of the nakshatras is quite profound and helps us understand the ancient star lore of many cultures.

Vedic astrology divides the lunar month of 29.5 solar days into 30 equal lunar days or *tithis*. This amounts to 371 tithis in a solar year of 365 days. The number of deities in the Rig Veda are 3,339, or 371 times the mystic number 9, reflecting the importance of the influence of the moon. The Vedas were oriented to astronomical influences of a profound order and at perhaps a much earlier date than that of Babylonia.[12]

Vedic vaastu, its architectural and directional science, shows how the great forces of the universe impact us through the orientation of our rooms and buildings and the direction that we face. Ayurvedic medicine preserves many Vedic secrets of herbs, foods, subtle physiology, and keys to rejuvenation. It is still widely practiced in India and becoming recognized worldwide.

Vedic mantras themselves have a tremendous power to change the psyche and bring in higher cosmic influences into our minds and hearts. Vedic mantras like Gayatri (Rig Veda III.62.10) to the sun god are still practiced by millions in India and are now being taken up by many in the West as well.

A few salient points about ancient history and Vedas:

Besides the knowledge side of the Vedas, there are also important historical implications of the Vedic literature. Vedic literature along with the current state of archaeology and genetics suggests a much longer history for the Vedas in India, perhaps extending into the ice age period. It suggests that the Vedic idea of previous cycles of civilization may indeed reflect ice age cultures. For example, the Puranas regard agriculture the

creation of Manu Chakshusha, the fourth Manu, before the fifth Manu
Vivasvan of the flood. We do note that agriculture began already in the
late ice age period more than ten thousand years ago. Many of these points
are mentioned in *Underworld: Flooded Kingdoms of the Ice Age,* by Graham
Hancock. Hancock quotes my work and that of other Vedic scholars like
N. S. Rajaram on several issues, particularly in his sections on India.

Ancient India of the third millennium BCE presents us with the
largest urban civilization of the ancient world and the most uniform,
with hundreds of sites from Afghanistan in the northwest to across the
Ganga in the northeast, to the coast of Iran in the southwest, and nearly
to Mumbai in the southeast. This civilization is usually called the Indus
Valley civilization, as the main sites were found by the Indus River; it is
also called the Harappan civilization after the city of Harappa, which it
was centered around.[13]

Mohenjodaro and Harappa are the two most famous and best excavated of the Harappan sites. Today, there are five sites larger in size than
Mohenjodaro and Harappa, though not as well excavated, and over two
thousand smaller sites, the largest being Rakhigari in the Kurukshetra
region west of Delhi. This Harappan or Indus civilization is the largest
in size and the greatest in uniformity of all ancient civilizations, and
India at the time, as India today, hosted a much larger population than
the arid regions of the Near East.

However, modern scholars portray this Harappan culture as a civilization without a literature, a mysterious civilization that arose and disappeared with little connection to the later history and peoples of India.
Meanwhile, the Vedas, which, as we have already noted, represent the
largest literature from the ancient world, are portrayed by scholars as a
literature without a civilization. In other words, the largest urban civilization of the ancient world is portrayed as civilization without a literary
record, while the largest literary record of the ancient world is regarded
as a literature without a civilization, though both come from the same
part of the world and are traditionally linked together.

Yet if we simply combine these two, the Harappan ruins and

the Vedic literature, we can end the mystery on both sides. Both the Harappan ruins and Vedic literature speak of the same region and reflect many of the same artifacts and practices. For example, the most common symbol found in the Harappan ruins is the swastika, which is the most sacred symbol of Hindu and Buddhist thought. Indus sites also contain fire altars, sacred water tanks, and images of figures seated in meditation (proto-Shiva) or performing yoga postures, such as Vedic and Hindu thought has always given prominence to.

Moreover, the so-called Indus Valley civilization is not located on the banks of the Indus River. The great majority of ancient urban ruins in India have been discovered on the dried banks of the river traditionally called the Sarasvati, which flowed to the east of the Indus. Landsat satellite photography has revealed that the Sarasvati was once a huge river system, up to five miles wide in northwest India, east of the Yamuna River, that dried up around 2000 BCE.

Vedic literature also mentions the Sarasvati River, the most revered of all the Vedic rivers and the great mother of the Vedic people. The Vedas and later literature locate the Sarasvati east of the Yamuna. The Vedic river hymn starts with the Ganga, Yamuna, and Sarasvati rivers and then identifies other rivers to the west. The sacred land of the Vedic people in Vedic literature (Rig Veda III.23.4) and Manu Samhita is situated between the two divine rivers, Sarasvati and Drishadvati, in the Kurukshetra region west of Delhi, where the Mahabharata War was fought at the time of Krishna. Both Sarasvati and Drishadvati were great rivers in ancient times before largely disappearing around four thousand years ago except as occasional run-off streams. That the Vedas speak of these rivers as their immemorial homeland is a strong evidence of their antiquity.

Moreover, the Rig Veda speaks of the Sarasvati as the largest river of the region, pure in its course from the mountains to the sea (Rig Veda VII.95.2). Later texts, like the Mahabharata, speak of the Sarasvati as a broken stream drying up into a series of lakes in what are now Rajasthan and Haryana.[14] Disasters along nearby rivers like the Shutudri (Sutlej) are mentioned in the Mahabharata, with the river breaking into a hundred streams, reflecting the changing of rivers in the region.

The Vedas as a lost civilization rest upon these lost rivers. After the ice age ended, the melting of glaciers kept the river flows in north India much higher, until the bulk of the glaciers melted. Most notably, *to date there is no archaeological evidence of any Aryan invasion or migration into India.* No one has ever been able to locate the so-called Aryans in the archaeological records. The attempts to do so, like that of Mortimer Wheeler and his proposed massacre at Mohenjodaro, have proven erroneous and are no longer accepted. There are no Aryan skeletons, no Aryan horses or chariot remains, no Aryan encampments or any identifiable special Aryan artifacts, no remains of cities destroyed by the Aryans, and no memory or literary records of any such invasion in the history of India, whether in the Vedas, Puranas, or Buddhist and Jain literature. In other words, apart from linguistic speculation, which itself has many variant opinions, there is nothing in the archaeological record to show any incoming Aryans at all.[15]

The whole idea of an Aryan race has been discredited, along with most of the nineteenth-century views it was connected to. The Aryan race idea was a product of European nationalism, not of Vedic thought, for which *Aryan* was a term of nobility only, not ethnicity. It is much like the swastika, which is a Hindu and Buddhist symbol of the wheel of dharma, which the German Nazis perverted into a Nazi symbol.

The Indus or Harappan culture came to an end owing to geological and climate changes, along with the drying up of the Sarasvati River. The decline of the river began by 3000 BCE before ending around 1700 BCE. But the same peoples remained and continued the same types of arts, crafts, and customs until the next urban phase began on the Ganga a few centuries later.

Relative to natural history and genetics, it is now known that the people of India have been continuously occupying their country for more than fifty thousand years. India's subtropical climate enabled them to remain in India throughout the ice ages, unlike Europe and Central

Asia, which became largely uninhabitable during the ice age glaciations. There is to date no genetic record of any incoming Aryans. The main genetic markers are of a movement of peoples outside Southeast Asia after the ice age ended and displaced the populations there. The so-called incoming Aryans have failed to turn up in the genetic record as well. Rather, we see the continuity of the same peoples in India going back into the ice age period.[16]

Curiously, the Vedic and Puranic view is that the Vedic people hailed from the south of India after a great flood. The Puranas relate that Vedic Manu, a great yogi, came from Kerala (Malaya) in the south (Matsya Purana I.13–14). Vedic rishis and sages like Vasishta and Agastya are connected to the south. In fact, the Bhrigus, one of the two main families of the Vedic rishis, are descendants of Varuna, the god of the ocean. The Rig Veda itself has over 150 references to the ocean (*samudra*), as well as to ocean travel and crossing oceans and rivers, though Western scholars claim the Rig Veda is a product of land-locked nomads from Central Asia! The Vedic people likely came from the south of India, perhaps connected to the fabled Kanya Kumari continent, which was said to have existed before the waters rose at the end of the ice age and submerged it.

Implications

If the Vedas do contain such spiritual and yogic secrets, this affirms the idea found not only in Vedic literature but throughout the ancient world that in ancient times people were more spiritually evolved than today. We find a similar myth of a primordial spiritual golden age in the Taoist literature of China, in Babylonian ideas of earlier ages, and in Hopi and Mayan literature. In this way, the Vedas are a record of that golden age and provide a direct link to the wisdom of that more evolved era.

If Vedic civilization is indigenous to India, then we would need to rewrite world history, particularly the history of the Europeans. We would find that the Indo-European groups of Europe, which include

Greeks, Romans, Celts, Germans, Slavs, and others, must have had a great cultural affinity with India before their connections to the Near East or their dispersal throughout Europe.[17] This would be just one aspect of connecting ancient cultures with still older cultures that perhaps extended back into the ice ages.

Clearly, there are many secrets of lost civilizations, and in seeking these out, we cannot forget the role of India, where the ancient world still lives. The history and literature of India, reflecting a knowledge of lost civilizations, should be given greater attention—not only the Vedas but also the Puranas and various yogic texts.

Conclusion

The Vedas are not the only ancient culture or the sole repository of wisdom, though they are certainly much more important than our current historical accounts indicate. Probably, all the main ancient cultures in the world are much older, more evolved, and more spiritually based than what modern history ascribes to them. Similarly, ancient populations and languages may be much older than current estimates indicate, such as the Proto-Europeans and Persians, who are also regarded by modern scholars as products of nomadic invasions from the north and east.

Our current human history of 5,000 years makes little sense if our species is over 150,000 years old, as current science estimates. The destructive effects of the end of the ice age, which saw huge land masses and coastlines submerged, the destructive influence of long periods of time, and the lack of attention by modern scholars used to a short historical time line may explain why such ancient and pre–ice age cultures have not been better discovered or recognized, even though in the case of India, they are still alive among us.[18]

True, history, not as mere technology but as the development of enlightened cultures, likely goes back tens of thousands of years on all the continents. The great civilizations of the early ancient world that we find, such as the Sumerians, Egyptians, Maya, or ancient Hindus, are more likely the remnants or survivors of yet earlier great cultures that our history has so far failed to uncover. Indeed, all the great ancient cultures that we have found do not present themselves as the founders of something new but as connected to earlier cultures going back into the ice age and before.

To go forward as a species into a real planetary age, we need to reclaim this spiritual and yogic heritage of ancient humanity. It provides much of the wisdom we need to help us deal with our global challenges. Our great gurus, elders, and ancestors can still be called on. A few remain. Their voices can be heard. Their words have been recorded. But unless we approach them with respect and seek to uncover the deeper meanings behind their mantras, symbols, and myths, we will not be able to access their wisdom or gain their blessings and the blessings of the greater universe that they carry.[19]

In light of such issues, we can discuss both the spiritual and historical implications of the Vedic literature. I can hopefully present the reader with a view from inside the Vedic tradition, reflecting the deeper Sanskrit meanings and Vedic yogic practices that the reader, otherwise, may not find easily.

Notes

1. David Frawley, "The Vedas and Ancient Egypt," *The Hindu,* April 14, 2003.

2. For the role of fire in ancient religions and as a cosmic symbol, see David Frawley, *Yoga and the Sacred Fire: Self-realization and Planetary Transformation* (Twin Lakes, Wis.: Lotus Press, 2004).

3. Notably Sri Aurobindo, *Secret of the Veda* (Silver Lake, Wis.: Lotus Press, 1996) and Sri Aurobindo, *Hymns to the Mystic Fire* (Silver Lake, Wis.: Lotus Press, 1998).

4. David Frawley, "Sanskritization: A New Model of Language Development," in *The Rig Veda and the History of India* (New Delhi, India: Aditya Prakshan, 2001).

5. David Frawley, "Secrets of the Yugas or World-Ages," adapted from David Frawley, *Astrology of the Seers* (Twin Lakes, Wis.: Lotus Press, 2000).

6. For a discussion of Vedic deities and their meaning, see David Frawley, *Wisdom*

of the Ancient Seers: Mantras of the Rig Veda (Salt Lake City, Utah: Passage Press, 1992).

7. Frawley, *Yoga and the Sacred Fire.*

8. David Frawley, "The Secret of the Soma Plant," American Institute of Vedic Studies, www.vedanet.com/component/content/article/16-ayurveda/173-the-secret-of-the-soma-plant (accessed July 9, 2012).

9. Frawley, "Vedic Yoga, the Oldest Form of Yoga," American Institute of Vedic Studies, www.vedanet.com/index.php?option=com_content&task=view&id=28 (accessed July 9, 2012); note also Frawley, *Yoga: the Greater Tradition* (San Rafael, Calif: Mandala Publishing, 2008).

10. Subhash C. Kak, "Knowledge of the Planets in the Third Millennium BC," *Quarterly Journal of the Royal Astronomical Society* 37 (1996): 709–15. See also Georg Feuerstein, Subhash Kak, and David Frawley, *In Search of the Cradle of Civilization: New Light on Ancient India* (Wheaton, Ill.: Theosophical Publishing House, 1995).

11. Frawley, *Astrology of the Seers.*

12. Frawley, "Vedic Origins of the Zodiac: The Hymns of Dirghatamas in the Rig Veda," American Institute of Vedic Studies, www.vedanet.com/index .php?option=com_content&task=view&id=31 (accessed July 9, 2012).

13. Feuerstein, Kak, Frawley, *In Search of the Cradle of Civilization.*

14. For a discussion of the Saraswati River and Vedic references to it see Frawley, "The Saraswati River: The Homeland of Civilization," part 1, chap. 2 in *Gods, Sages and Kings*: *Vedic Secrets of the Ancient Civilization* (Salt Lake City, Utah: Passage Press, 1991).

15. Frawley, *Myth of the Aryan Invasion of India* (New Delhi, India: Voice of India, 1994).

16. Navaratna S. Rajaram, "History in Our Genes: The Situation in Ancient India."

17. Frawley, "Vedic Origins of the Europeans: The Children of Danu," American Institute of Vedic Studies, www.vedanet.com/component/content/article/20-ancient-india-and-historical-issues/162-vedic-origins-of-the-europeans-the-children-of-danu (accessed July 9, 2012).

18. For a good discussion of these issues, see David Frawley and Navaratna Rajaram, *Hidden Horizons: Unearthing 10,000 Years of Indian Culture* (Ahmedabad: Swaminarayan Aksharpith, 2007).

19. Frawley, "A Call for a New Sacred Fire," in *Yoga and the Sacred Fire.*

FOUR

A Cosmological Journey

HOW MODERN SCIENTIFIC DATA IS TAKING US BACK TO THE WISDOM OF THE ANCIENTS

DR. MANJIR SAMANTA-LAUGHTON

A Realization of Galactic Proportions

"Okay, that's it! I can't keep this to myself anymore."

It was early 2004, and I looked up from the report in *New Scientist* magazine. Antimatter had been found pouring from the heart of our very own Milky Way galaxy, and astrophysicists did not know why.[1] But strange though this was, it was totally predictable from the theories I had published in a paper the previous year.[2] How was it that I knew something that the astrophysicists themselves did not? And why me? Why was a female, British Asian, medical general practitioner (GP) without even an A level in physics and barely out of her twenties coming up with all these ideas about the cosmos?

It was that moment that prompted me to overcome my reservations about writing the book that eventually became *Punk Science: Inside the Mind of God*.[3] I was in the middle of something big. I didn't know why—I just had to go with it and see where this road was leading me. It was as if I wasn't in control any more; this theory had begun to take over my life.

The Road to Eureka

Believe me, this is not where I thought I would end up—putting forward a new theory in physics. I am from a medical family and have trained as a GP like my parents. But after a spontaneous spiritual awakening, which happened in my first few weeks of medical school, I added a burgeoning mystical life to my medical studies. Pretty soon, I realized that the principles of the universe I was experiencing mystically must have their correlation within scientific realms.

To start with, I simply wanted to explain these esoteric principles in terms of modern physics. Like authors who had published before me, I could see the links between esoteric principles such as distant healing and nonlocality in quantum theory. So I started learning about ideas in cutting-edge physics and comparing these with traditional esoteric principles. My aim in the beginning was to provide better care for my patients. I had a (perhaps naive) belief that if doctors simply understood the physics behind energy healing modalities, then maybe they would lose their fear of including them in medical practice, and patients would then benefit from these powerful but nontoxic treatments. But this journey took me somewhere quite different.

Gradually a different path emerged, and as I firmly stepped onto it, the universe moved around me creating extraordinary events leaving me free to study and write full-time. I started writing a book, even though I had no publisher initially, highlighting the links between cutting-edge biology and physics and esoteric ideas. But how did I end up going from being a GP wanting to help her patients to making predictions about the universe that were rapidly being proved right?

At the Heart of Every Galaxy

It was the autumn of 2003, and I had become captivated by the field of cosmology, which had been in turmoil since around the turn of the century with many long-held beliefs becoming obsolete as data came pouring in from telescopes. Cosmologists had just faced one of their biggest challenges for years: the unwelcome arrival of dark energy—a mysterious force that seemed to be blowing the universe apart and accelerating its expansion.

Images from Hubble and other telescopes were throwing open some of our long-cherished beliefs and making us question our theories and expectations about the universe. I became particularly fascinated by black holes. The concept of black holes started life as a conclusion of Einstein's theory of relativity—that if space and time curved beyond a certain point, they would create a point of infinite gravity. Initially, it was thought that certain stars collapse at the end of their lives and produce these points of infinite density and gravity, with a pull so powerful that not even light can escape—hence a so-called black hole.

For decades, these objects remained a theoretical concept, and although they sparked the imaginations of science-fiction writers, it was not known if black holes really existed. It was not until the dawning of the twenty-first century, when our telescopes were picking up black holes everywhere, that we realized that not only did back holes exist, but they were actually quite common.[4] How is a black hole detected if no light can escape it? One of the ways is to look at the material around them, called an accretion disc, which spins so fast that only the gravity of a black hole could be creating it.

The amazing thing was that when we turned our telescopes on neighboring galaxies, we found a supermassive black hole at the heart of each one. We even found a black hole at the center of our own galaxy! So instead of being rare exotic creatures, it turned out that black holes are actually quite common. As well as appearing in the heart of each galaxy, smaller black holes appear throughout the galaxies. Sometimes, they are associated with objects such as quasars, which give out bright radiation.

Hold on a minute: Why would a quasar, which has a black hole associated with it, give out such bright radiation? Surely the black hole would suck up all the light so that we can't see it? In fact, the more we looked, the more the data indicated surprises that contradicted our current theories.

The Great Annihilators

It was in studying objects called microquasars, which are smaller versions of quasars, that I started to find some answers. Microquasars also have a black hole associated with them, but their behavior, again, is peculiar. They, too, are spewing out material very fast, despite the black hole associated with them.

Sometimes they give out gamma ray radiation, sometimes electrons at close to the speed of light, and sometimes the antimatter opposite of electrons—positrons. Because we know that within microquasars, antimatter and matter combine to form light in the form of gamma rays in a process called annihilation, *New Scientist* magazine dubbed them the Great Annihilators.[5]

What was the cause for this strange behavior? Why was this very fast material being spewed out by microquasars? Why aren't the black holes associated with the microquasars sucking everything up? Astronomer

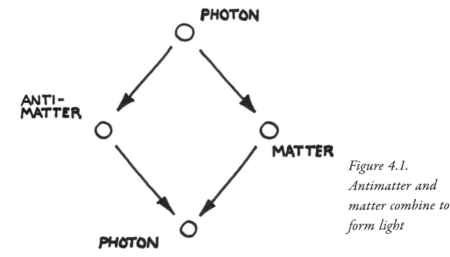

Figure 4.1. Antimatter and matter combine to form light

Sir Martin Rees commented that we should study microquasars. There was a general agreement that black holes all probably behave in the same way, just at different scales, so what we find out about black holes of this size will inform us about larger black holes.[6]

The Universe Speaks

I was pondering all these conundrums—black holes, dark matter and dark energy, and microquasars—as I took a walk with my dog in the woods in the autumn of 2003. I also wanted to find out how everything fitted together with the notion that consciousness is fundamental to the universe, which has arisen out of the work of quantum physicists such as Amit Goswami and Fred Alan Wolf.[7,8] Radical scientists such as these have looked at the conclusions of quantum physics, which tell us that a subatomic particle only comes into existence when it is measured. They realized that the act of conscious observation has a role in creating reality. Some physicists have gone further and concluded that, in fact, consciousness is fundamental to the universe.

Mulling this all over in the woods, I decided to take a rest on the branch of an oak tree and remembered something I had seen years ago in a video featuring the mathematical cosmologist Brian Swimme.[9] He recommended that we take time to tune into the rotation of our own planet, and for some reason, here on this branch of an oak tree, was the first time I tried it.

What came next is something I find hard to describe, but it was if I had been thrown into the very fabric of the universe and caught a glimpse of its secrets. Everything seemed to be made up of the most exquisite geometry and mathematics, which was at the same time both infinitely complex and ever so simple. And I suddenly understood how black holes work, and it wasn't at all how we had previously theorized. I had been shown what I now call the black hole principle, and it was a discovery that would profoundly alter the course of my life.

Dimensions of Consciousness

To understand the black hole principle, I need to first discuss a few other scientific ideas. One is that the universe is made up of many dimensions. This concept started in physics after Einstein had successfully united space and time. Einstein did the equivalent of climbing up a hill to gain an overview of a seemingly disorganized crowd. From this higher perspective, the scene becomes unified; you can see the big picture instead of just seeing the chaos on the ground.

This is effectively what Einstein did in mathematical terms, and ever since, people have been trying to find a way to unite all the forces of nature. Sometimes they do this by creating higher dimensions, such as string theory. These higher dimensions are all around us, but we can't see them because they have different geometrical qualities. Physicists used to think that these dimensions are very small, but changed their minds and started realizing that these dimensions could be worlds of their own.[10] So, according to physics, we live in a universe of many dimensions.

Another concept that has come out of academic physics in recent years is that the speed of light is not the speed limit of the universe. It sounds crazy, but some radical thinkers, such as Joao Magueijo, have been postulating that the way to solve some of the problems we have in cosmology, such as the horizon problem and the flatness problem, is to realize that the speed of light is variable and was faster in the early universe.[11] Magueijo even goes on to say that light is infinite and is curled up in higher dimensions.[12] So what we see as the speed of light is actually a small fraction of its actual speed, which is infinite. Naturally, these ideas have caused a storm in the world of physics, with some people branding Magueijo and his colleagues as heretics.

These two notions, of multiple dimensions and infinite light, when combined with ideas coming from quantum theory present a universe alive with consciousness. And all this has come from physicists themselves in the academic world—not from New Age postulations—which makes these ideas all the more remarkable.

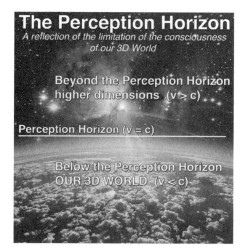

Figure 4.2. The perception horizon

When I started to piece all this together, I realized that what we call dark matter and dark energy is not actually dark at all—it is superbright![13] What we have been calling the speed limit of the universe is not a speed limit at all; it is simply a reflection of the limitations of consciousness in what we call our reality—three spatial dimensions and one of time. The speed of light then becomes the perception horizon, beyond which we don't perceive anything with our normal senses and or our instruments, which are attuned to this dimension alone. However, the areas of the universe that lie beyond this perception horizon are the realms that mystics have been discussing throughout the ages—the light perceived in deep meditative states.

Black Holes: The Source of Infinite Light

So what does this have to do with black holes? Well, in that insightful instant during my walk, which only lasted a few seconds but imparted volumes worth of books to me, I realized that black holes are not dark guzzling monsters at all. We have got it all wrong. They are actually the source of infinite light. This infinite light lies at the heart of black holes. It spirals from the center, down through the dimensions to the edge of our perception, where the light then splits off into a particle of matter such as an electron and a particle of antimatter—a positron.

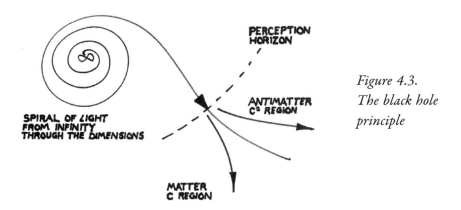

Figure 4.3.
The black hole
principle

This is why we see electrons spewing out of black holes at the speed of light because they have only just reached our dimension and therefore our perception.

And that is not all. This is a breathing process, and it works both ways. Positrons and electrons recombine to form gamma rays. Black holes are therefore the source of the gamma ray bursts that we have seen coming from even the furthest regions of our cosmos and have puzzled scientists for over fifty years since they were first discovered. We even have evidence of this breathing process happening near our own Milky Way galaxy. High-energy gases close to the center of our galaxy have been observed moving in and out, and nobody seems to know why, but this finding totally fits our theory.[14]

Burping Black Holes

We may also be able to account for the strange patterns we see coming from black holes. A lot of astrophysicists think that the emissions from black holes are the result of explosions or black holes guzzling up matter such as stars, causing matter to be ejected in the process. But instead of a steady decay of emissions, as would be expected after an explosion, the pattern is more erratic, leading to bizarre concepts such as the one that black holes burp up their food.[15]

Once we understand that a deeper process is occurring in black holes than just an explosion limited to our dimension, then we will no longer need to create bizarre explanations as we will have a simple, elegant theory that can make some powerful predictions.

I also realized that the black hole principle does not just end with black holes in the cosmos; this same signature behavior is present at every level in a fractal fashion—from objects as small as atoms and quarks to supermassive black holes and even structures in between, such as stars and planets. If I am right, we would see the following types of behaviors in structures:

- Emission of electrons at almost light speeds
- The presence of antimatter and matter annihilation
- Emission of antimatter
- Gamma ray radiation emissions
- Patterns that are unpredictable—with hours or maybe days between flares
- A bipolar jetlike concentrated pattern of emissions (see color plate 1)

The Fractal World

After publishing my initial ideas in a journal in the winter of 2003, I spent the next two years researching and verifying this theory, which I called the black hole principle. Sure enough, a lot of the unexplained behaviors of various objects in the cosmos, from red dwarfs to planets, fit this pattern. Even comets were throwing up surprises for astrophysicists, but not for me—their behavior fit the black hole principle perfectly.[16] Behavior that we have known about for a long time, like radioactivity and the quantum jumps of an electron within an atom, can now be seen in a new perspective.

Even planets and stars show the same pattern of periodic ejections and emissions of high-energy electrons and light. Just look at the X-ray and gamma ray radiation found around the planets of our solar system, the mysterious plumes given off by Jupiter, and solar flares, which remarkably display the same cycling of antimatter and matter that we see in supermassive black holes.[17,18]

Our own planet Earth is the site of some astonishing evidence of the black hole principle. Now surely, our own planet cannot be full of fractal black holes? But if you remember, the term *black hole* is now a misnomer as they are actually the source of infinite light and are the creative forces in the cosmos. It is something that cosmologists themselves were forced to announce in 2010 mainly because the size of each galaxy has such a direct correlation to the size of the supermassive black hole at its center that it was no longer possible to deny the creative role of black holes.[19]

Bolt Upright

So let's look back at some of the criteria for black hole behavior and compare it to our own planet. Where do we see high-energy electrons moving at very fast speeds? In lightning! We are often given the impression that lightning is created by a sort of static electricity that builds up in the clouds, but nobody has been able to prove this. The measurements that have been taken actually show that the power buildup is not nearly enough to cause a bolt of lightning.[20]

When a lightning bolt hits Earth, it is traveling at one-third the speed of light. Amazingly, recent discoveries have shown that gamma ray flashes that exist in Earth's upper atmosphere are associated with thunderstorms and lightning bolts, and just this year alone (2011), NASA has also found that antimatter is being emitted too (see plate 2).[21,22] So now we have periodic ejections of electrons, gamma rays, and antimatter as well as the presence of matter and antimatter annihilation, just as we find in a supermassive black hole at the center of a galaxy.[23] But it is happening not in outer space but in our own atmosphere! This same black hole principle is happening at every single level. There are many more examples given in the book *Punk Science,* which includes DNA, quarks, and the long-derided concept of chakras.[24]

We live in a fractal black hole universe with the signature of creation happening at every single level in everything. Every level of the universe is being created in every moment via spirals of light from infinity. When they reach our dimension, delineated at what we are currently calling the speed of light but is really the limitation of our perceptions in our dimension, they split into the antimatter and the matter that make up our universe and a mirror universe to ours. The matter universe is the one that we are mostly aware of in our daily lives.

Bang Goes the Theory

This means that creation is happening at every single level, not just at one single point fifteen billion years ago; there was no big bang. Astonishingly, the very evidence that was supposed to support the big bang theory is showing up its deficiencies, and this has prompted a group of cosmologists to form the Alternative Cosmology Group, protesting that unless you work on the big bang theory, you will not get academic funding.[25]

However, the more we look at the evidence, the more the big bang theory disintegrates. For example, when we started looking deeper into the universe, we expected to find that we would see only younger stars; as it has taken a longer time for the light to reach us, we should be looking into the early universe. But that is not the case. No matter where we look, the universe looks the same—old stars and young stars appear everywhere.[26]

The other piece of evidence that was supposed to cement the big bang theory but, instead, derailed it was the measurement of microwave background radiation. Discovered by accident in the 1960s by Penzias and Wilson, this radiation has been interpreted as the remnants of the big bang. We even faintly pick it up as the snowstorm picture on our television sets.

But strange features started to appear in the microwave background. Curious alignments and axes were seen that relate to current structures.[27,28] This meant that instead of being related to an event that happened billions of years ago, the microwave background shows alignments to current objects. With microwaves being emitted by our very own Milky Way black hole, it could be that the microwave background is aligned to current structures because it is being emitted by them in the here and now![29]

Time and time again, findings that were puzzling to astrophysicists were perfectly fitting the black hole principle. The predictions I have outlined above can be applied to structures as small as a quark and as unexpected as a brown dwarf.[30,31]

So when I found that antimatter was pouring out of our own Milky Way galaxy in a veritable fountain, to the surprise of many but totally predictable by this theory, I realized that too much evidence was accumulating for me to keep this theory to myself; it needed to get out there.[32] So I collated the data together and published it in the book *Punk Science,* which provides many references for further reading. Since then, of course, we have discovered massive bipolar gamma ray emissions coming from our own galaxy, too: another iteration of the theory.[33]

Nothing New under the Black Hole Sun

It has been a difficult journey, at times requiring me to leave behind the familiar life of a medical doctor and step into uncharted territory. The discovery of similar theories from groups around the world has just reiterated that we are in the middle of a massive scientific revolution. In fact, many scientists even a hundred years ago were formulating similar theories but did not have the astrophysics data that we have acquired in the last few decades to express them in this way.

Going even further back, we realize that the concept that the centers of galaxies are a creative force in the universe has been described by many earlier cultures. The Maya described the center of the galaxy as the Great Mother or cosmic womb. The gnostics had a creation myth, possibly inherited from earlier cultures, that describes a goddess from the center of a galaxy swirling around and falling through some sort of cosmic boundary before creating our world. Maybe this knowledge has something to do with spirals appearing in ancient art, such as at New Grange in Ireland.

I get a sense that the time for this theory has come and that we are simply rediscovering what we used to know. Maybe we had to move away from this ancient knowledge in the cycles of time so that we could rediscover it now with the benefit of our current technologies, which brings us right back to what our ancestors knew—that everything is a spiral of living breathing creative light from infinity occurring at every level and at the heart of every spiral is the same infinite oneness that connects every structure in the universe from the very large to the very small.

Notes

1. E. S. Reich, "When Antimatter Attacks," *New Scientist,* April 24, 2004, 34–37.
2. Manjir Samanta-Laughton, "QBC: The Science of Auras and Chakras," *Holistic Health* 79 (winter 2003–04): 16–21.
3. Manjir Samanta-Laughton, *Punk Science: Inside the Mind of God* (Ropley, Hampshire, U.K.: O Books, 2006).
4. J. R. Minkel, "Bye Bye Black Hole," *New Scientist,* January 22, 2005, 29–33.
5. Nigel Henbest, "The Great Annihilators," *New Scientist,* April 1, 2000, 28–31.
6. Ibid.
7. Amit Goswami, with Richard E. Weed and Maggie Goswami, *The Self-Aware Universe: How Consciousness Creates the Material World* (New York: Tarcher/ Putnam, 1995).
8. F. A. Wolf, *Starwave: Mind, Consciousness, and Quantum Physics* (New York: Macmillan, 1984).
9. Brian Swimme, *Canticle to the Cosmos,* DVD.
10. J. Lykken, *The Physics of Extra Dimensions,* quick-time video associated with lecture at Enrico Fermi Institute, February 15, 2003.
11. Joao Magueijo, *Faster Than the Speed of Light: The Story of a Scientific Speculation* (New York: Penguin, 2004).
12. Magueijo, *Faster than the Speed of Light.*
13. John V. Milewski, "Superlight: One Source, One Force," The Wonderful World of Advanced Materials, November 17, 1996, www.luminet.net/~wenonah/new/ milewski.htm (accessed July 9, 2012).
14. P. Richter and B. P. Wakker, "Our Growing Breathing Galaxy," *Scientific American,* January 2004, 28–37.

15. G. Schilling, "Do Black Holes Play with Their Food?" *Science NOW,* August 18, 2005, 4.

16. Stuart Clark, "Tails of the Unexpected," *New Scientist,* September 10, 2005, 32–35.

17. Jeanna Bryner, "Giant Storms Erupt on Jupiter," Space.com, January 25, 2008, www.space.com/4878-giant-storms-erupt-jupiter.html (accessed July 9, 2012).

18. H. Muir, "Celestial Fire," *New Scientist: Inside Science* 161 (June 21, 2003): 1–4.

19. Marcus Chown, "Supermassive Black Holes: The Fathers of Galaxies," *New Scientist,* January 6, 2010, 30–33.

20. Anna Gosline, "Thunderbolts from Space," *New Scientist,* May 7, 2005, 30–34.

21. Ibid.

22. "NASA's Fermi Catches Thunderstorms Hurling Antimatter into Space," NASA website, January 10, 2011, www.nasa.gov/mission_pages/GLAST/news/fermi-thunderstorms.html (accessed July 9, 2012).

23. Douglas P. Finkbeiner, "WMAP Microwave Emission Interpreted as Dark Matter Annihilation in the Inner Galaxy," January 8, 2005, www.arxiv.org/abs/astro-ph/0409027 (accessed July 9, 2012).

24. Samanta-Laughton, *Punk Science.*

25. E. Lerner, "Bucking the Big Bang," *New Scientist,* May 22, 2004, 20.

26. Marcus Chown, "End of the Beginning," *New Scientist,* July 2, 2005, 30–35.

27. G. D. Starkman and D. J. Schwarz, "Is the Universe Out of Tune?" *Scientific American,* August 2005, 36–43.

28. Zeeya Merali, "'Axis of Evil' a Cause for Cosmic Concern," *New Scientist,* April 23, 2007, 10.

29. Finkbeiner, "WMAP Microwave Emission."

30. Amanda Gefter, "Liquid Universe," *New Scientist,* October 16, 2004, 35–37.

31. R. E. Rutledge et al., "Chandra Detection of an X-ray Flare from the Brown Dwarf LP 944-20," *The Astrophysical Journal* 538 (August 1, 2000): L141–44.

32. Reich, "When Antimatter Attacks."

33. "NASA's Fermi Telescope Finds Giant Structure in our Galaxy," Nasa website, November 9, 2010, www.nasa.gov/mission_pages/GLAST/news/new-structure.html (accessed July 9, 2012).

FIVE

Megaliths, Shamans, and the City Builders

THE HIDDEN CONNECTIONS

LUCY WYATT

We all share certain assumptions about the ancient past. There are many commonly held presumptions about megaliths, shamans, and city builders. In this article, I challenge those presumptions, as well as explain what the hidden connections are and why they are hidden. I provide a brief overview of civilization that goes right back to the end of the ice age and so gives an alternative interpretation of how living in cities came about—in particular, by exploring the links between megaliths, shamans, and city builders. This article is based on research from my book *Approaching Chaos*.

The first point to make is that we do not normally link megaliths and shamans with city builders. Indeed, there are no ancient cities associated with well-known megalithic sites in the United Kingdom, such as Avebury or Stonehenge. If you mention megalith to anyone, Avebury or Stonehenge are normally the images that spring to mind; and if you say shamans, then people think of Peruvian medicine men in the jungle or Mongolians in smoke-filled yurts. When we Westerners talk about our ancient pagan "primitive" past, we usually refer to nature and nature spirits, sacred groves of oak trees, temples and zodiacs in the landscape, energy lines, and rocks and springs. We think of Druids; we think of Stonehenge. It is all wild, elemental, and powerful. We do not think of pharaohs, nor do we think of places like Washington, D.C.—and yet they are all linked.

One reason why we do not make these associations is because of the Romans. They, along with the Greeks, were the most powerful of all the Indo-European tribes, and they continue to dominate us in the West. So much of what we understand about the ancient past is mediated through these people: it is filtered through their mind-sets, their way of thinking, because we have inherited their languages. They both provide access to the past—because we can learn about life two thousand years ago by read-ing the material they left behind—and form a barrier.

This may sound bizarre, but the Greeks and Romans themselves did not understand everything about the times they were living in. In fact, they were quite capable of getting it wrong. More particularly, they did not fully understand the group of people we call the Egyptians—in spite of living with them for several hundred years.

The Greeks, of all the Indo-European tribes, were the closest to the Egyptians, and it is mostly through the Greeks that we know as much as we do about ancient Egypt. But after the end of the fourth century CE, even that possibility disappeared, and we lost all ability to read hiero-glyphs. For a long time, Egypt remained mysterious, a closed book.

So what are these connections that have remained hidden for so long?

The Ice Age

To answer that question, I want to go right back, back to the beginning as it were—back to the end of the ice age more than twelve thousand years ago. (The dashed line in figure 5.1 represents the extent of the ice; the other line, the lower sea levels. You can read about the clans

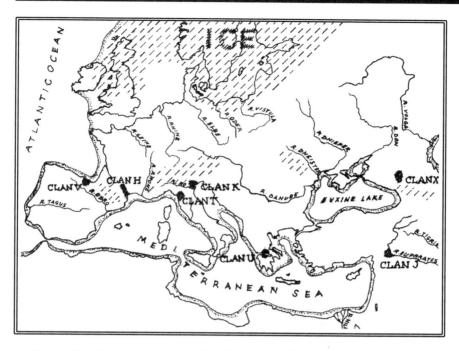

Figure 5.1. Ice age map, reproduced courtesy of Bryan Sykes, The Seven Daughters of Eve *(London: Corgi, 2001)*

in *Approaching Chaos.*) We tend to start the story of how civilization began during the ice age; how we came to be modern, progressive people with all our urban comforts and sophistication, leaving behind the wild, woolly, elemental stuff.

And the story we tell ourselves is that it all starts with the farming experiment. You can read about it in the British Museum: Paleolithic man instead of sitting in his cave begins to throw seeds around outside; he finds he has a crop surplus, and being clever, he decides to exchange it for something else. Primitive people were then on their way to becoming civilized with towns and cities growing out of early marketplaces. They could leave behind their hunter-gatherer cave-dwelling past and evolve into modern man, with the help of the Greeks and Romans, of course. Lots of people continue to believe that civilization only really starts with the Greeks and Romans.

The Farming Experiment?

But unfortunately, we have been telling ourselves the *wrong* story. This is not what the prehistoric record shows. There was no farming experiment. The Natufians, for instance, who were around from about 12,500 BCE onward, cultivated wild seeds for three thousand years. During this time, there was no change from a wild seed to a domesticated seed. Even when the change from wild to domesticated did occur after 9,500 BCE, it is not plausible to suggest that it was an evolutionary process.

The difference between wild and domestic seeds is expressed in a single gene: one that relates not to taste but to convenience; convenience being one of the hallmarks of civilization. Figure 5.2 shows a barley seed head with its rachis—the little hinges that connect the seed heads to the stalk. Wild seed rachis break when the seed heads are ripe; the domestic version waits to be picked.

Figure 5.2. Barley seed head

The chances of a rare genetic mutant wild cereal turning into domesticated cereal have been calculated at once or twice in two to four *million* seed heads—according to Gordon Hillman who is cited by Steve Mithen (a well-respected prehistorian academic). For this change to have occurred naturally would take 20 to 30 cycles, that is 20 to 30 years.[1] No one is realistically going to wait around that long for an "experiment" to work; they would return to trapping and say, "Dad, can you forget your farming experiment?" The obvious conclusion is that this change was deliberate: someone knew how to interfere genetically with cereals.

What is also suspicious is the climate and geography of those places where the change to farming apparently took place. One such place is Machu Picchu, high up on the altiplano in the Andes in South America, shown in color plate 3; another is the Fertile Crescent near the Mediterranean Sea—often referred to as the cradle of humanity because so many "firsts" happened here The first fully morphologically domesticated cereals occurred at Halula in the northern Euphrates Valley in about 7000 BCE. The map of the Fertile Crescent in figure 5.3 shows the Taurus Mountains in the west, in Turkey, and the Zagros Mountains in the east, in Iran, with both the Tigris and Euphrates rivers coming from a mountainous area in the middle of the crescent.

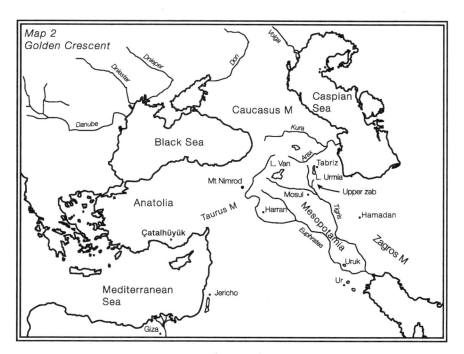

Figure 5.3. The Fertile Crescent

If farming really were the stimulus for the creation of civilization, why were the earliest examples of it located in such agriculturally difficult places? Jacquetta Hawkes is one of the few to draw attention to this curious situation in her comment that civilization "was not inevitable, for on the one hand men have lived on well-watered and fertile land without creating civilization, and on the other hand they have created civilizations in apparently poor environments."[2]

Hawkes is not alone in her comments. Diana Kirkbride, a one-time director of the British School of Archaeology in Iraq, commented about one site dating to 7500 BCE that she excavated in the 1970s in the Mosul-Sinjar region in northeastern Iraq (in a place called Umm Dabaghiyah) that it was "singularly uninviting"—even allowing for change over time and degradation of habitats. Likewise, Charles Maisels discusses another site dating to 6000 BCE to the east of Mosul at Yarim Tepe on the Upper Zab, describing it as a zone of rocky limestone hillocks "not really suitable for farming, yet there is plentiful evidence of it here."[3]

It is also in the Fertile Crescent that we have the remains of a series of well-built settlements dating to between the tenth and eighth millennia BCE—the most famous being the end of the eighth millennium at Çatalhüyük in Anatolia, southern Turkey. Çatalhüyük is another site hailed as an example of humanity on its way to a civilized life.

What is significant about Çatalhüyük is that well-constructed storerooms are the central feature of the settlement—better built than the human dwellings around them. Çatalhüyük is carefully laid out with a proper street pattern and all the houses have the same floor plan; yet it did not develop into any kind of city. The diet of the inhabitants is also resolutely Stone Age, consisting of wild animals, aurochs, and such like. This contradicts the idea that farming leads to surplus, which leads to markets, towns, and so on. None of this makes sense.

Here in the Fertile Crescent, we have the earliest evidence not only of farming but of metalwork and pottery—not civilization, as such, but the fingerprints of the civilizers. So what were they doing in the mountains? I will return to this question later.

Bronze Age Secondary Products Revolution

Then, suddenly, around 5000 BCE, the time of the Bronze Age, the first cities started to appear in Mesopotamia (southern Iraq)—about as far away from the mountains as is possible in that part of the world. By 3600 BCE, Uruk, for example, was a great city with over ten thousand people. We know that these are cities because they have the recognizable infrastructure of a city and evidence of activities like administration and record keeping. These skills are not innate. We only have to look at our own modern difficulties with teaching well-known civilized techniques like writing to know that even after thousands of years of civilization, these skills have to be retaught.

And coincidently, not just cities appeared, but something happened in farming too—what the archaeologists call the secondary products revolution. It is around this time that people milked cows (and made butter and cheese), plowed the soil, rode horses, took wool from sheep, planted vines, and so on—the kind of farming that we would all recognize. Before this moment in time, it was not possible to take wool from a sheep: sheep had coats like deer, even though there is evidence of sheep/goat ovricaprids having been eaten by humans as far back as 10,500 BCE.

How odd and how useful that, just when lots of people start to live in cities, the production of food becomes more organized. This shift had to be deliberate because no self-respecting hunter-gatherer would give up providing for himself and his family to live in a city until he could be sure that he could rely on someone else for food production and that he had a skill that would be useful in a city.

In particular, farming skills had to be taught. Farming is not natural. Anyone who thinks it is easy should try it. The hunter-gatherer was not used to staying in one place; he followed the herd. He was more used to killing than keeping stock alive, especially through the winter. Farming is a completely different skill set that requires knowledge of the soil and the calendar.

What is notable is that people did not make the transition from nomadic hunter-gatherer to nomadic pastoralist. The shift to farming always involved a settled pattern first, usually identified by the presence of pigs, which cannot be herded long distance. Take the example of the Ferghana Valley in Central Asia, which is in the eastern part of Uzbekistan and is famous today for its Kirghiz tribes who herd massive flocks of sheep over long distances. The evidence of older patterns of Bronze Age farming, the Chust culture—which can be seen in the museum in Tashkent, capital city of Uzbekistan—is still of the settled pattern first.

What this suggests to me is that the early farmers were not necessarily hunter-gatherers who took up farming because of some environmental change or other external pressure. They were actually a different people with a different knowledge base. First cereals were genetically interfered with, and then animals. This was not a natural evolutionary process. Even Julius Caesar knew that aurochs could not be domesticated. In any case, how would Neolithic man know what would make a "good" cow, just from observing them at waterholes?

I would argue that this change in farming happened because of cities and not the other way round. The first evidence of a city's existence isn't a marketplace but a shrine. One of the oldest cities in southern Mesopotamia, Eridu, has a shrine dating to 2000 BCE that has seventeen layers underneath it that possibly go back as far as 5000 BCE. Hawkes has also commented that the key group of people who are involved in cities from the start are not farmers but priests.

So, what has this got to do with megaliths and shamans? The connection lies in what these cities represent as a total concept of civilization—a concept in which megaliths and shamans were an integral part. Cities did not develop out of farming but arrived as preplanned artificial constructs on the landscape. They have identifiable characteristics that link them to a specific archetype, which includes the knowledge of how to move big stones and has shamanic ritual at the heart of it.

The Total Civilization Concept

I refer to this archetype as the Ur concept of civilization. The Egyptians called it living in *ma'at* or truth—the goddess Ma'at having the feather of truth. But I prefer Ur, which in this context doesn't just mean the famous city that Sir Leonard Woolley excavated in the 1920s in southern Iraq (and in my opinion mistakenly identified as the biblical Ur of the Chaldees, as I have good reason to believe that was another Ur elsewhere); Ur in this context has a meaning of foundation and as such can be found in names like Jerusalem (*oru-shalem* or foundation of peace).

The best way to describe this Ur concept is to imagine a color wheel plus white. The archetype was based on all the usual aspects we attribute to civilized city living: straightness, accuracy precision, balance, design, infrastructure, organization.

If there is one part of the circle that is more important than any other, it is the temple at the center, which holds all the other parts in balance. It was the priesthood that supervised the foundation of cities, the construction of the great engineering works and monumental architecture. It was they who sanctioned the trading exchanges, determined the calendar and predicted the weather, educated the young, kept written records, and healed the sick and helped the dying on their way. They understood the importance of the soul (the psyche) and its role in reincarnation and immortality. Were they also the ones who bred wild animals into domesticated versions?

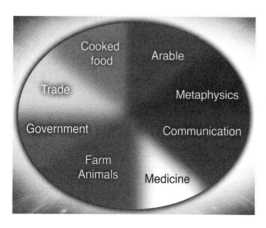

Figure 5.4.
The Ur concept of civilization

There are also the relationships across the wheel: all forms of *communication* (trade, travel, and education), the *individual* body (the art of cooking, and the link between food and medicine), *agriculture* (domestication of animals and organized arable production), and *power*. Power in this context refers to political power (administration, justice, architecture, and infrastructure) and religious power (the priesthood). The critical role is the melchizedek or priest-king.

This archetype exists for all time and in all places, which is why the same characteristics appear in the Near East as in the Indus Valley, in Phoenicia, in Minoan Crete, and in Central and South America (and possibly the Far East—but I haven't explored that aspect). Egypt, with its pharaohs, became the best example of it.

Proto-Indo Europeans

But what is truly extraordinary about the Ur concept is the confirmation of aspects of it among people who themselves were not civilized and who can be found living a long way away from the civilizers. They did not even live in cities. These people are the very early Indo-European tribes long before they came to Europe, the Proto-Indo-Europeans.

The location of the original homeland of the Indo-Europeans before the fourth millennium BCE is controversial. There is no universal agreement. My own personal view is that it was in the Pontic Caspian in the Ukraine—a long way away from the civilizers in Mesopotamia. And yet, there is evidence, based on an analysis of Proto-Indo-European language, that the civilizers came into contact with these early Indo-Europeans.

It is now a well-established idea that the Indo-European tribes (Celts, Romans, Greeks, and so on) once all lived together. What linguists have worked out is that Indo-Europeans last lived together over five thousand years ago—a time frame that relates to the Bronze Age civilizers. This link was discovered through the realization in the nineteenth century that Indian Sanskrit, although written in a different alphabet, has the same language roots as other European languages, such as Latin and Greek.

Etymology reveals what kind of environment they knew; what kind of dwellings they lived in; what skills they had; and, to a limited extent, what they thought. And, in my opinion, certain concepts that relate to the Ur civilization archetype have been embedded in the language for more than 5,000 years—2,500 years *before* they lived in cities.

Contact with civilizers is implied in that the Indo-Europeans knew about bronze and copper but not about tin, which suggests that they did not know how to make bronze but got bronze from elsewhere. They also picked up from the civilizers over five thousand years ago practical farming skills and benefited from the secondary products revolution. They knew about stock breeding; evidence of domesticated sheep and cattle and herding can be reconstructed and attributed to Proto-Indo-European, as can the secondary products of butter and cheese.

There is a very good reason why the civilizers would want to make contact with the early Indo-Europeans. There was a certain something that Proto-Indo-Europeans had, which the civilizers were keen to

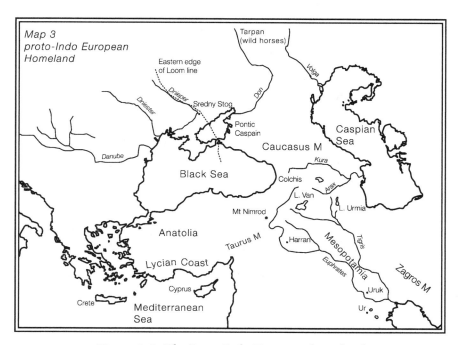

Figure 5.5. The Proto-Indo-European homeland

exchange skills and ideas for. It was this certain something that I think establishes the Proto-Indo-Europeans in a distinct time and place, and that something was the wild horse or the tarpan. The Indo-Europeans lived in the range of the tarpan.

Until the arrival of the civilizers, who knew how to genetically interfere with wild creatures for the benefit of humans, the tarpan had been of little use to the Proto-Indo-Europeans. The first domestic horse bones are usually claimed to be those dating from 4000 BCE, found at the Dereivka site in the Sdreny Stog region of the Ukraine. The breakthrough in the exploitation of the deep steppe did not happen until about 3500 BCE, and the first wheeled carts did not appear on the steppes north of the Black Sea and Caspian before 3000 BCE.

The civilizers would have brought horses down from the Ukraine, and although it was long before horses made an obvious impact on Mesopotamia, within a certain period of time there is evidence of their use. By 2800 BCE, 80 percent of Sumerians lived in cities and had wheeled carts.

The shift from wild to domestic horses had such an impact on the Proto-Indo-Europeans that they venerated the horse for thousands of years. They attributed godlike powers to them. Their attitude to religion was simple and nature based (sky god and earth mother). A term for religion can be reconstructed from *creed* based on two words, *cre dhe,* meaning "put into your heart."

One concept that particularly demonstrates the impact of the civilizers and is inexplicable to linguists is the concept of king (*reg*), which can be reconstructed to the earliest level of Proto-Indo-European language (*rex, raj, reich*). This is a remarkable concept as it underpins the rules, regulation, and accuracy aspect of the archetype. But at the time they learned this word, the Indo-Europeans were wild warlike tribes living in mud huts, where the central focus was the hearth. Linguists are forced to give the ridiculous explanation of two kings: one for war and one for ruling. Is it possible that the Indo-Europeans picked up a word that they did not understand the full meaning of?

Global Catastrophe: Fourth Millennium BCE

Then, around 3159 BCE, there was an appalling environmental catastrophe, which resulted in a massive migration of all peoples—the Proto-Indo-Europeans and the civilizers among them. It is after this catastrophe that ancient Egypt as we know it begins. At this point, the Proto-Indo-Europeans split up into their individual tribes, and the civilizers had no further common impact on them, although bits of knowledge remained with the individual tribes.

Celts, for example, went the farthest west, ending up in Ireland, and far to the east in the Tarim basin on the west of China, where they became Tocharians, tall four-thousand-year-old ginger-haired mummies wearing tartan have been found in the Chinese Taklamakhan desert.[4] The language of the Celts, who went the farthest, retains the most archaisms, and therefore more connections with Indians and Sythians, and is possibly the most interesting.

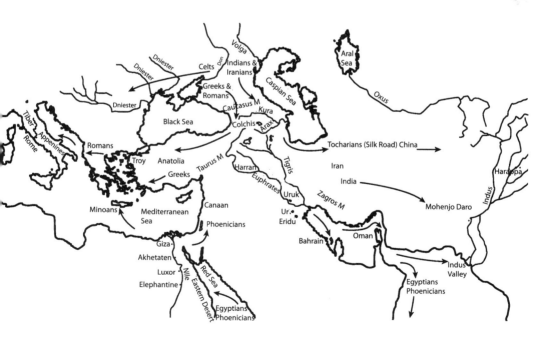

Figure 5.6. Diaspora

To give one example, the Celts possibly retained knowledge of the gods of the civilizers. They continued to refer to Tetates, one of the old names of Thoth, the Egyptian god of writing, when the Greeks and Romans had already changed him to Hermes and Mercury. The implication of this Celtic reference is that Egyptian deities could have been known to the Proto-Indo-Europeans *before* the start of Egypt. The name *Hermes* is in itself worth noting, as its root is possibly *ur-mes* meaning son of Ur (*mes* or *mos* are Egyptian words that mean "son of," as in Thutmosis, a pharaoh name that means "son of Thoth").

But in spite of the close proximity of the Proto-Indo-Europeans with the civilizers, there is no obvious evidence that they knew about shamanism in order to access the metaphysical secrets of the original archetype—which is perhaps why they never built cities themselves until much later. Even though the concepts of shaman and shamanism are well known, how they relate to civilization is less familiar.

Shamanic Ritual and Role of the Pharaoh

In essence, a shaman is someone who has an out-of-body experience in which he or she undergoes a journey as a spirit on behalf of a person or a community in order to find answers to particular questions. The kind of shamanism that is practiced these days is more usually on behalf of a sick person or child to identify remedies that will cure the patient. It is important to understand that the information thus obtained is not discoverable through experimentation, as it often involves the use of poisons that have to be treated in a particular way first, otherwise they would be fatal.

These shamanic journeys are trancelike, dangerous, frightening, near-death experiences that can result in the actual death of the shaman. They are, therefore, to be avoided by anyone who is not properly trained or prepared (one of the problems with modern drug taking is that it can result in mental damage from ignorant use). The initiation or training of the shaman is thus critical from an early age. In addition, the preparation of the substance that brings on the trance is key to the whole process.

How this applies to the original archetype of civilization is that the king had the responsibility of undertaking the special journey on behalf of his people. In the case of Egypt, that person was the pharaoh; this title, interestingly enough, could be a Greek corruption of the words *per ur,* the name of the place where the pharaoh's initiation took place (*per ur* means "house of foundation"), which might have been at Nekhen (or Hierakonopolis, its Greek name), possibly in its mysterious fort, which had no defensive purpose.

Every forty years, the pharaoh prepared for a highly important festival, sometimes referred to as the pharaoh's jubilee, or the Heb Sed Festival. The festival incorporated the Osirian rites—a reenactment of the death of the god Osiris and his revival at the hands of Isis, his wife—and took took place in a purpose-built courtyard adjacent to a specially constructed pyramid. There were public aspects and secret aspects. Citizens from all over Egypt came to the festival, and the purpose of it was to rededicate the country to civilization.

Figure 5.7. Pharaoh riding a serpent

In the public aspects, the pharaoh wore a special bull kilt and had to run around the courtyard. He also participated in a ritual meal called the *hotep.* After this meal, the pharaoh disappeared into the secret part of the festival, which took place inside the pyramid, where he entered the realm of the deity Sokar.

Sokar is interesting because of what he represents. Sokar had a more complicated association with death than just being dead. He was part of a triple manifestation of the gods Ptah-Sokar-Osiris. These gods represented the triple powers of animation, incarnation, and restoration, and thus were essential to the Egyptian ideas of cycles of life and death, in terms of the soul being immortal and reincarnated in a living body.

Writer Rosemary Clark describes Sokar as representing "the latent spiritual principle within all living things, the spirit embedded in the deepest regions of matter that await arousal," a description that implies the beginning of life rather than the end of it.

Pyramids—Not tombs

It is our cultural problem that we think of pyramids as tombs. Very few dead bodies have ever been found in them. The Egyptians buried their dead either in the royal tombs on the west bank of the Nile opposite Luxor or in mudbrick *mastabas*. The Egyptian word for pyramid is *mr*, which has the idea of an instrument for ascending, according to American Egyptologist Mark Lehner, who translates *mr* as "place of ascension" according to his belief that the pyramids were tombs for dead kings and where the dead kings souls ascended. A close examination of the structure of the Great Pyramid at Giza reveals another clue to their function.

First, some statistics: The Great Pyramid covers thirteen acres. It is built of 2.3 million blocks of solid rock with an average weight of 2 tons per block; some blocks weigh 50 tons. The four corners are true 90-degree angles to within one one-hundredth of an inch. It is aligned on the cardinal points and deviates by only 5 degrees.

What is remarkable about this pyramid is that it has clearly been constructed very carefully and deliberately, and it is devoid of any kind of internal decoration or ornamentation; whereas the mastaba tombs at Saqqara are beautifully decorated with the most exquisite bas-reliefs of life scenes that would help a pharaoh on his way in the afterlife.

Consider the most important chamber in the Great Pyramid: the

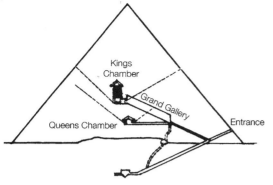

*Figure 5.8. Cross-section of
the Great Pyramid*

King's Chamber. An enormous effort was made to bring extraordinary granite slabs—megaliths that weighed up to fifty tons—five hundred miles from the quarry in Aswan. And then these slabs were used in the chamber in such a way that their function was not visually obvious. Furthermore, the chamber is deliberately constructed so that its walls and its ceiling are not connected. The ceiling is supported by walls beyond the internal walls. Above the ceiling are a series of hidden granite beams with bits taken out of them.

One plausible explanation for all of this is that the purpose of the chamber was to create an electrical field using vibration. The quartz in the granite has piezo-electric properties. The reason for not tying the walls to the ceiling was so that they could vibrate freely, and the explanation for the gouges in the beams above the ceiling could have been for fine-tuning the resonances.*

By way of reinforcing this idea of vibration in an electrical field, the pharaoh either lay in a sarcophagus of alabaster or granite or on a special Heb Sed Festival bed covered in gold leaf (Tut's golden bed can be seen in the Cairo museum)—gold being a good conductor of electricity.

---

*The importance of materials is not unique to Egypt and possibly explains the presence of a giant slab of mica found hidden in the Pyramid of the Sun in Mexico. One modern commentator, Christopher Dunn, who has a technical background, has worked out that the Egyptians knew about ultrasound and used it for carving and drilling (that is how he explains the amazing accuracy of Egyptian stonework and the fine carving on very hard stones like basalt and granite—exquisite examples of vessels can be seen in the British Museum). See Christopher Dunn, *The Giza Power Plant: Technologies of Ancient Egypt* (Rochester, Vt.: Bear & Co., 1998).

Before doing this, the pharaoh put on the *qeni* garment over his chest and participated in the Wepwawet Opening of the Mouth Ceremony. Was the point of using the qeni garment, which the pharaoh described as the embrace of Osiris, to protect the pharaoh's heart from the electrical field? And was the Opening of the Mouth Ceremony to stop him from swallowing his tongue during his trance?

What confirms my suspicions that this was all part of a shamanic ritual are the Pyramid or Coffin texts. These texts were discovered in the nineteenth century by Flinders Petrie, the Victorian archaeologist. Again it is our cultural problem that we think of them as describing the journey of the pharaoh's soul after death, whereas it is more likely that they describe his soul's journey in life. Dr. Jeremy Naydler, an Oxford academic, is one of the few who has come to this conclusion.

The Pyramid Texts frequently refer to the pharaoh taking the form of a bird and flying up or climbing a ladder. Chapter XX of the Egyptian Book of the Dead, for instance, talks of the pharaoh rising into the sky like the mighty hawk. The Antechamber Texts in the Pyramid of Unas at Saqqara refer to "a stairway to the sky [which] is set up for me that I may ascend on it to the sky, and I ascend on the smoke of the great censing. I fly up as a bird." Elsewhere, the same texts refer to the pharaoh flying up in the form of a falcon to the "imperishable northern stars"—an important point I shall come back to.[5]

Alchemy and the Solar Bread

If this was a shamanic experience, was the hotep meal the means by which the pharaoh brought on a trance? A significant element of the meal was the solar bread. And there are references to the solar bread in the Pyramid Texts. One Pyramid Text, which Naydler describes as an enigmatic food spell, is an utterance for the offering bread to fly up.

So what was the solar bread? This essential ingredient of the Hetep meal clearly had special properties. This is where the story gets really interesting. It is at this point that the Greeks, through whom we know as much as we do, got confused. They confused a process with an outcome; as a result, we know about the process without being aware of its purpose and that process was what we call alchemy.

Have we been misled about alchemy? Maybe alchemy isn't the changing of another metal into gold, or even a spiritual transformation, but the purification of gold to achieve an even purer gold (the four-thousand-year-old Mesopotamian golden ram caught in a thicket—now in the British Museum—is an example of very pure gold). There are several methods for achieving purification, and one of them is to expose gold to a high electrical charge to remove impurities. It is also possible to use this process to turn pure gold into a white powder with levitational properties.

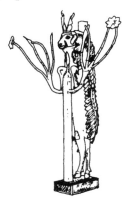

Figure 5.9. The golden ram

The usual source for the word *alchemy* is *khem,* which is the description of Egypt as the black land, but this definition doesn't work in this context. What makes more sense, to me at least, is that alchemy is derived from *khemi,* the Egyptian word for the fixed stars, and so alchemy means a journey to the fixed stars or the imperishable northern stars. The Egyptians possibly used the levitational properties of the white powder in the form of solar bread as their means of entering a trance.

Because of the Greeks' misunderstanding, we use the term to identify only one part of the process, the means by which the Egyptians made that journey—the preparation of the gold. The Greeks were ignorant of the outcome, the astral flight to the fixed stars. The circumstantial evidence that confirms my interpretation that the preparation of the gold was key to the whole operation is the link between the solar bread—the substance consumed during the hotep, the pharaoh's ritual meal—and the cow goddess Hathor.

Hathor and Gold

Hathor the cow goddess had many roles, mostly to do with nurturing. She is sometimes attributed with lending her cow horns to the goddess Isis when tending the infant Horus. Hathor is also the one who nurtures the soul of the pharaoh on his journey.

Figure 5.10.
Hathor the cow goddess

Even more significantly, it is in her temple at Serabit el-Khadim in the Sinai Peninsula where, in the nineteenth century, Flinders Petrie found vast quantities of a mysterious white powder hidden under slabs in the floor. Furthermore, another of her names is Nub-t, the word for gold, and her connection with gold is obvious at her temple at Denderah on the Nile, which has the hieroglyph of gold on its back wall. It is in the Denderah temple where there are the strange "lightbulb" reliefs in the crypt.

Mouni Sadhu, who wrote a fundamental work on the tarot in the late 1950s, alludes to the role of electricity in his summary of a typical alchemical process, albeit repeating the widespread deception that gold results from other metals.

Sadhu notes that "[i]n order to transform another metal into silver or gold, we must first destroy the imperfect combination of its components, that is to separate the subtle from the gross in that metal, and then to establish a new, perfect combination, passive or active. . . . The Emerald Tablets speak about this separation of the subtle from the gross." Sadhu goes on to explain in more detail the stages that an alchemist might follow to create the philosopher's stone, which he identifies as being a powder.[6] The first phase is the preparation of the "universal solvent" or mercury using a mineral called the "magnesia of the sages." The second phase is the operation, which produces a "dazzling white color" after slow heating in the athanor (the alchemist's oven). There are several points to note in his account: his view that the philosopher's stone is a powder; that the universal solvent is called the magnesia of the sages, which he later identifies as some kind of electrical charge; and the specific description of the powder being a dazzling white color. Is this the powder that Flinders Petrie discovered in the Hathor temple at Serabit el-Khadim?

*Figure 5.11.
Reliefs in the crypt at
Denderah*

Writer Lawrence Gardner also describes the electrical process of purifying gold, which results in a white powder with levitational properties. According to Gardner, when the molecular structure of the gold changes, some of its matter turns into energy and becomes pure light.

Not only does the powder weigh less than the original metal, but it is capable of transferring some loss of weight to the container in which it was originally weighed.

Snakes Communicating with DNA

So, now we have all the ingredients. There remains one more piece of the jigsaw puzzle to add: What was it that the pharaoh was communicating with? Who were the *netr,* the Egyptian gods? Were they sometimes giant snakes? And is it just coincidence that netr, the Egyptian word for god, is identical to a Proto-Indo-European word for snake, also netr (*natrix* in Lation; *nathir* in Old Irish; and *naeddre* in Old English, where it became adder). Is that the reason that Thoth or Hermes is associated with the twin snakes of the caduceus?

The modern experience of Jeremy Narby, which he describes in his book *The Cosmic Serpent: DNA and the Origins of Knowledge,* provides some corroboration.[7] Narby traveled to the Peruvian Amazon in 1985 to study a native community, the Quirishari, as part of his Ph.D. in anthropology from Stanford University. Here he undertook a shamanic experience using the ayahuasca vine in which a pair of enormous snakes communicated with him. What particularly struck Narby was the visual parallel between the image of entwined snakes, such as in the caduceus, and that of the double helix of DNA.

Narby then came to the fascinating conclusion that the parallel was more than visual: it was actual. Shamans, he concluded, were communicating at the level of molecular biology, of DNA itself. He was surprised to discover in the technical literature that the shape of the double helix of DNA is "most often described as a ladder . . . or a spiral staircase," which compares with the worldwide frequent references made to climbing a ladder during a shamanic trance.

Narby thus discovered how native people acquired their knowledge of medicinal plants. These plants were often highly toxic and required critical special preparation before use; otherwise, they would kill you

Figure 5.12.
Thoth as Hermes with caduceus

before you had chance to experiment with them and find out their healing properties. Native people knew precisely which plants to choose out of *eighty thousand* Amazonian plant species. And the means by which they knew this nonempirical knowledge, he was told and personally experienced, was through shamanism.

Pharaohs—Sophisticated Shamans

What the pharaohs of ancient Egypt were doing was much more sophisticated than the Peruvian jungle version. And knowing the importance of gold to the whole process also explains why civilization appears to start in mountains—that is where the gold is. Çatalhüyük was part of a supply chain of emporia to support operations elsewhere in the mountains, and so the storerooms for this emporia were better constructed than the human dwellings; these storerooms were more important than how the locals lived.

Mesopotamia had no gold reserves, and yet its ancient name of *ki-en-gi* translates as "land where gold is king." Mesopotamian gold came from the Fertile Crescent. The hairs stood on the back of my neck when I realized that the sites where the earliest pottery was found in the Fertile Crescent are near gold mines and important routes for gold.

The links between megaliths (the ability to move massive stones weighing fifty tons or more over vast distances and hundreds of miles), shaman (wise men who can take their souls on journeys for the benefit of others at great personal risk to themselves), and the original cities should now be clear; they are all integral to each other.

We don't realize any of this because of the barrier the Greeks and Romans created for us—a barrier that grew even greater after the Romans came under the influence of a monotheistic religion we call Christianity from the fourth century CE onward. I would personally argue that it was at that point that civilization collapsed, and that we have been living in a dark age ever since, struggling to reconnect with the original archetype that appeared in the Bronze Age over five thousand years ago.

Romano-Christian Destruction

It was in the fourth century CE that fanatical Romano-Christians massacred the last Egyptian priests at the temple of Isis on the Island of Philae in the Upper Nile. These same people destroyed the site of the Eleusian mysteries in Greece near Athens in 396 CE and burnt down the famous library at Alexandria in 415 CE, brutally murdering Hypatia, its last priestess.

The Egyptians had realized long before that the writing, as it were, was on the wall and that the end lay ahead. The shift that marked the start of Egypt's long decline was the change from Bronze Age to Iron Age in about 1200 BCE, characterized by the fall of Troy. It was at this time that the Hekla volcano in Iceland erupted in 1159 BCE, causing twenty years of poor harvests, famine, and appalling social destruction, including a form of child sacrifice.

There is a particularly sad prophecy in the Hermetica:

> If truth were told, our land is the temple of the whole world; . . . a time will come when . . . . Egypt will be abandoned. The land that was the seat of reverence will be widowed by the powers and left destitute of their presence. When foreigners occupy the land and territory, not only will reverence fall into neglect, but . . . a prohibition . . . will be

enacted against reverence, fidelity and divine worship. Then this most holy land, seat of shrines and temples, will be filled completely with tombs and corpses . . . only stories will survive and they will be incredible to your children. Only words cut in stone will survive to tell your faithful works. . . . Whoever survives will be recognized as Egyptian only by his language; in his actions he will seem a foreigner.[8]

Egypt had become increasingly vulnerable to invasion, which happened first with the Persians in about 600 BCE, followed by the Greeks under Alexander the Great in 333 BCE. The Romans, who were so desperate to get hold of Egypt, did not succeed until 30 BCE, at the time of Anthony and Cleopatra. Before the arrival of Alexander, the Egyptians had decided to open themselves up a little to the Greeks from about 500 BCE onward—which explains why all of a sudden the Greeks knew everything (mathematics, geometry, geography, medicine). Pythagoras, for example, is reckoned to have spent twenty-five years in Egyptian temples being taught. He was not the only Greek to do so.

When the Romano-Christians killed the last Egyptian priests at the temple of Isis in 394 CE, all knowledge of hieroglyphs was lost to be rediscovered fifteen hundred years later in the nineteenth century, with the translation of the Rosetta stone by Frenchman Champollion. As a result, one means of accessing Egyptian wisdom and knowledge was soon forgotten. By the end of the fourth century CE, the Romano-Christians had symbolically and literally cut us off from the ancient past. Not surprising, then, that we knew nothing about the shamanic ritual of the pharaohs or the connections between megaliths and cities.

The Egyptians were especially keen that their secrets should not fall into Roman hands. The Romans were powerful enough as it was, but they never knew how to move the big stones. And if anyone still falls for the explanation that megaliths are moved by teams of slaves, then they need to consider the point that Rome was the ultimate in slave society and still couldn't move megaliths. The Romans *had* to invent the pulley and mortar for constructing their large buildings. Roman building is either smaller dressed stone or many bricks laid on a spectacular scale.

Roman Power

We might mistakenly think that the fourth-century massacre on the Island of Philae occurred because the Christianized Romans saw the light and realized the need to eliminate pagan practices. The truth is, however, that the Romans had been attacking pagans for years before they converted to Christianity.

The military campaigns that the Romans waged against pagans all had something in common: Those pagans all knew about aspects of the original archetype of civilization. The Romans threw out the Pythagoreans; they banned alchemy; they invaded Britain to destroy the Druids; they fought in central Turkey to destroy the Chaldean Magi; and they attacked the Essenes at Qumran on the Dead Sea. All this happened long before Christians infiltrated the Roman state.

Indeed, Constantine decided to adopt Christianity in the fourth century CE because he could see the political advantages of it. The Romans were used to uniting behind the glory of Rome, and now they could use religion and the one God as another tool of unification. This monotheistic religion then became a useful weapon for attacking those pagan pockets that had metaphysical secrets that were denied to the Romans. And so it was that the connections between megaliths, shamans, and cities were hidden for such a long time and perhaps needed to be—given that the knowledge was for peaceful purposes only. Alchemy was the missing link.

The secret knowledge did not entirely die out after Egypt collapsed but went up the trade routes, appropriately to the northern Euphrates to Harran, where it was kept alive by alchemists and a people known as the Sabians. The story of how we gradually began to reconnect with that hidden knowledge is explained in more detail in my book *Approaching Chaos*. I hope I have managed to give a brief overview of the connections between megaliths, shamans, and city builders—why they are hidden and why we have not realized them until now.

Notes

1. Steven Mithen, *After the Ice: A Global Human History 20,000–5,000 BC* (London: Phoenix, Orion Books, 2004), 36–37.

2. Jacquetta Hawkes, *The First Great Civilisations: Life in Mesopotamia, the Indus Valley and Egypt* (London: Hutchinson and Co., 1973).

3. Mithen, *After the Ice,* 432–34; and Charles Keith Maisels, *Early Civilisations of the Old World: The Formative Histories of Egypt, The Levant, Mesopotamia, India and China* (London: Routledge, 1999), 126.

4. Elizabeth Wayland Barber, *The Mummies of Urumchi* (London: Pan Books, 1999).

5. Jeremy Naydler, *Shamanic Wisdom in the Pyramid Texts* (Rochester, Vt.: Inner Traditions, 2005).

6. Mouni Sadhu, *The Tarot: A Contemporary Course in the Quintessence of Hermetic Occultism* (London: George Allen & Unwin, 1962).

7. Jeremy Narby, *The Cosmic Serpent, DNA and the Origins of Knowledge* (London: Phoenix, Orion Books, 1999).

8. Timothy Freke and Peter Gandy, *The Hermetica: The Lost Wisdom of the Pharaohs* (London: Piatkus, 1997).

SIX

Atlantis and the Cycles of Time

JOSCELYN GODWIN

Ever since Plato described his Atlantis, many authors have claimed to have found it. Some say it was in the Atlantic Ocean, with the Azores as its former mountain peaks. Others prefer the Mediterranean: Malta, Crete, Cyprus, Santorini, and Troy all have their champions. British Atlantologists find its legacy in Cornwall or the Irish Sea; Germans, in the sinking isle of Helgoland; Swedes, in Sweden. Some favor the Arctic, others the Antarctic. Still others turn to the New World, finding Atlantis in Cuba, San Domingo, Central America, Bolivia, even Wisconsin. All these authors must have finished their books with a serene smile and the certainty that they, and they alone, had put a stake through the heart of the matter. The fact that it now looks like a pincushion gives one pause. Since these theories cannot all be right, it is quite probable that many are wrong.

So I search for Atlantis in a different way. To begin, I see a wiser group that takes a global perspective. Rather than planting the Atlantean flag in a single location, it finds evidence in the worldwide "fingerprints of the gods" for a prehistoric seafaring culture, expert in mathematics and astronomy and given to moving large stones. Some of the particularists, to give them their due, find their place as contributors to this broader vision. Plato aside, each has found something of value and added in some way to knowledge of the distant past.

Anyone who keeps abreast of the "new archaeology" is well aware of all this. He or she may also have noticed that the new archaeology has a New Age aura about it. Among its prime movers, Colin Wilson is one of the most popular authors on occult traditions. John Anthony West has written a defense of astrology and an exposition of the Hermetic adept Schwaller de Lubicz. Graham Hancock writes about experiences with entheogens. Robert Bauval's theories touch equally on Hermetic doctrines of astral immortality. Robert Schoch is concerned with parapsychological research. However, their prime material is still the monuments themselves; their prime intent, to understand why they are as they are. The only explanation that satisfies them is that prehistoric peoples experienced states of being incomprehensible through the materialist paradigm. The reasonable course, then, is to try a different paradigm.

Another type of Atlantologist has been doing this all along, by taking a suprarational approach to the question of prehistoric high culture. It is wrong to call them irrational, because they do not reject reason. However, they consider other avenues of knowledge supplementary if not superior to it. The traditionally minded put their faith in scriptures and sacred authorities, while those open to the paranormal rely on intuition, initiation, clairvoyance, or mediumship. One might call them occultists, but only in the sense that they all claim access to knowledge that is "occulted" or hidden from the rationalists.

The occultists' Atlantis is a colorful and often beautiful tapestry, woven by visionaries, prophets, and receivers of divine revelation. But I cannot leave it at that. I want to turn the tapestry over to see how the knots are made, then snoop around in their workrooms.

One of the first facts to emerge is that there are distinct national schools. The first Atlantologists of the modern age were two Frenchmen of the Enlightenment—the astronomer Jean-Sylvain Bailly and the theosopher Fabre d'Olivet. Together, they launched a particularly French strain, carried onward by Saint-Yves d'Alveydre, Edouard Schuré, Papus (Gerard Encausse), René Guénon, and Paul le Cour. After World War II, this spawned a more popular genre with Louis Pauwels's and Jacques Bergier's *Morning of the Magicians,* the review *Planète,* and the books of Robert Charroux, who blended it with the ancient astronaut theory.

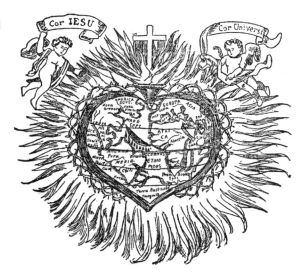

Figure 6.1. The heart crest, a representation of the French view of Atlantis, has a map at its center showing the location of the lost continent.

Gravure allemande de 1708.

The French Atlantologists tend to give information *ex cathedra,* keeping their sources to themselves, as though what they have to say about prehistory is obvious to any reasonable person. Reason does not exclude immaterial or even spiritual realities, but once these are accepted as part of the natural order of things, certain consequences follow. From the start, they envisaged prehistory in a context of the variously colored races (yellow, red, black, white), to which they attribute separate origins. Each arose on a different continent or, according to some, on a different planet. This is a constant of French occultism, together with the caution that no race is deemed superior or inferior to the others. One of the later writers, Jean Phaure, says that we are all of mixed blood, but "whether we are yellow, white, black, or red, we possess that fragment of the divine Spirit that makes us humans and not animals."[1]

The Germanic strain of Atlantology is rather different, and its earlier proponents have harmed our subject, and occultism in general, by association. The Ariosophists of the pre-Nazi era were racial supremacists, and their Atlantean theories conformed to that outlook. In 1904, Lanz von Liebenfels, a "new templar," set the trend in his *Theozoologie,* writing of how the tall, white race of Atlantis interbred with apes. The result was a hybrid race of "sodomitic apelings" that survived into classical times and left its genetic stain in almost all of us. Lanz's solution was a rigid eugenics program that would, in time, breed out the animal element, though he added that purified humanity would still need some subhuman creatures as slaves. Few of the Ariosophists veered so far toward the lunatic fringe as von Liebenfels, but none of them challenged his authority.

After the German defeat in World War I, Ariosophical doctrines were in place to comfort the battered German soul and hold out a glorious future for it. Here is one version of the myth, which I paraphrase from Hermann Wieland's *Atlantis, Edda und Bibel:* The Arctic region, where a temperate vegetation flourished, was home to the Aryans, a blond, blue-eyed, brachycephalic race. They lived there happily until a regularly recurring alteration of the earth's axis brought on an ice age, then were forced to migrate southward. Leaving their polar homeland, the Aryans settled on the island-continent of Atlantis, setting up a twelvefold nation that would later become the model for the zodiac and the divisions of time by hours and months. They were forbidden to kill animals and lived whenever possible as vegetarians, unlike the lower races who already inhabited the land and were little better than beasts themselves. The Edda and both Testaments of the Bible are really chronicles of the Aryans' history. Whenever the Bible speaks of Beasts, it refers to lower races, as do all the laws of Moses and injunctions of Jesus.[2]

Readers of my earlier book *Arktos: The Polar Myth in Science,*

Symbolism, and Nazi Survival will be familiar with much of this and with later developments.[3]

Germanic Atlantology also included some who were caught against their will in the maelstrom of events. Herman Wirth, for instance, was busy with his own theory of a prehistoric Arctic culture that left its symbols in petroglyphs throughout the circumpolar regions. Anticipating later anthropologists like Marija Gimbutas, Wirth believed that this was a matriarchal society and that the trouble began later with patriarchy and its aggressive monotheistic religions. Wirth was co-opted by the Ahnenerbe (the think tank of the Schutzstaffel or SS) because his theories superficially seemed to support the Nordic-Aryan myth, but he disappointed them. Himmler fired him, and Wirth was forbidden to publish for the remainder of the Third Reich.

One who managed to keep out of trouble was the little-known occultist known as Peryt Shou. His career spanned both world wars, during which he ran a small and secretive group, teaching methods

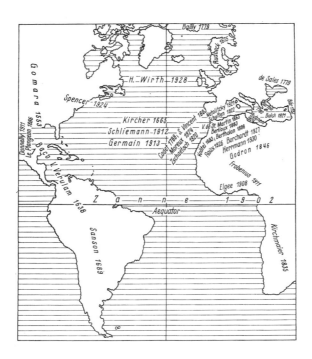

Figure 6.2. German map of the Atlantic

for regaining one's spiritual birthright through a mixture of astrology, posture, and mantra. He wrote two books on Atlantis and is probably the first to have seen any significance in the names Plato gives for the ten Atlantean kings. He analyzes them into their phonetic contents and tabulates their correspondences with star names, the Egyptian decans, the Sephiroth of the Kabbalah, the antediluvian patriarchs of Genesis, and the multiples and divisions of the "mother number" 432.[4]

Shou's object was to retrieve the spiritual awareness and autonomy that were lost with the fall of Atlantis. In his words, "Man forms himself, creates himself, for he possesses the divine guardian, the angel in his breast, who watches lest he thereby violate the divine law. . . . In the course of his development, man grew ever further from this primordial religion. He believed that the Godhead was there to care for him, and so he should entrust everything to it. . . .Through the Fall, man lost the right to free self-determination. He had to lean on God for everything and thereby forgot that God burned with its holiest rays in his own breast."[5]

After Germany's second defeat, anything occult was shunned owing to its associations, real or attributed, with the Third Reich. Rare exceptions were Rudolf Steiner's Anthroposophic movement, which was obviously innocent of any complicity with Nazism, and the Externsteine circle. This was founded in the 1960s by Walther Machalett, a schoolteacher enthralled by the genii loci (spirits of place) and by a theory of prehistoric geodesy (earth measurement). His scheme linked Atlantis and the pyramids with the Externsteine, an awe-inspiring natural formation in northwest Germany. Meeting each year on Ascension Day in the shadow of those towering rocks, the Machalett forum brings together psychics and engineers, scholars and eccentrics, in a nondogmatic exploration of prehistoric cultures and Earth mysteries.

Each of the major strains of occult Atlantology has its own style. The Germans are more indebted to theosophy and its concept of root races (see below), which the Ariosophists developed in one direction, the Anthroposophists in another. They almost never claim supersensible powers themselves but believe that such existed in ancient times and may be revived in the future. The third major national strain is the British, which differs from the French and German by its openness about its methods and the great variety of them.

From Britain, we have accounts of Atlantis from self-trained trance mediums (Dion Fortune, Margaret Lumley Brown); dictation by an inner voice (H. C. Randall-Stevens); visions of the past induced by meditating at an ancient site (Paul Brunton); open-eyed visions onsite by a medium (Olive Pixley); manuscripts made available during initiation into an arcane order (Lewis Spence); a discarnate entity who takes the subject on a tour (Daphne Vigers); the return of a well-known nineteenth-century medium (Mandasoran); another medium who acts as mouthpiece for his controlling entity (Anthony Neate); a person who has a single flash of inspired vision from which she develops a system (Katharine Maltwood); an enthusiast for outlandish theories who constructs his own eclectic model (Brinsley Le Poer Trench); and another whose enthusiasms lead to a geometric revelation of his own (John Michell). The variety of methods is matched by the variety of Atlantises thus received.

Besides these three principal strains, there are undoubtedly Russian Atlantologists, and certainly some scientific interest there and in Eastern Europe, but apart from Nicolas Zhirov and Zdeněk Kukal (who have been translated), these await researchers who know the relevant languages. In any case, to classify modern Atlantology by national schools overlooks the biggest contributor of all. None of the twentieth-century authorities, whatever their alleged sources, could avoid the influence of theosophy.

Modern theosophy has passed through two distinct eras, often mistaken for a single one. The earlier one is represented by the writings of H. P. Blavatsky and her contemporaries; the later, by Charles Webster Leadbeater and Annie Besant. Blavatsky made some remarks on Atlantis and prehistoric cultures in *Isis Unveiled* (1877), but it was

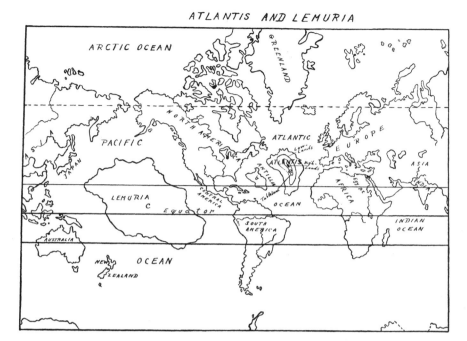

Figure 6.3. Map showing Atlantis and Lemuria

a series of letters signed by the Mahatmas Koot Hoomi and Morya that outlined the definitive scheme of human evolution from the occultist point of view. Blavatsky amplified it in *The Secret Doctrine* (1888), which chronicles five "root races" that have nothing to do with the colored races of French Atlantology but are large-scale stages of human evolution. They begin with humanity in an ethereal or gaseous state (the first two root races) and devolve through a gradual coagulation and division into sexes (the third, called Lemurian) into full physicality with the fourth root race (Atlantean). With the fifth (Aryan, our current state), we are on the long return journey to spiritualization.

In Blavatsky's scenario, every root race except the first suffered one or more cataclysms. Continents disappeared, new lands appeared, mountain chains rose. "The face of the Globe was completely changed each time; the *survival of the fittest* nations and races was secured through timely help; and the unfit ones—the failures—were disposed of by being swept off the Earth. Such sorting and shifting does not happen between sunset and sunrise, as one may think, but requires several thousands of years before the new house is set in order"[6] (italics in original). The immediate cause of these cataclysms was not an outside agency, such as a comet, but changes in the inclination of Earth's axis (another topic treated at length in *Arktos*).

As to the dating of these events, Blavatsky was aware that the most advanced scientists of her day allowed an age of Earth of 500 million years. Humanity is virtually coeval with the planet: the first root races appeared in the primordial and primary periods, the Lemurians in the secondary period (age of reptiles), and the Atlanteans in the tertiary period (age of mammals). There is no fossil evidence because early human bodies were not fully materialized. Most of Atlantis was destroyed 850,000 years ago, leaving a fragment that finally vanished as recorded by Plato. As for him, he was an initiate who was forbidden to tell the whole truth about the human past. "Aiming more to instruct as a moralist than as a geographer and ethnologist or historian, the Greek philosopher merged the history of Atlantis, which covered several million years, into one event which he located on one comparatively small island."[7]

After Blavatsky's death in 1891, the theosophists kept the basic structure of root races while seeking to improve on the details. They tended to move the Atlanteans closer to the present day so that they could be made responsible for Stonehenge and the pyramids. One such was Alfred Percy Sinnett, to whom the Mahatmas Koot Hoomi and Morya addressed their letters. After the correspondence ceased, he started his own private circle in which an entranced medium gave out further information. Sinnett's friend Leadbeater, in contrast, used his own clairvoyance to penetrate the distant past, the astral plane, past lives, and so on. The most popular book of occult prehistory, Walter Scott-Elliot's *Atlantis and the Lost Lemuria*, derives its Egyptian material from Sinnett's medium (whom Scott-Elliot married) and the rest from Leadbeater.

Scott-Elliot's book includes four maps of Atlantis, first published in 1896, which have been reproduced countless times since. Sinnett, in his preface, says that these maps come from "records physically preserved," and Scott-Elliot describes them as "a globe, a good bas-relief in terra-cotta, and a well-preserved map on parchment." From later sources, we learn that they are in Tibet, in the Museum of Records of the Great White Brotherhood, and that Leadbeater was given permission to visit it in his astral body and copy the maps there.

The Atlantis myth carries a powerful psychic charge and has served many groups and individuals in its manipulation of people's belief systems. I am not in the business of debunking, but I like to get to the bottom of tall tales like Scott-Elliot's maps. Other popular clichés would be James Churchward's *mu;* the last words of Jesus, reputedly spoken in "pure Mayan"; Katharine Maltwood's Glastonbury zodiac; the Lemurians of Mount Shasta; and the various Atlantean scenarios put out by Rosicrucian orders. By clearing away such growths, one has a better chance of tackling the genuine enigmas of human origins and evolution.

Whom, then, should we trust? I listen to them all: Rudolf Steiner; Alice Bailey; the ill-matched traditionalist couple of René Guénon and Julius Evola; the Avalonians from Dion Fortune to John Michell; the excruciating *Oahspe;* wily Gurdjieff's Beelzebub; Phylos the Tibetan, who starts the Mount Shasta business; Edgar Cayce; the "I AM" folk (see "The I AM Discources" by Guy Ballard); William Dudley Pelley of Silver Shirts fame; Maurice Doreal (Claude Doggins) with his Emerald Tablets; the teasing trio of George Adamski, Richard Shaver, and George Hunt Williamson; wise old Seth; tough old Ramtha (J. Z. Knight); James Merrill with his Ouija board—and quite a few others.

Am I laughing at them, or with them? It depends on the degree to which they were deliberately putting one over on their disciples or audiences. And having said that, who is meant by "they"? The channelers themselves, or whatever is communicating through them? Most channelers seem sincere: almost all of them started their careers unwillingly after a transcendent irruption into their lives. But I am suspicious of their sources, which, when they are not total bores, often seem to be stretching our credulity for their own amusement. Since they do not agree with one another, they cannot all be right: for example, they date the Great Pyramid at anything from 200,000 to 6,000 years ago. Yet each source has an amazing consistency and personality and a seemingly inexhaustible fund of knowledge.

In former times, possession by a god, demon, or spirit was the only explanation for this phenomenon. Once those were eliminated, it seemed that everything had to come from the channel's subconscious mind, or conscious fraud. I offer a lightly held alternative hypothesis. It combines Buddhist doctrine with the allegory of cyberspace and goes as follows: When sentient beings die, they release mental energies that may form congelations of intelligence, perhaps combining with other free-floating energies in resonance with them (note that in Buddhism no immortal soul exists to keep them together). These act like files containing a mishmash of information, memory, dogma, and speculation, ordered as in life by a logical program akin to language. Given a suitable recipient, they download into it, blending with the recipient's own information, beliefs, and so forth. The way it emerges—through trance, automatic writing, and so on—is merely a matter of style. This suggestion somewhat resembles the idea of the "egregore," a wandering influence that takes on a pseudopersonality and may be nourished by attention, belief, and sacrifice. But it does not hold out much hope for finding the truth about Atlantis.

If we are sincere in our desire for this, we have to face the mystery of time and its connection with human consciousness. To be brief, it is a question of whether sequential time exists at all outside our minds. The metaphysical doctrines of East and West suggest rather that time, like space, is part of the illusion inherent in human consciousness. We feel caught in its coils and rhythms, but from a higher point of view, past and future coexist. Some channeled communications do help us understand this and so does (I'm told) quantum physics. There is the further possibility that the Atlantis visited through clairvoyance, astral travel, or entheogens might be not in Earth's past but in a parallel and present universe.

Coming down to Earth, there is an idea that time proceeds not in a straight line but in cycles. There are two main schemes: the four ages or *yugas* and the astrological ages based on the precession of the equinoxes. The weightiest chapters of *Atlantis and the Cycles of Time* survey the origins and permutations of these theories. My object is to give the reader solid information, properly sourced, so that it is clear where the various claims come from and what assumptions (cosmological, historical, metaphysical) underlie them. For instance, Hindu orthodoxy puts us in the Kali Yuga, which began in 3102 BCE and lasts 432,000 years, getting worse all the time. Others reject these figures, especially the French traditionalists who have made time cycles their particular study. René Guénon, Alain Daniélou, Gaston Georgel, and Jean Phaure all come up with a reduced duration for the Kali Yuga of something over 6,000 years. Their calculations of its end date and the consequent return of the golden age vary: CE 1999, 2000, 2012, 2030, 2160, and 2442 are all mentioned.

There are also contrarian theories. Fabre d'Olivet reversed the yugas, convinced that the Kali Yuga was not the worst period but the best. Some Buddhists, Jains, and the modern guru Sri Yukteswar have them going alternately up and down, like a sine wave. Each of these conflicting theories needs to be examined for its roots and motives, rather than accepted on anyone's authority.

There is similar disagreement about the end of the age of Pisces and the dawning of the Aquarian age. The earliest date I have found is 1760, one of four dates suggested in Godfrey Higgins's *Anacalypsis*. The year 1881 was once a popular choice, seeming to agree with another cycle: that of the reigns of the seven archangels, which was part of the teachings of the Hermetic Brotherhood of Luxor.

Carl Jung took the trouble to consult astronomy and pointed out that dating the age of Aquarius depends on which star marks the beginning of the constellation. That gives a wide range, from 1997 to 2154, but the actual year does not matter much: it was the whole period of transition that interested him.

Calculating the Aquarian age also depends on whether you take the traditional precessional number, 25,920 years, giving 2,160 years for each age, or whether, like Jung, you follow the current scientific estimate of about 25,770. Furthermore, you may divide it into twelve ages according to the astrological constellations, which are exactly 30 degrees each, or the astronomical ones, which are of unequal length and whose borders may shift along with the proper motion of their component stars.

To put the final wrench in the precessional machinery, many traditional texts assert that Earth's axis used to be perpendicular to the ecliptic, so that in former times there was no precession and no seasons. Some connect this with the golden age and with human habitation in polar or arctic lands. If precession is a recent phenomenon, large-scale cyclical theories based on its invariance are null and void.

All of this may seem mean-spirited, for it undermines many cherished assumptions, but that is not the case. There is a positive joy in this kind of research. The material is philosophically challenging, the parade of characters fascinating. Some of them may be rogues, paranoiacs, deluded and deluding, but what else do we find in profane history? This study, like

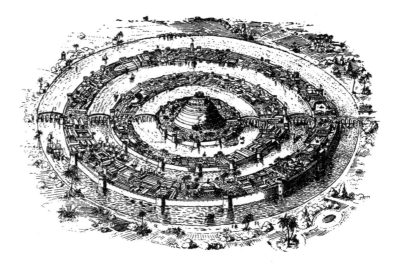

Figure 6.4. City of Atlantis

no other, stretches the imagination over all of space, from Mediterranean islands through crustal shifts and crashing moons, right up to the center of the galaxy. It ranges over all of time, from the dawn of the historical period back to the birthday of this present Earth. And as we reimagine the past, so we help to form our future.

Notes

1. Jean Phaure, *Le cycle de l'humanité adamique* (Paris: Dervy, 1988), 273–74.

2. Herrmann Wieland, *Atlantis, Edda und Bibel* (Weissenburg, Germany: Roland facsimile Bremen, 2001).

3. Joscelyn Godwin, *Arktos: The Polar Myth in Science, Symbolism, and Nazi Survival* (Kempton, Ill.: Adventures Unlimited, 1996).

4. Peryt Shou, *Esoterik der Atlantier in ihrer Beziehung zur aegyptischen, babylonischen und jüdischen Geheimlehre* (Leipzig: Theosophisches Verlagshaus, 1913), 40–42, 59–61.

5. Peryt Shou, *Atlantis: Das Schicksal der Menschheit* (Germany: Schleierwelten-Verlag, 2008), 78.

6. H.-P. Blavatsky, *The Secret Doctrine,* vol. 2 (London: Theosophical Publishing Co., 1888), 636–37.

7. Ibid., 760–61.

SEVEN

Bring Back the Sun

GREGORY SAMS

Imagine living in a culture where people spent more time deciding what brand, color, and flavor of condom to buy than they do considering prospective candidates and the act of sex itself. Something would be out of balance. Yet, we live in a culture where most people will have spent more time in their lives contemplating which style of sunglasses to purchase than they will have spent contemplating the most important thing in those lives, the sun itself. Something is out of balance.

It was once absolutely common to give the sun a great deal of thought, respect, and appreciation. Many of the greatest monuments that survive from ancient civilizations were built to honor the sun. Yet we are raised with the built-in assumption that ancient people were primitive and uncivilized savages. As modern researchers such as Graham Hancock and Michael Cremo have clearly shown, nothing could be further from the truth. Though in many ways we now enjoy an advanced technology to that which existed thousands of years ago, it is not so certain that our understanding of the cosmos and our spiritual development have advanced at the same pace.

Many modern researchers have explored what remains of the civilization of ancient Egypt, recognizing the cosmological alignment of ancient pyramids and calculating where their shafts would have originally pointed toward in the night sky. Others have studied the Mayan calendar and been amazed at the understanding it displays of solar and stellar activities taking place tens of thousands of years earlier. Tens of thousands make the pilgrimage to Stonehenge every summer solstice to touch and absorb the energy of the hallowed stones of this Celtic monument. We acknowledge our social and scientific debt to the ancient Greeks, whose rediscovered knowledge helped fuel the Renaissance and lift Europe out of the Dark Ages.

Yet as we explore the history of these cultures, we all too easily overlook the one underlying principle common to the Egyptians, Maya, Celts, and Greeks, not to mention the Sumerians, Chaldeans, Assyrians, gnostics, Khmer, Norse, Inca, Aztecs, natives of South and North America, and countless other cultures throughout the world, including today's Hindu and Shinto religions. This is the recognition that our local star is a conscious entity—a celestial being. It remains one of the most powerful and unspoken taboos of the Western world and one that even modern researchers of the above cultures are often reluctant to breach.

Many of us have finally let go of the biblical mind-set that placed humans on planet Earth as the be-all and end-all and raison d'etre of God and the universe. Since 1975, we have been seeking other intelligences across the galaxy, looking for telltale radio signals, incorporating technology that enlists the brainpower of idle computers throughout the world. Though I quietly came to the realization that there was intelligence in residence at our local star in 1966, I only really "came out" on the subject when talk about the search for extraterrestrial intelligence (SETI) came up. I would then feel compelled to point out that this search was being conducted in complete ignorance of the most intelligent character in the neighborhood—our local star. And no special tools or techniques are required to spot this one—just an open mind that has let go of an old taboo. It should really be called SSLU—the search for something like us.

Our culture is infused with the notion that the sun worship once practiced throughout the world was born out of ignorance. When SETI got me going on the subject, I would often get "Are you kidding?" and "Who is this crazy man?" looks—just the sort of looks that my brother and I received in the 1960s when introducing people in Britain to the radical freaky notion that what we ate affected our health and well-being. This unfounded assumption came up recently on a Sunday morning spiritual radio program when I was asked, "But they were primitive then. Don't we know better now?" That is an interesting question, and I must reply with a question: Is there anything we know today, from the latest in solar science and astronomy, to physics and quantum mechanics, that has any bearing on the issue of solar consciousness?

We will return to that question later, but we first must ask what we know about our own consciousness that would assist us in the evaluation of whether such a phenomenon could exist elsewhere, whether in bacteria or thousand-year-old trees, in volcanoes or stars.

What is this stuff that we are forever talking about raising or lowering? What is this quality that distinguishes our complex body with being alive and vital? What do we know about *this*?

We know that many scientists actually doubt its existence. Since they have no tools with which to weigh it or measure it, and there seems to be no formula that can express consciousness, this group finds no alternative but to deny its existence. They believe consciousness to be an illusion that is constructed by our brain to gain some, as yet undetermined, evolutionary advantage. Some in this "grand illusion" camp have a corollary to their belief, which is that human beings have no free will and that every single thing we do or think (every rhyme, each wink and stink) is somehow predetermined by the arrangement of particles immediately after the big bang.

For scientists who do acknowledge the existence of consciousness, it was assumed, until very recently, that human beings were the only vessel that it could possibly inhabit. Nothing else was deemed to be aware of its own existence, or functioning on anything other than the level of a biological machine driven by nothing more than the need to propagate the species. Descartes had a lot to do with this, but now a debate is going on, as some scientists devise tests for consciousness, such as recognizing yourself in a mirror or playing for no apparent reason other than to have fun. This camp is arguing that orangutans and dolphins and a handful of other species, mainly primates, might just share this rare facility.

But scientists are not getting very far, perhaps not trying very hard, in understanding what consciousness is or from whence it arises. And that isn't surprising, considering what a tricky word it is to define— right up there with *God* and *infinity*. There is no accepted standard definition for consciousness. Mystics and philosophers have devoted entire books to it or summed it up with the two words: *consciousness is*.

Without the need for proof or measurement, we know of our own consciousness because we feel its existence. It was enough for ancient civilizations to know of solar consciousness because they felt its existence. I do not suggest that because we feel something it is true. But when a near universal belief is sustained for thousands of years, it merits consideration. It does not matter which continent we look at, or which century, or which culture. Our pre-Christian ancestors believed that their basic intuition was correct, notwithstanding any explanations and baggage that might thereafter have been added to the picture by organizing priests.

We might well experience this connection to solar consciousness intuitively when, as children, we put smiling faces on drawings of the sun. But by the time we leave school, there is little hint of it left, as we adopt the "we know better now" attitude. Which brings us back to that question of just what it is that we now know better. And who were the original "we" that we know better than? Is it science that has taught us that sun worship was primitive and irrational?

If we could have told a Mayan or Egyptian sun worshipper about the fusion reaction in the core of the sun, described the very different functions of the next six layers, and explained the corona and the solar wind that spins from it, his or her jaw would have dropped in delighted awe. Our science would give that worshipper greater cause to revere the character bringing light and the power of life to our Earth. The knowledge of anatomy does not diminish our living status.

Was it the church that told us sun worship was primitive and irrational? Yes. They knew better because the Old Testament told them so. They had it on God's authority, written in his own book, that the sun was just a convenient ball of light placed in the heavens for the benefit of humankind. And since most of the religions that had been replaced by the new church were big on sun worship, it was very much not OK to persist with such ideas. Neither philosophers, scientists nor variants of Christianity were excluded from papal control of such thinking.

The Christianity of the Cathars, influenced by Mary Magdalene's transmission of Christ's teachings, incorporated sun gazing and elements of solar appreciation into its practice. This, and other unauthorized deviations from Catholic creed, prompted the Vatican to organize twenty years of the brutal Albigensian Crusade (1209–1229) and to create the dreaded Inquisition, dedicated to eliminating every last trace of the Cathars religion and its followers.

Nearly four centuries later, in 1593, they were again alarmed, this time by the teachings of one Giordano Bruno. Copernicus who came before, and Galileo who came later, recognized that the sun and planets did not revolve around Earth, believing instead that the whole universe revolved around the sun. Unlike them, Bruno also recognized that our sun was but one of countless stars populating an infinite universe. He also recognized that the sun and stars were all living beings—still something of a blind spot for modern astronomers. He was lured back to Italy, arrested by the Inquisition, and imprisoned for seven years, during which time he refused to recant, even under torture. When finally sentenced to death, he responded to the judges: "Perhaps you, my judges, pronounce this sentence upon me with greater fear than I who receive it." His tongue was tied before he was tied to the stake, lest he try to spread his inflammatory ideas to the assembled crowd.

The scientific aversion to considering the question of solar consciousness stems, in essence, not from solar experimentation, technical investigation, or application of the scientific method. It stems from little more than habit, and a religious habit at that.

Obviously, we are not going to be able to apply our normal consciousness tests to the sun, with mirrors, questionnaires, and analysis of playfulness. But we can take a look at what solar scientists have been able to find using telescopes, helioseismology, spectral analysis, and some pretty brilliant thinking and deduction. I am not in the business of knocking scientists or their discoveries, but I am intolerant of the unfounded taboos that most of them embrace and to which all of them must conform, or face ridicule.

Let us take a very cursory look at a few features of the sun's seven distinct levels, to see if these are the sorts of features you would expect to find in an inanimate, unintelligent, accidental agglomeration of simple matter. And the sun's matter, in common with over 99 percent of matter in the universe, is not in the simple states of solid, liquid, or gas with which we are familiar on this planet. Most matter does not have an even balance of electrons and protons and is thus highly fluid and conductive to the transmission of electromagnetic energy. Plasma is very active. Those plasma gas balls that are sold for visual home entertainment almost look like living things.

The hot inner *core* is where the nuclear fusion reaction takes place, converting five million tons of the sun's mass into energy each second. This reaction has been going on steadily for some 4.5 billion years and is estimated to have at least as long a future. With the equivalent of billions of hydrogen bombs going off every second, some containment around this first layer of the sun is obviously necessary. This second level takes the form of the *radiation zone,* a region of very dense matter that is twenty-five times as thick as Earth's diameter. Traveling at the speed of light, a photon would pass through this layer of the sun in about one second, but they have to bounce around a bit on the journey outward, and it takes them more like a million years to make the transit. Photons enter this zone as deadly gamma rays vibrating at high frequency and

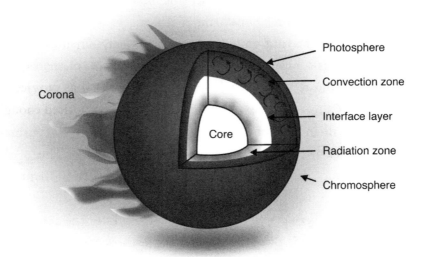

Figure 7.1. The sun's core

low wavelength and exit it as safe visible light—the stuff that reaches our planet and sustains all life.

Outside the radiation zone is the third, and relatively thin, *interface layer,* described as being like giant twisting ropes of electromagnetic energy. It is thought to be here that electromagnetic energy is produced to power the sun's invisible outermost seventh layer, the corona—about which more later. This energy is believed to be generated by the differential rotation of the *convection zone,* which surrounds the radiation zone and turns at a different speed, producing a dynamo-like effect.

Huge bubbles of charged matter carry the photons from the core through the convection zone to the photosphere with a fractal turbulence compared to that of water in a fast boiling kettle. While the density of the plasma at the beginning of the radiation zone is that of gold, by the time we reach the convection zone, the density is that of water. It will emerge into the next level in about a week, where the density of the sun is now far thinner than Earth's outer atmosphere.

At just 100 to 300 kilometers deep, the visible outer surface of the sun is relatively as thin as an onion skin. The *photosphere* provides the setting or base for many of the sun's most visible, intriguing, and dramatic features, from sunspots to solar flares, coronal mass ejections to coronal prominences. Isaac Newton was the first to spot sunspots and track their activity. Records have been kept ever since of their cyclical, though inconsistent, nature. Solar scientists are still as puzzled as Newton was by their meaning and mechanism, but have noticed enough of a correspondence with coronal activity to believe that they are managed or controlled by the corona. The same is thought to be the case with flares, coronal mass ejections, and prominences, each of them fascinating and powerful events that defy any straightforward explanation.

We have burst forth from the light-producing core and bumbled through the light-processing radiation zone, twisted through the electrical interface layer, bubbled through the seething convection zone, and shot out of the photosphere, adding another spark to the universe. We have not reached the outer levels of the sun, but already it seems curious to believe that such structured, complex, coordinated, and sustained activity is all going on by accident with nary a drop of intelligence involved. Were solar scientists to step outside the bounds of their religiously rooted taboo, I strongly suspect that they would recognize this complex and energy-rich assembly of active plasma to be another life-form and quite probably one higher than us.

I have rushed through describing the processes taking place in the five inner layers of the sun to give more space in this article to explaining the energetic outer level. The temperature of the sun progressively drops as photons travel from a 15-million-degree core to the 5,800-degree photosphere. We would expect the temperature to drop even further as we travel outward from the surface into the coldness of space. But instead, the temperature rises—one of many unexplained aspects of solar behavior. The "atmosphere" of the sun is so thin in matter content that it would be considered a near vacuum by our standards, but it is rich in energy and activity.

The lower level of the sun's atmosphere, the *chromosphere,* is populated by what look like long thin needles or jets of red light shooting upward at high speed. First spotted in 1851, they are called *spicules,* and there have been various theories as to what they are. The big bubbles of the convection zone may be sending sound waves into the chromosphere, powering their upward trajectory at supersonic speeds. One must wonder about the purpose of this activity in the system of a living sun. At the top of the irregular chromosphere, the temperature has jumped from 5,800 to 20,000 degrees, and at the other end of the wafer-thin transition to the outer atmosphere, the heat runs to a million degrees.

Now we reach the least understood feature of the sun, and perhaps, its crowning glory. The energy-rich and matter-light *corona* is bigger than the sun's physical "body," stretching two or three million kilometers into space. Temperatures have become hundreds of times hotter, ranging from 1 to 5 million degrees Kelvin. Why hasn't the heat emanating from sun's surface just dissipated into the cold surrounding space? Scientists still struggle to understand why this is.

The corona is an invisible electromagnetic phenomenon, but the power of its activity and associated events are awesome. It only manifests during a total solar eclipse, as even 1 percent of sun's light will completely overwhelm that of its corona. What we see at this moment is its eponymous crownlike shape outlined by light released by free electrons streaming off the sun, excited by the corona's powerful magnetic field lines. Its shape is not constant, changing along with the sunspot cycle on the photosphere. Although solar scientists hold it responsible for many of the sun's features, they describe the corona as the most mysterious feature of the sun. Interesting.

While scientists grapple with the very real difficulties of explaining the nature and existence of the sun's corona, permit me to hypothesize about the possible relevance of this fascinating phenomenon. Perhaps the invisible corona is the most important feature of the sun—that to which all else is geared and that which is responsible for some of its most far-reaching effects. It is difficult to resist the temptation to compare aspects of a living conscious sun to our own existence, relating its fusion-reactor core to our own heart or its chromosphere full of spicules to our seeing apparatus. But it is, of course, a completely different nature of being, and in some respects, one might as well be looking for the nose of a cauliflower or the nipples of a trout.

It does seem reasonable, though, to look for the mind of a conscious sun, and here, I suggest, one need look no further than its corona (see plate 4). Like our own mind, the corona is essentially an invisible extension of the sun. As with the force lines of a magnet, all we can ever see is the effect of the corona on particles that are in its presence. Some scientists will no doubt continue to debate the existence of a human mind until tools are developed sensitive enough to register and measure it. In the perfect darkness of a total solar eclipse, does it not seem likely that we are witnessing the image of a mind infinitely more powerful than our own—without the need for any special tools?

We will leave the sun now, hitching a ride out on the solar wind, a rarefied stream of charged particles that spins from the corona at speeds of 300 to 900 kilometers per second. As the sun turns, the solar wind twists into a huge spiraling electromagnetic bubble called the *heliosphere,* which holds the entire solar system in its embrace, cushioning its planets from the potentially disruptive effects of cosmic rays. Isn't that thoughtful?

Recognition of the sun and other stars as living beings changes the way we look at everything, not just galaxies and a universe awash with them, but everything from subatomic particles up to light itself. Could there be similarities on different scales between the 100-plus-billion neurons in own brains and the 100-plus-billion stars in our galaxy, all of them sending electromagnetic signals in the direction of their neighbors? How do molecules of water become a thundercloud hurling bolts of lightning earthward? Can a tree be tickled by the ripple of a breeze, an ocean know its currents' flow, a mountain feel its majesty? How could clouds of hydrogen and helium atoms assemble into something as complex and finely tuned as a light-producing star?

Could energy have been the original raw material of matter? And is it energy that holds it all together? Is it, too, the architect? For us, it is energy that provides the spirit of life. Without energy, we do not live or think. Without energy, there is nothing that we call living left. Yet, we are brought up with the assumption that it is us who brings life to energy, and not the other way around.

Why do so many of our linguistic expressions for intelligence rely on light-related words, using phrases and terms as we *shed light on the matter,* enabling us to *see the light,* after which we may be *illuminated on the subject, in the light of* the *brilliant* new insights gained from the *dazzling* ideas of the *bright* author of an article on *enlightenment*? Isn't it *delightful*?

Why are there so many questions? Perhaps it is because we are curious. An open and curious mind drove and directed me along the journey of seven years that was the writing of *Sun of gOd.* The solar path led in many directions, illuminating an unexpectedly coherent whole as the book progressed. Within its pages, the dogma has been stripped from science and the faith removed from religion to reveal the compatibility of ancient beliefs with cutting-edge science.

Relieved of its unfounded antispirit prejudice, science can help us to recognize a universe that is designed from the bottom up, not the top down. This universe is intelligent and well designed without needing an intelligent designer pulling all the strings behind the scenes. *Sun of gOd* underwrites the ancient wisdom of "all is one" in a refreshing and up-to-date manner, neither rejecting science nor relying on revelation to make the point.

Today's marvelous technology enables us to probe the far reaches of the universe and to wonder on the mysteries of matter at a quantum level. Yet, we have still to rediscover the most elemental aspect of our sun, the most important character in our lives, even though no technology is required. Like us, it is alive. And the knowledge of that improves forever our relationship with the universe.

EIGHT

Was Our Solar System Designed to Produce Humans?

CHRISTOPHER KNIGHT AND ALAN BUTLER

It is strange where research can lead you. More than a decade has passed since we joined forces to try and find out if there was any reality to a claim that highly accurate units of length had been in use during the British Neolithic. We found that these supposedly primitive people were using a highly developed science that connected them to the rhythms of Earth.

This led us on to realize that the science used by these Neolithic people did not die out as we first assumed. In our most recent book, *Before the Pyramids,* we uncovered rock-solid evidence that the powers that be in Washington, D.C.—in the White House, the U.S. military, and the highest levels of the Scottish Rite of Freemasonry—are aware of and secretly celebrating this ancient system of science.

But our biggest personal challenge has been to face up to the consequences of our own findings; because they have brought us to the point where we have found compelling evidence that our planet and its environment have been carefully designed for us. Stranger still, there appears to be a message built into the very fabric of the solar system itself.

This was not a finding that we had looked for, or even cared for. We are very pragmatic people working in an area of ancient research that is specialized and very sober. Here was an idea that was apparently outrageous—but apparently inescapable.

In early 2009, we had decided to revisit all our findings, which had resulted in three joint books plus one still in manuscript form (now published). We were troubled because, despite one of us being an agnostic and the other an atheist, we could not escape the conclusion that we were looking at a message from what we called the UCA (unknown creative agency) that had designed our solar system and all life on Earth.

Then in late November 2009, we were contacted by David Cumming, an expert in AI (artificial intelligence), who had studied our evidence in great detail and independently come to the same conclusion. He claimed that it formed an equation with a very clear message from the creator.

That equation has been refined to:

$$\frac{Hl_f.1}{\Omega} = C_0$$

We describe the mathematics at the end of this article, but the important point is this:

$Hlf.\pi$ is the specification of the SETI (search for extraterrestrial intelligence) communications frequency for extraterrestrial messages based on a galactic aspect of the hydrogen atom. This shouts, "Pay attention—this is a message." Omega (Ω) represents the numerals of the base ten counting system. The equation states "ten-fingered humans I am talking to you."

The left-hand side of the equation equals the right-hand side, which is the speed of light in a vacuum measured in Thoms per second (harmonic units of Earth, moon, sun harmonic). This says, "The message is from the creator"—because the speed of light is the most significant physical reality in the universe.

Is this credible? The facts behind it certainly are. But we thought we should go back to retrace some of our key findings over the years to help you decide.

The Origin of the Megalithic Yard

The starting point of our joint research was simply to consider whether Alexander Thom had been right or wrong in his identification of a prehistoric unit he called the megalithic yard. He was a professor of engineering at Oxford University who surveyed British and French megalithic sites over the course of half a century until he died in 1985. Thom's approach was entirely different to that adopted by any archaeologist. Looking at the scale and obvious planning involved in megalithic sites, Thom had been forced to conclude that the planners and builders must have been highly skilled engineers—just like himself. He, therefore, carefully analyzed what remained of each megalithic site and then tried to imagine what it was the builders had set out to achieve. Once he had a picture in his mind of what he thought their plan had been, he went away to create his own solution to the assumed problem. Having drawn up his own design, he then returned to compare the site layout to his own blueprint. He deduced that the builders had all been working to a common set of units based on his megalithic yard that was 2.722 feet plus or minus 0.002 feet (829.7 mm plus or minus 0.5 mm).

Thom was viewed as an unwelcome outsider by nearly all archaeologists, and even today most believe, quite erroneously, that he has been proved largely wrong.

Our starting hypothesis was that, if the megalithic yard were real, then it is highly probable that its apparent accuracy can best be explained by it being derived from nature rather than an invented unit. If we could identify a natural origin, then Thom was probably right; if we couldn't, the debate will continue because it is impossible to prove a negative.

It did not take too long for us to realize that there is only one aspect of nature that delivers up a near-perfect means of creating measures, and that is the revolving of Earth on its axis—something it does every 86,164 seconds. This provides the potential for creating a unit of time, which can then be used to make units of length, weight, and capacity—and potentially everything else from frequency to temperature.

The most obvious way to observe the turning of Earth is to watch the stars, which appear to pass overhead once for each rotation. They also move across the sky in an annual rotation due to Earth's orbit of the sun. Megalithic astronomers could not help but notice that there were 366 daily star movements to one annual one.

To create a repeatable linear unit from the turning of Earth, the only tools one needs is a length of rope, a few poles, a ball of clay, and a piece of string.

We knew that ancient peoples from all across time have liked to create patterns in which the same values work upward and downward. And we had good reason to believe that early peoples had used a 366-day calendar and a 366-degree circle. These astronomers knew that there are 366 star rises (any star such as Sirius) over one circle of the sun, so it was logical to divide the horizon into 366 parts to measure the time in 1/366 part of a day.

They measured time in the same way that all clocks did until recent times—with a pendulum. A handheld ball of clay on a string is a perfect instrument. When stationary, it is a plumb line to gauge verticals, and when swinging, its beats measure time with great accuracy. The only factors that have any significant effect on the beat are the length of the pendulum from fulcrum to the centerline of the weight and the mass of Earth (gravity). The energy put into the swing by the user has no effect; if the swing is made more vigorous, it just swings faster in a wider arc but the rate of beat remains exactly the same.

Our first and most obvious assumption was that the megalithic people had divided the horizon up into 366 equal parts and then used a pendulum length that beat 366 times.

This proved to be spot on. A pendulum that beats 366 times during one 366th of Earth's turn was, much to our joy and amazement, half a

Figure 8.1. A basic pendulum is a very accurate tool to measure time.

megalithic yard in length! A circle scribed by such a pendulum would have a diameter of one megalithic yard. Archie Roy, emeritus professor of astronomy at Glasgow University (and a friend of the late Alexander Thom), joined us to give a public demonstration of how the megalithic yard is a product of measured observational astronomy.

Figure 8.2. A frame 1/366th of the horizon angled to time a star

We later refined the timing method, having realized that the megalithic astronomers had improved their own accuracy by using the movement of the planet Venus at certain times rather than a star. Gordon Freeman, a distinguished professor of chemical physics and a much published amateur archaeologist specializing in megalithic structures was impressed with this saying: "Tying the my [megalithic yard] to Venus path arcsecond is a major discovery. I'm an admirer of Thom, but was neutral about the my. Now I'm a convert."

Alexander Thom had been right all along because the chances of this technique producing a perfect fit for his unit could not be a coincidence. But there was more—much more to this system. Given that the builders of these megalithic sites some five thousand years ago used a 366-degree circle caused us to look at Earth itself. Taking the polar circumference as the text-book 40,000,000 meters, we turned it into megalithic units and discovered the following:

- Earth's polar circumference   =   40,000,000 meters
- 1 megalithic degree (1/366)   =   109,290 meters
- 1 megalithic minute of arc (1/60)   =   1,822 meters
- 1 megalithic second of arc (1/6)   =   303.6 meters

Now, 303.6 meters for a second of arc may look a little boring, but it is 366 megalithic yards. The actual figure is 829.5 mm, which fits nicely with Alexander Thom's definition of 829.7 plus or minus 0.5 mm.

We now call this beautifully geodetic unit from the 366 system a Thom to differentiate it from the arguably very slightly less accurate megalithic yard.

The megalithic second of arc appears to have been adopted by the Minoan culture of Create some four thousand years ago. The palaces of Crete were carefully surveyed by Canadian archaeologist J. W. Graham, who identified a standard unit he called the Minoan foot, which was 30.36 cm. It follows that one thousand of these feet make precisely one megalithic second of arc—a decimalized version of what was already an ancient measure.

Even earlier, the Egyptian culture had adopted units driven by the same thinking. They took the megalithic yard and made it the circumference of a circle. The diameter of that circle was called a royal cubit, and the hypotenuse of a square from that diameter was called a *remen*.

Artifact-based Evidence

When we wrote *Civilization One,* we stated that the people who created the megalithic yard must have built very large circles and divided the circumference into 366 parts to be sure that they were viewing 1/366 part of the night sky. We suggested that they may well have understood a quick method to do this by making a circle with a diameter of 233 units (any length would do if they didn't already have a megalithic yard). They then knew that they would have a circle of 732 units, which is twice 366; so they could take every other pole on the circumference. This is a 99.999 percent accurate means of using pi in a practical manner. For all engineering purposes, this means perfect.

Several years later, we found that structures even older than the megalithic structures demonstrated the use of the 233/732 circles—exactly as we had predicted. These are henges—large circular mounds such as the group near Thornborough in North Yorkshire, England. They were built around 3500 BCE, well before the megalithic builders began their stonework phase. What is more they were using the megalithic yard, or the Thom, as we now call the geodetically refined value of the same length. At Thornborough, there are three interlinked henges that are 233 Thoms across and 732 Thoms around their outer perimeter. These structures with units and ratios are about 366 megalithic rods between the centers of the first two and 360 between the second. The trio, which are also exactly three megalithic seconds of arc apart by latitude, have also been identified as being laid out as a copy of the stars of Orion's Belt—exactly like the Giza pyramids (see plate 5). The difference is that these are a thousand years older. We also explain in *Before the Pyramids* how Khufu's pyramid builders came to this location in England to get instructions on how to plan this star pattern on the ground!

Weights and Measures

Having established that the people of the British Neolithic had units of lengths and time, we wondered if they had other units, such as capacity and weight. We knew (or so we thought) that the metric system was devised by the French in the late eighteenth century when they used a pendulum that beat at the rate of one second to create a unit they called the meterre (meaning to beat out time). They later made a very small adjustment so that their meter was 1/10,000,000 of the distance from the equator to the North Pole. To create a unit of capacity they took a 1/10 part of the meter (10 cm) and made a cube. Filled with distilled water, this cube's capacity was called a liter, and its weight was designated a kilogram.

We applied the same logic to the megalithic yard (which Alexander Thom said was divided into forty megalithic inches). So we calculated what a four-megalithic-inch cube would contain. The answer is one pint—to an accuracy of one part in five thousand as defined by the British government in 1601. And when carefully filled with any unpolished grain, such as barley, it weighed just one imperial pound.

This was odd in the extreme, but it appears that (unknown to history) Imperial units were indeed based on cubes because doubling the sides of the cube to eight megalithic inches is equivalent to one imperial gallon and doubling again produced a unit equivalent to a bushel, which was used as a dry weight until recent times.

Next, we found some truly bizarre connections. We thought for thoroughness that we ought to consider the volumes of spheres with megalithic dimensions in addition to the cubes, and a 6-megalithic-inch sphere held a liter and a 1.5-megalithic-yard-wide sphere of water weighs a metric ton. The level of accuracy was not spot on, but at a level of 99 percent fit, we were surprised, to put it mildly.

We are used to modern measurements that are ad hoc, but the 366 system works in depth. Take just two examples:

1. Earth mass
    * 1 megalithic degree (1/366) slice of Earth $= 360 \times 10^{20}$ pounds
    * 1 megalithic minute slice of Earth $= 6 \times 10^{20}$ pounds
    * 1 megalithic second slice of Earth $= 10^{20}$ pounds

2. Temperature (hypothetical scale)
    * Water freezes at 0 degrees
    * Water boils at 366 degrees
    * Absolute zero at −1,000 degrees

The Sumerian Meter

It is well known that the Sumerian culture had a 360-degree circle and a 360-day year. They knew perfectly well that this was wrong and that there are 366 star turns in a complete year, but it made their system of numerical notation and they built in compensation. They also invented the hour, the minute, and the second—or at least they are the earliest people to be known to have used it. (In fact we now know that the second of time was in use in the British Isles at least 2,500 years before the Sumerians adopted it.)

The Mesopotamian cultures, at various times, used a range of linear measurements, depending on the item being measured, but there is a general consensus that a linear unit known as the *kush* or barley cubit was the main unit of length for during Sumerian times.

The kush was made up of 180 *se*, meaning barley seed, and was equivalent to 49.94 cm and the often-used double kush, which Professor Livio Stecchini stated that he believed should be 99.88 cm. It follows that this double kush was made up of 360 se, just as their year had 360 days and their circle 360 degrees. It is no coincidence that the double kush is almost identical to the modern meter because they were both based on a pendulum that swings at the rate of once a second.

The Sumerians and later cultures of the region around the Tigris and Euphrates rivers used a sexadecimal counting system of base tens and sixties. Their divisions of time were very neat, indeed:

Year	=	360 days
Month	=	360 hours
Day	=	360 *gesh* (a gesh was 4 minutes or 240 seconds)

Each of the Sumerian hours represented 1 degree of the moon's journey around Earth and every degree of the moon's journey was split again, by 60 to give minutes of the arc and by 60 again to give seconds of the arc.

Today, we use seconds to measure many things, including the speed of light, which is 299,792,458 meters per second. If we change that to kush per second, we get the amazingly round figure of 600,000,000—which is a beautiful sexadecimal value (99.95 percent accuracy).

The Jefferson Paradox

Thomas Jefferson, one of the Founding Fathers of the United States, was an amazing polymath. He set out to create a new system of units for his fledgling country, which—apart from the dollar—were never adopted. He started by looking at what means nature provided for producing a repeatable unit, and like us, he quickly identified the spinning of Earth. Furthermore, he used a pendulum that beat at the rate of once per second as his starting point, completely unaware of its ancient origins. He recorded the following statement:

> A pendulum, vibrating freely, in small and equal arcs, may be so adjusted in its length, as, by its vibrations, to make this division of the earth's motion into 86,400 equal parts, called seconds of mean time. Such a pendulum, then, becomes itself a measure of determinate length, to which all others may be referred to as a standard.[1]

Jefferson also carefully looked at the units of measure from Europe, and he was surprised to find that they were not in the least haphazard as generally thought. He wrote:

> This seems to have been so combined as to render it indifferent whether a thing were dealt out by weight or measure; for the dry gallon of wheat, and the liquid one of wine, were of the same weight; and the avoirdupois pound of wheat, and the troy pound of wine, were of the same measure.

Another remarkable correspondence is that between weights and measures. For 1000 ounces avoirdupois of pure water fill a cubic foot, with mathematical exactness.[2]

He was bemused by the obvious science that lay hidden behind old measure:

> What circumstances of the times, or purposes of barter or commerce, called for this combination of weights and measures, with the subjects to be exchanged or purchased, are not now to be ascertained. But a triple set of exact proportionals representing weights, measures, and the things to be weighed and measured, and a relation so integral between weights and solid measures, must have been the result of design and scientific calculation, and not a mere coincidence of hazard.[3]

Jefferson concluded that some very ancient but long-forgotten science was behind these unexpected correspondences. He concluded: "but the harmony here developed in the system of weights and measures . . . from very high antiquity."

When Thomas Jefferson had finished creating his own new system of measures, his use of the pendulum and the second of time had connected him directly back into the system from prehistory. Though he could not know it, the following is true:

- 1,000 Jefferson feet = 360 megalithic yards
- 366 Jefferson furlongs = 1 megalithic degree of arc of Earth
- 366^2 Jefferson furlongs = exact circumference of Earth

This is a case-winning piece of evidence.

Megalithic yard deniers or those who wish to casually dismiss the 366 system as all being a strange set of coincidences have to explain away the Jefferson paradox. Why is the ancient measure (still described in textbooks as ad hoc) connected in the way Jefferson described and how could his "new" system harmonize perfectly with a system employed five thousand years earlier some 6,000 kilometers away to the east?

The Sun and the Moon

Have you ever wondered how marvelous total eclipses are?

It is a very strange quirk of fate indeed that the disc of the moon should seem, from an earthly perspective, to be exactly the same size as the sun. While we casually take it for granted that the two main bodies seen in Earth's skies look the same size, it is actually something of a miracle. Most people are fully aware that the moon is tiny compared to the sun, but that it is much, much closer to us, which causes the two to appear equal in size. To be precise, the moon is 400 times smaller than the star at the center of our solar system, yet it is also just one 400th of the distance between Earth and the sun.

The odds against this optical illusion happening at all are simply huge—but how bizarre that both values are the same, perfectly round number. Experts are deeply puzzled by the phenomenon. Isaac Asimov, the respected scientist and science-fiction guru, described this perfect visual alignment as being "[t]he most unlikely coincidence imaginable."

This perfect fit of the lunar and solar discs is a very human perspective because it only works from the viewpoint of someone standing on Earth's surface. And it only works at this point in time because it was very different in the past, and it will change again as the moon moves away from Earth.

The magic of the moon's movements above our heads goes to even more astonishing levels. By some absolutely incomprehensible quirk of nature, the moon also manages to very precisely imitate the movements of the sun. It imitates the perceived annual movements of the sun each month.

The full moon is at its highest and brightest at midwinter, mirroring the sun at midsummer, and at its lowest and weakest at midsummer, when the sun is at its highest and brightest.

The strangeness of the Moon continues when one considers its structure. It is either hollow or made up of extremely low-density material at its center. It has its great centers of mass distributed in various places at

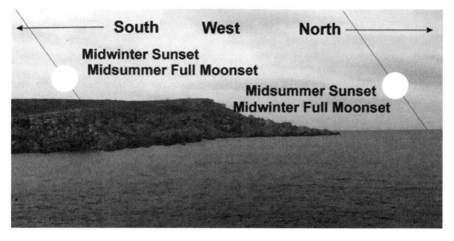

Figure 8.4. Midwinter and midsummer sunset and moonset; this drawing shows the peculiar relationship of the sun and moon throughout the year as seen from Earth. At midsummer in the Northern Hemisphere the sun sets north of west, whereas the full moon sets south of west. At midwinter the situation is reversed, with the sun setting south of west and moon setting north of west.

relatively low points just below its surface. This is odd in the extreme.

Its origin is also mysterious. The material that forms the moon came from the surface of Earth, but there is no satisfactory explanation for how this happened. The so-called double-whack theory seems unlikely in the extreme.

Applying the megalithic 366 system of geometry and Thoms to the moon and the sun produces an astonishing result:

- Polar circumference of the moon   =   13,162,900 Thoms
- 1 megalithic degree (1/366)   =   35,964 Thoms
- 1 megalithic minute (1/60)   =   600 Thoms
- 1 megalithic second (1/6)   =   100 Thoms

The sun produces:
- Polar circumference of the sun   =   5,271,967,000 Thoms
- 1 megalithic degree (1/366)   =   14,404,281 Thoms

- 1 megalithic minute (1/60)   =   240,071 Thoms
- 1 megalithic second (1/6)   =   40,011 Thoms

Given it is impossible to establish an exact circumference for the sun's surface, this result can be considered to be 40,000—as one would expect, given that the sun is four hundred times the diameter of the moon.

How peculiar that the sun and the moon comply with the same system that defines Earth so well? It is almost as though we are looking at the blueprint of the solar system.

The Rhythm of the Solar System

The fact that the 366 system worked so perfectly for Earth, the sun, and the moon caused us to look at every other planet and moon in the solar system. Nothing. None of our neighbors come close to fitting the system. We even tried using each planet's own spin-to-orbit value rather than Earth's 366, but this also drew a blank. There seems to be something very special about our planet and our moon's relationship with the sun.

We stated to look closely at every aspect we could and the following values fell out:

366
- The number of complete rotations of Earth in a year
- The number of Thoms in a megalithic second of arc on Earth
- The percentage size of Earth compared to the moon

100
- The number of Thoms in a lunar megalithic second of arc
- The number of times Earth rotates faster than the moon

400
- The number of times the sun is larger than the moon
- The number of kilometers the moon turns on its axis in a day
- The number of times the moon is closer to Earth than the sun

Plate 1 (above). Bipolar emission
Plate 2 (below). Terrestrial gamma ray flashes

Plate 3 (above). Machu Picchu, Peru

Plate 4 (below). The sun's corona

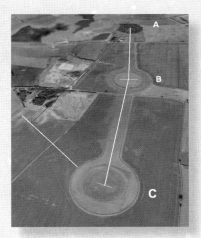

Plate 5. The Thornborough henges, a perfect copy of the stars of Orion's Belt. A to B is 366 megalithic rods, B to C is 360 megalithic rods, and the true north–south latitudinal distance (shown in red) is three megalithic seconds of arc.

Plate 6. A Hopi drawing of a mudhead *katsina* (also spelled *kachina*, associated with the nether realm) wrestling with Pálulukang, the horned water serpent, which is akin to the Mesoamerican deity Quetzalcotl.

Plate 7. View from a koppie near Kimberley in the northern Karoo. Barely visible on the horizon is Platfontein, one of the final relocation settlements of the San. A giant red anthill is seen in the foreground.

Plate 9. Hopi corn *kachina* doll, Kriss Collection, Museum of Northern Arizonan

Plate 8 (above). Anthropoid with staff and striped helmet, Driekopseiland, South Africa

Plate 10 (right). Hopi drawing of their sky god Sótuknang. Because of his control of lightning, he is associated with Pálulukang.

Plate 11 (below). The Step Pyramid

Plate 12 (above). Entrance to the Serapeum

Plate 13 (below). An almost unreal view of a corridor in the Serapeum

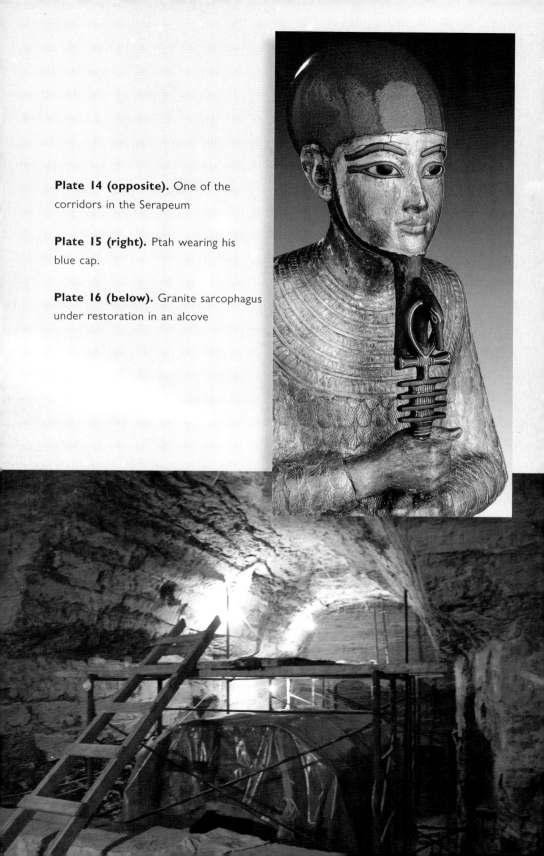

Plate 14 (opposite). One of the corridors in the Serapeum

Plate 15 (right). Ptah wearing his blue cap.

Plate 16 (below). Granite sarcophagus under restoration in an alcove

Plate 17 (right). One of the huge granite sarcophagi in the Sarapeum

Plate 18 (left). Funerary mask of Prince Khaemwaset

Plate 19 (below). Gigal and the cobras of Saqqara

10,000

- The number of times faster that light travels in a vacuum compared to Earth's speed of orbit around the sun
- The number of Earth turns in an orbit of the sun times the number of Earth turns in one lunar orbit of Earth
- The exact number of times that the time difference between a sidereal and solar day fits into one orbit of the moon

40,000

- The number of kilometers to Earth's polar circumference
- The number of Thoms in a solar second of arc

1,000,000

- The number of times faster that light travels in a vacuum compared to the moon's speed of orbit around Earth

109.25

- The number of Earth diameters to the sun's diameter
- The number of solar diameters across the maximum diameter of Earth's orbit around the sun

27.322

- The number of times Earth turns in one turn of the moon
- The percentage size of the moon to Earth
- The number of megalithic seconds of time it takes the moon to pass across one megalithic second of arc in the sky

The Message

Are we looking at God's blueprint? These integer numbers could not possibly fall out of the Earth-moon-sun relationship by accident when every other solar system body appears to have no rules whatsoever.

SETI, originally set up by NASA, spends a vast amount of energy searching for radio messages from a nonhuman origin, based on the belief that we are probably not alone. SETI has been criticized by a number of physicists who argue that radio is not a viable means of communicating across the vast amounts of space and time involved in the universe. Some have suggested that a message is more likely to come by means of large physical objects.

Consider these words by Professor Christopher Rose and Dr. Gregory Wright: "Rather than transmitting radio messages, extraterrestrial civilizations would find it far more efficient to send us a 'message in a bottle,' some kind of physical message inscribed on matter. And it could be waiting for us in our own backyard."

Could the moon have been constructed as a message by integrating ratios and values of both the sun and the moon? The problem is that all these values only work now—at this point in time, which means that the message sender intended for it to be discovered right at this point in time. Did they know that humans would have developed the intelligence to read the message at this point?

It all sounds very weird; especially to us because we are hard-nosed pragmatists and certainly not wishful-thinking believers in exotic ideas. Until now that is, because evidence should not be ignored just because it is not what you expected to see.

Could humans have been "seeded" on a planet that would sustain us? It is a fact that the Moon has been a very accurate "incubator" to nurture life at all of its stages of development. If Earth did not have our unique Moon there would be no humans. That is certain.

Which brings us to David Cumming's idea that all of this can be expressed as an equation that formally identifies that there is a message:

$$\frac{Hl_f.l}{\Omega} = C_0$$

The equation describes a relationship between the hydrogen fine transition line, the ratio between the circumference and diameter of a circle, and the speed of light in a vacuum.

Cumming first realized the importance of the equation when he recognized the equation produced the number 361,449—a very accurate value for the speed of light expressed in the Thom units of an ancient Stone Age measurement system.

First, why is the top line of the equation, Hlf.π, significant? SETI searches on a frequency equal to the frequency of the hydrogen line multiplied by pi (Hlf.π). This frequency was suggested by Pyotr Makovetsky, for various reasons, as the best potential transmission frequency that should be searched for signs of extraterrestrial intelligence, and this frequency was adopted by SETI. The search frequency equals 1420.405751 MHz multiplied by 3.141592653 (pi is chosen to 10 significant figures to match Hl_f) equals 4462.336272. If you check what frequencies members of the SETI alliance are listening on currently, you'll find that Makovetsky's frequency features in many of the lists SETI researchers are using.

Second, why is the value of omega significant? This is the number 0.0123456789—all the characters of the base 10 number system. Cumming states the message originator would know that this is a very likely number system for any life-form to use. At the same time, using all the consecutive characters of any number system at all, in a message, is a very direct sign that this is a message, an ordered intelligent communication and not, he says, a random occurrence.

Take pi/omega (π/Ω) and work this out. Our value for pi is 3.141592653 (ten significant figures are used for pi, as this is what we're using for omega), divided by the omega value of 0.0123456790 (using more significant figures won't affect the calculation), this gives us the result of 254.4690072. The result of the calculation is actually a value in Thoms, namely 254 milli-Thoms, or more conveniently expressed as 0.2544690049 Thoms.

Standard physics says that the frequency of a wave, multiplied by the wavelength of that wave, is equal to the speed of the wave. In the case of the equation, when you divide out pi/omega, the answer must be equal to the wavelength of the hydrogen line, because the hydrogen line frequency multiplied by the hydrogen line wavelength must equal the speed of light.

When we look at the overall equation, we know in advance that the equation will give the value for the speed of light very accurately because what we're doing is multiplying the frequency of the hydrogen line by the wavelength of the hydrogen line. But remember, we've divided pi (3.141592653) by omega (0.0123456790) to get a result for the hydrogen line wavelength expressed in Thoms, so the fact that we get a highly accurate answer appears to be nothing short of a miracle.

The speed of light calculated using the equation is 1420,405,751 cycles per sec (frequency [Hz]) multiplied by 0.2544690072 Thoms (wavelength). This works out at 361,449,241.3 Thoms per sec. This equals 299,804,073.2 meters per sec. This result for the speed of light is 99.996 percent correct.

Applying Occam's razor, Cumming claims that we are left with the simple conclusion that Earth, the sun, and the moon must have been created to accord with the equation of creation.

Ancient Knowledge

One question that needs to be asked is: How did the people of the British Neolithic come to know all about the 366 system and the magic of the sun, moon, and Earth? Presumably, they were told. The Sumerians, who did leave written records, say they were told by strange outsiders who taught them the secrets of astronomy and science.

But among the many surprises we have endured over the last few years, it is one we came across in early 2009 that stumped us. As we explain in *Before the Pyramids,* there can be no doubt that the Founding Fathers of the United States secretly designed Washington, D.C., using megalithic seconds of arc for every detail of the city plan. It is still happening. The Pentagon is a perfect and inspirational exposition of Stone Age knowledge—using the 366 system and the Thom with as much perfection as Stonehenge or Thornborough.

And this was driven by the 33rd Degree of the Ancient Scottish Rite of Freemasonry. Presidents and people unknown have been driven to build a city using God's own values—a city fit for God's great purpose.

Do the powers that be in the United States already understand this message? Are they preparing to respond? We believe that something very special is about to happen, and the world needs to know what it is.

Notes

1. John P. Foley, ed., *The Jeffersonian Cyclopedia* (Funk and Wagnalls, 1900).
2. Ibid.
3. Ibid.

NINE

Science versus Religion

FROM GENESIS TO ATLANTIS AND THE MEASUREMENTS OF THE GODS

HARRY SIVERTSEN AND STEPHEN REDMAN

This article introduces the two intimately related books of over five hundred pages each by Harry Sivertsen and Stephen Redman, which, under the project name of Megalith, Masonry, Myth and Measure, *are individually titled* Deluge: From Genesis to Atlantis *and* Measurements of the Gods.

In 1971, Keith Thomas of St. John's College Oxford published a fascinating book titled *Religion and the Decline of Magic*. In the course of the work, he gave examples of commonalities between the two subjects. Today, we have a different debate, not religion versus magic but religion versus science. So how are these two seemingly diverse subjects defined? The word *science* is ultimately derived from the Latin word for knowledge, *scientia*. Hence, science can be described as knowledge. Of course, given what is generally known as the scientific method, we can add the words "gained by experiment or experience" or something similar to knowledge for a clearer description. However, knowledge is the dominating factor.

Religion, on the other hand, as described in 1535 and contained among numerous other similar descriptions in *The Oxford English Dictionary,* is seen as: Recognition on the part of human beings of some higher unseen power as having control of his destiny, and as being entitled to obedience, reverence, and worship.

Yet such a description, while perhaps being suitable for the commonly accepted perceptions of Christianity, Judaism, and Islam, does not necessarily fit the multitude of beliefs that have blossomed among the world's cultures. Further to this, the primary arguments of today revolve around the concept of creation ex nihilo, or out of nothing, versus the scientific approach of physics and evolutionary biology. Yet, while the physics concept of the big bang is as well known as Darwin's and Wallace's ideas regarding evolution, the source for the creation side of the argument appears in most arguments to be derived solely from the biblical account. But from where did this concept arise? Is this a Hebrew construct or can the source be found elsewhere?

Ultimately, the creation concept of the primary religions of today is derived from Indic sources, long predating any Hebrew writings. In fact, much of the early Bible is drawn from such foundations, but this has passed unrecognized by most.

Religious critics claim that religion is based on belief and not knowledge, but could not knowledge have led to belief in a similar fashion as scientific endeavor has led to beliefs of a whole variety of types of knowledge in the modern world? People had to ask questions to arrive at the conclusion that Earth was created; they had to have knowledge to raise those questions. This being the case, religion, as science, is based on knowledge. Perhaps the knowledge was of a different variety to that today perceived as valid, or possibly there is little difference, and that lacking the learning that has evolved during the past century, human beings arrived at the only logical answer they could find, an answer that in fact was a very much simplified version of today's ideas.

Conceivably, as many of the writings of the religious works stem from earlier oral traditions, from a time before writing was developed, the meanings of some of the works have been misunderstood. Possibly, much is allegory for something else. Just maybe, the strange tales in fact make references that originally would have been understood in a similar fashion as do the science reports of today. All it would take is for science fact to be disguised in a story to make the memorizing of the important elements easier than it otherwise would be. What would result is what we term allegory, and indeed, this was a common ploy before the development of writing.

The well-known scientist Richard Dawkins is vociferous in his condemnation of religion. Dawkins, along with the British Humanism Association, has been involved in a campaign that uses London buses to carry the slogan "There Probably Is No God." We agree, and in fact would go further; we are convinced that the principles of the major religions sprang out of what today would be termed scientific enquiry. Dawkins, in his much acclaimed work *The Selfish Gene,* developed the theory of memes, a concept later taken up and popularized by Susan Blackmore in her book *The Meme Machine.* A meme is an idea, a tune, a concept that takes over one's thinking, in Dawkins's words, "parasit-izes" the mind. One example Dawkins uses is the concept of life after death.

Yet, Dawkins, in his blanket negative treatment of religion, has allowed his own mind to be taken over by the meme of religious con-demnation. He has not applied the scientific enquiry of his training to make a value assessment of the works that influence the believers. In other words, Dawkins's adamant refutation makes him equally as guilty of unfounded belief as he asserts applies to religious believers. Both are directed in their thinking by memes of beliefs, the religious of their faith, and Dawkins in the nonexistence of any value in the religious works.

Let us steer a middle road and reveal what both Dawkins and the religious believers have missed. We shall show where early thinking in fact was based on what today would have been accepted as logical deduction and not merely faith in a religious concept; the religious element that embodied such information came later. Our source is ancient Indic material from which, as becomes apparent in our book *Deluge: From Genesis to Atlantis,* eventually all the primary religions took their guide; indeed, there are even commonalities in Egypt. The information from which the following was developed is derived from this book and reveals the type of analysis contained between its covers.

Creation

The questions of today also perplexed the minds of the sages of ancient times, the most prominent query being from where did all derive? In humanity's experience, all grew or was made, except Earth and what was in the skies. Animals mate to produce offspring, flowers need pollinating insects to reproduce, but the stars did not reproduce, except for comets, in the form of meteorites, which were flung away from the parent body. Strange. The stones of Earth were just there. Like the sun and the moon. The moon has its phases, which were reasonably well understood, and the sun moved north and south during the course of a year—knowledge, scientia, gained via simple observation. All except comets and meteorites were regular and steady. One knew what was to happen in the skies; they were predictable, and one could prophesize what was going to happen generations into the future. The heavens give accurate counts of time—of days, months, and years; of numbers; of math. All was confirmed via repeated observations, what today would be termed the scientific method, and was understood more than twelve thousand years ago, at the end of the last ice age, which is approximately when our story commences.

But while reproduction and heavenly movements were generally understood in principle, it was not known for where or what it was all derived. Given that the stellar movements were as steady as a mark on the rim of a wheel, even if that wheel was a section of a log, which, when rolled, brought the mark regularly back to its starting point, the whole of the universe must have been created or fashioned to work so accurately; nothing else observed had such symmetry. So from a sequence of logical deductions, it was determined that, lacking another satisfactory explanation, the whole of the universe had to have been created; the sun, moon, and stars would not have merely grown as neither did the ground upon which these thinkers stood, but neither could they have emerged from nothing.

Hence, we have knowledge, scientia, determining that all that is known had to have had a creator. Fine, but from where did the creator's raw materials derive, from what did this creator fashion not only Earth but the sun, moon, and stars? Taking this further, if there was a creator, who or what created the creator? This line of investigation was getting into a bit of an eddy, so an invention was made, a power greater than the creator, a power that was just that, power, a power that willed a creator into being.

Here we have the Indic Brahman, the overarching power, that which is in everything and is everything—from thought to rock, from bird to fish, timber to water, from flame to ice—is the overarching indescribable, omnipotent ever-present abstract entity that is in all and is all. Effectively, the only word that adequately describes Brahman is *energy*. Brahman is simply pure energy, and as modern science has shown, it is from energy that all in the universe is derived. However, Brahman could not make the visible, physical elements; something had to happen to turn this energy into an observable universe. Brahman required a creator, a builder, to turn ideas into reality, a catalyst that turned energy into action. Brahman willed the creator Brahma into being to turn Brahman's desires into realities—the creative moment, the source of all; from raw energy came the explosion of creation, from raw energy came the universe and all within.

Invention? Yes, it was. Satisfactory explanation? For the available information at the time—yes. Complies with modern interpretations? Take away the elements that describe characteristics that would apply to human personality and yes. Creation based upon logic, effectively an early description of what we think of as the big bang, an interpretation that suffered only from a lack of the scientific information available today and that made no allowance for the vast time lapses involved simply because there was no comprehension of this, but nevertheless, a definition that in fact preempted the modern concept. This was a theory based upon logic that in fact has stood the test of time but has been grossly misunderstood and ignored. Religious? No.

The Flood

Demonstrating close observation of the skies since the end of the last ice age, we here relate a little of what constituted the flood story.

It was noticed that the whole of the cosmos appeared to rotate around a specific point in the sky, the northern end of the axis of the universe. The closest to this point was a particular star that (as we know today) got no closer than circa 4.7 degrees. This was Vega in the northern celestial hemisphere. Opposite this star in the southern skies, at the other end of the imaginary axis in the cosmos, was a similar situation; however, the star there, Canopus, was farther from the southern imaginary axis endpoint; here we find a bright light in the sky that circles 7 to 8 degrees from the axis end or due south.

The northernmost of these stars, when seen in position at the end of the universal axis, became the seat of creation, the home of the creator Brahma, as all revolved around the creator. From this north polar position, Brahma controlled the strings of all the stars and planets, keeping them in their allotted positions. Brahma in that polar position was recognized as the pole star.

Then, shortly after 12,200 BCE both the north polar star Vega and its counterpart in the south, Canopus, started moving away from their allotted positions. Simultaneously, the sea level rose; the farther away from the ends of this axis the stars moved, the higher the waters rose. These stars had been direction-giving entities for hundreds of years, and now they were moving; the heavens were not quite so stable after all. Something was wrong; the creator had moved out of position or the whole universe had moved, as surely the creator would stay in position? The stars were no longer linked to the central point, as the guiding star of the extreme northern skies was no longer in place relative to the remainder of the universe. The invisible strings that held all together were broken. Not only that, but Earth was no longer the stable place it once was, as coastal flooding was now the norm. Something must have gone wrong for Brahma to allow this destruction to happen.

This flooding, coupled with the loss of pole stars, continued for many years, and records were kept of the movements of the heavens. As time was denoted by the movements of the sun, moon, and stars, the years were counted. People were flooded out of their homelands, and one particular group who had observed the movements of both stars from their vantage point on the equator at Sundaland (south Malaysia) eventually found themselves in northwest India in what is now Pakistan at Merhgarh. Other groups from coastal regions adjacent to Sundaland moved northward to China and adjacent regions.

After many years, another star came to replace the closely circling northern light, although this did not happen to the south. By 8100 BCE, 3,600 years after the loss of Vega, the star Tau Hercules of the constellation Hercules was very close to the polar position, in fact within 3 degrees or, in terms of time, 500 years, and the skies were steady once more.

Brahma, although appearing different and not so bright, was back in place, albeit in a different constellation. By 7600 BCE, Tau Hercules was as close as it would get to the polar position, within about 0.75 of a degree, and shortly after this, before 7100 BCE, there was a turndown in the climate, and the seas stopped rising. The floods even reversed, and there was a new pole star. Here was an apparent correlation: lose a pole star, and there is coastal flooding; gain a pole star, and after a while it stops. Once a different pole star is in place, all is new; the constellation surrounding the star is different—a new creation of the heavenly realm, the northerly abode of the god of creation.

The climate change was not to last, however, and soon the waters started rising again, just as Tau Hercules was leaving the polar position. This change further correlated loss of the pole star with flooding. Once more the specter of destruction put fear into people's minds. There was destruction, not only on Earth, but devastation in the heavens. Once more people moved away from the rising seas, roughly the region of south Malaysia, as applied to the specific people of which we write, between Hong Kong and Borneo. There was little of their original homeland left. Other refugees from the rising waters of adjacent areas found themselves eventually moving to regions such as China and Japan; others found a new home in the Middle East, and some as far afield as Europe.

Calendars were kept, the years counted, and once more, in 3300 BCE, along came Thuban in the Draco constellation as a pole star, after millennia of chaos in the heavens and ever increasing flooding. Sundaland was now underwater; the plain between Hong Kong and Borneo, where the people who moved to Merhgarh once lived, was now under many feet of water. This time, however, the floods stopped completely; the sea level had risen about one hundred meters and was now reasonably stable, and there was a new pole star, a new creation to confirm cessation of flooding. Cause and effect: lose a pole star, and there are floods; gain one, and the floods stop and all goes back to normal. This was pure logic, scientia gained via observation and thought.

Here is the basis of the flood story in the religious works. The familiar tale started in India but later spread across most of the world to China, the Middle East, Greece, and eventually even to Europe. Almost certainly there are elements of native versions telling the same tale hidden in localized myths that have yet to be deciphered. The counts of thousands of years were diligently recorded with a flood period being a canonical 3,600 years and the creation epoch an era of 1,000 years. Manu, the Indian Noah, was a manifestation of Brahma the creator and created all anew after the flood, whereas the Hebrew authors claimed that God's chosen family, that of Noah, carried the essentials of creation in a boat.

Maharaja Druva or Druva-loka is the generic Indian term for pole star and is also an alternative name for Manu. Manu lasts until he is created anew, then his son (also Manu) takes over. The constellation Hercules is seen as a depiction of Manu conducting austerities standing on one toe (the pole star Tau Hercules) on the banks of a river. The river is the Milky Way in its most northerly position, similar to the way the Nile was seen in Egypt. Plato based his Atlantis tale on this description, with the flooding being that which occurred before the onset of Tau Hercules, before the Pillars of Hercules. He was referring to a time, not an earthly location.

So why the tales of boats? There is little invention without good reason. Rain came from the skies, hence the source was a heavenly ocean, as noted in the Genesis account; after all, no one had observed water going upward. Rain fell from the skies; the heavens pivoted around the pole star (the seat of creation), and when this moved, the heavenly ocean was disturbed, a heavenly flood ensued. A heavenly ocean meant the gods or lights in the sky needed boats to get around, and they had to move about to organize a new heavenly creation, a new constellation with its pole star in place. All is astronomical; even the forty days and nights of rain is, in fact, a reference to the loss of view of the Pleiades, as recorded by classical authors, and the date of the flood so described can be ascertained to the day—twenty days before the vernal equinox in 2300 BCE. The new year commenced at the first new moon after the winter solstice, meaning the count of days given in Genesis for this description is correct.

This flood has had great influence, as Noah's "boat"—a strange rock formation on Mount Nisir in Turkey, precisely where the Chaldean legend states it is to be found (the region is now known as Durupinar after the Turkish flier who photographed the formation)—was surveyed in antiquity, as well as recently, and it was emulated within the Pyramid of Khufu, albeit in a scaled-down fashion. The funerary boat of Khufu has its length the same as the width or beam of the mythical boat of the gods in Turkey, and this is not a coincidence; it is a very odd measure.

So as it was observed that all revolved around the pole star, the pole of the ecliptic was not understood when the flood tale was developed; it was a logical assumption that if the pivoting point was knocked out of place, then all would run amok. As there was a celestial ocean from which came rain, any travel in the heavenly realms would by necessity be by boat. The sun traveled in a boat pulled by fish in Egyptian lore; boats appear in Indian lore where Varuna is afloat in the vessel in a similar fashion to Ra, although here there is mention of oars, and it is notable that while Ra's boat is towed by a fish, so also is that of Manu. There is logic in these stories, a logic not even noted by most of the readers of the works.

A different and seemingly unrelated version of the sun's traveling vehicle from India is the chariot, here pulled by seven horses, in fact the Pleiades. This is seasonal and datable as the Pleiades reference applies loosely to the spring period circa 3500 BCE, when the Pleiades rose about thirty-eight minutes before the sun and hence were seen to be "pulling" the sun over the horizon. While horses are a little imaginative, here we are moving toward an Earth-in-heaven concept and not as commonly portrayed the other way around, the heavenly sea and boats along with the pivot of the world are logical deductions, given the limited amount of information available to the seers of the day. That they are illogical to us today is immaterial; they were derived from logical deduction and limited knowledge.

By the time of the New Testament, the whole pole star sequence of seven stars was known, and it is replicated in the Book of Revelations under the guise of kings, some fallen some standing. Of course by this time, religious fervor had overtaken reason; although some, such as the author of Revelations, obviously were aware of the truth behind the tales. It seems certain that a succession of wise men, a small minority, perhaps a priesthood, handed down the original interpretations to successive generations.

Hence, we see that a creator, later to become, via the machinations of human imagination, God, was originally a necessary part of ancient science, definitely not religion. These people were logical and developed some sound philosophies; in many ways they were very clever. The Indian sages laid the foundations of the science of today (see *Measurements of the Gods*).

Logically, while many cultures seemingly worshipped their ancestors, the principle religious concepts of the modern world were developed primarily for political reasons, laws from God via Moses and the Ten Commandments being a typical example. Lacking further knowledge, the average person would, of course, accept what the elders stated, and their minds would be taken over by the meme of religious faith. One cannot break God's laws, which is somewhat different to those of a tribal leader, but he now has God on his side, and miscreants have to answer to and be punished by God through him. Different cultures developed a variety of laws, but in essence, it was relatively easy to keep the peace through fear of God. The Christian message turned this on its head, and one was now supposed to love God, as his laws were good. Yet the "love one another" message of the Sermon on the Mount exists in an early Buddhist interpretation—not as a religious concept or dogma but as a philosophical way to peace. Most ideas have a predecessor, and with Buddhism, we again are heading back toward India.

Numerous hints and clues to the astronomical elements of the flood tale can be found in the religious (science?) books. What was initially merely a suspicion of greater knowledge being hidden in the ancient texts has been confirmed by in-depth research, including the results of archaeological investigation. In fact, the familiar measures of premetrication are many thousands of years old, and there is much information regarding these units and their use among the pages of the Bible.

Perhaps historians of science should take a long hard look at what are generally dismissed as valueless religious texts; as seen above, these tell a tale of questioning and endeavor, a quest to understand the universe, an investigation that is still ongoing today.

The Books

The two works here are irrevocably linked. The original concept was for a single book, but the volume of information unearthed dictated that two books were required. *Deluge: From Genesis to Atlantis* deals primarily with the subjects of its title, while *Measurements of the Gods* explores ancient measures and finds much that has escaped conventional learning. This latter work reveals a great deal that is very easily checked by the reader and shows how the enquiry can be, as we hope it is, extended by others. Both books commence in modern times and have as their ultimate destination the same place on Earth, Sundaland. It is to this specific location that the evidence has led the enquiry.

Measurement systems, one would think, would be the province of the historian of mathematics. Yet, the subject has hardly been touched by those who logically would understand the subject area. Perhaps as textually much has been shrouded by myth, one could understand this, but again, the work of John Michell, the researcher who gave the principal author of this work his first insight into the units in use in the past, has been in the public domain for nearly thirty years and academia has not taken it on board. In *Measurements of the Gods,* we trace the uses of the measures through Europe, classical Greece, Egypt, and Mesopotamia to India, where the development of the systems took place. There are links seen between India and China, which again confirm Michell's Earth dimensions.

In the process of this exploratory journey, much is revealed that seemingly has not been published elsewhere, including the use of Michell's interpretation of the anciently accepted Earth circumference in the scales of medieval maps and charts. The development of the unit measures is far older than most would imagine, and the proof is in the archaeology of Merhgarh, now in Pakistan, but the measuring of Earth, an essential prerequisite for the development of the values, took place elsewhere—and even earlier than the dates of 7500 to 8000 BCE that archaeologists have ascribed to the remains at Merhgarh.

Effectively, this work reveals a great deal that convention has missed with abundant evidence to reinforce the arguments involved.

Deluge: From Genesis to Atlantis

In this book, the flood evaluation seen above is relayed with, of course, far more detail than presented here in this article. The work commences with a brief overview, which leads to an examination of the arguments that ensued with the onset of the discipline of geology and the realization that, in fact, Earth is very old. From there, the book moves to the Mountains of Ararat and eventually, after revealing (and refuting) the ideas of some others, arrives at the object of the tale in Genesis, the ark of Noah. This is a geological anomaly at what is now known as Durupinar in Turkey, at the precise location recorded in the Epic of Gilgamesh.

But there was a second ark, the ark of the covenant. This is connected to the tale, as much revolves around information hidden by the use of numbers and measures, and here it is revealed that the same cubit value applied to Noah's vessel was in use for this ark. A smaller derived unit applied to the tabernacle and moving from there to Solomon's Temple, it is seen that this smaller unit applied to all except the temple surrounds and the mysterious oblation to the Lord. The measurement values are explained in the text.

This oddity, the oblation to the Lord, this allocation of a large tract of land, is, in fact, quite informative, as numerically, as indicated by its dimensions, it is a representation of the ark of Noah. Here we have an explanation for ark representations, paintings, and carvings being of a boat shape with what cannot be described as anything else but a stone built temple aboard. The oblation, the grossly oversized ark depiction contained Jerusalem, itself a representation of Earth and its attendant temple. There are hints in the descriptions of this temple that much is of an astronomical nature, and as seen above, this is correct.

The measures seen here were originally developed from biblical texts—purely as an exercise in possibilities. It emerges that they are correct; they link to numerous other unit values as discovered by Michell and, in fact, were used by the designers of religious buildings in medieval times in Europe. In fact, surveys of such structures seen in *Measurements of the Gods* confirmed the validity of the assessment.

Deluge develops its themes over a number of chapters and includes some Indian astronomy and a completely new and verifiable interpretation of the India *yugas;* traditionally vast time periods of many millions of years. The concept was based on a lunar construct. These values then link to the pole star periods seen in earlier chapters. The dating seen here is confirmed via Indian descriptions of climatic events that are recorded in ice cores and are well documented. Hence not only dating, but the whole interpretation of the yugas, is confirmed as well as the ability to record accurate observational astronomy in the distant past.

A number of concepts of creation are included, such as those from China, Mesopotamia, and Egypt, for comparison to the biblical and Indian interpretations. It is noted that, once more, there are a number of values associated with lunar counts—as indeed can be seen in the Genesis flood tale where Noah was afloat for a synodic year or lunar period.

A chapter dealing primarily with biblical verses from the Books of Daniel and Revelations is quite revealing, as here we see that the whole pole star sequence was understood, not the timing between all the stars, but nevertheless, while this period was a canonical 3,600 years, it is seen that after the demise of Polaris, a shorter period ensues to the next star. We also show why the concept of the number of the beast is erroneous. The operative value here is 36, which is the last to count to reach 666. The punctuation in the King James version of the Bible is clear in this respect, and the triple value does not apply to the number of the beast. This "beast" is the flood period, devised because the seas had ceased rising and an evil was still required to explain when a pole star was misplaced. Much of Revelations, in fact, revolves around the demise and reinstatement of a pole star.

Plato's Atlantis is seen for what it is, a replication of the same story with his "beyond the pillars of Hercules" being a reference not to a location but to a time, a time before 7600 BCE, a time when Vega had moved out of place and Tau Hercules had yet to take position as the pole star. Here there is much detail that irrefutably confirms the evaluation.

In essence, this book reveals the truth behind the mysteries of both the flood recorded in the religious annals and Plato's tale of Atlantis. The work reveals that this is a cyclic situation (three floods are mentioned in Genesis), but the sequence and allegory has to be understood before these cycles are comprehended. The imaginative father of Western philosophy, Plato was giving a historical astronomy lesson in his Atlantis story. A great deal of other directly related information is revealed via the investigations given in this five-hundred-plus-page work, but in a nutshell, this is *Deluge: From Genesis to Atlantis.*

Measurements of the Gods

It's clear that observational astronomy was a reality in the distant past, with written records of events in the seventh millennium BCE (in the Mahabharata) and correlations in myth that show the skies were closely watched around 12,000 to 13, 000 BCE. What else is there to be derived from these distant epochs?

Deluge takes us from recent centuries back to 12,000 to 13,000 BCE. *Measurements of the Gods* commences in the twentieth century and ends just the other side of 9000 BCE. The journeys end again at Sundaland. As with *Deluge; Measurements of the Gods* confirms the abilities of the sages of India, long before Egypt became a coherent nation. What follows is a very brief overview of the contents of this book.

As the title suggests, the primary subject is measurement, and here we have further evidence of the abilities of our distant forebears. This book covers much that contradicts conventional thinking; the work brings together disparate bits and pieces and shows them as parts of a coherent whole. Measurements have been frequently used symbolically, as is revealed in *Deluge; Measurements of the Gods* gives the history of these measurements. The book reveals the ancient source of the British imperial system (extended from John Neal's evaluations) and the numerous other units that were in use up to the onset of the metric system in France and their use on ancient buildings, such as in Egypt, and not so ancient, including the American White House and the George Washington Monument. Also reviewed is the application of these measurements in maps and charts used by people such as Piri Reis and Columbus.

We relate the confusion that reigned in Greece regarding the size of Earth and steer a course through that recorded chaos of measurement. Also reviewed is the Indian weights system, the basics of which spread to the rest of the world. Of course, we reveal the most fundamental elements of all: the relationships of measurements to the lights in the sky—the gods—which is the source of all calculations. Measurements of the Gods, indeed.

Sequentially, *Measurements of the Gods* commences with suggestions of allegory and calendars, a description of ancient measures and methods, the onset of metrication and modern Earth measure (with a comparison to John Michell's evaluation) and hence to the records from Greece of Earth dimensions.

From here, we move to maps and their scales as used by Columbus and Piri Reis followed by a more in-depth look at the ancient systems, which in turn is followed by a return to Noah's ark and its representation in the Great Pyramid, a shortened version of the section in *Deluge* for those who may only read this work. There is some repetition of historical material later in the work for the same reason.

In the same chapter is a section on Stonehenge, its measurements and a calendar previously missed. The latter supplies a sound reason for the odd sarsen stone classified as number 11 and also a periodicity for the occasional winter celebrations, which have recently been discovered to have taken place there. Silbury Hill is also analyzed in this chapter;

our astronomical argument supplies a sound reason for the vast effort entailed in building the structure. Note that this does not involve sighting to any other point and accommodates some other ideas that have recently emerged regarding the Stonehenge environs.

The following three chapters deal mainly with measures and alignments across the landscape in South Gwent, with notes to the effect that our investigations have found similar situations in Somerset and Fife. These chapters are profusely illustrated. Once more, little of this nature has been revealed in the past. One interesting facet here is the replication on the ground via two stones and some hilltops of the forty days of rain in the Genesis flood myth, the loss of view of the Pleiades, here dated via alignments of other sites to 2500 BCE against the biblical 2300 BCE. This is followed by an examination of numerous buildings, including the aforementioned famous American structures, and of course, in this we reveal the use of the ancient measures once more.

Moving slowly back toward India, the following three chapters are of a historical nature, albeit with some new explanations, and these then lead us to archaeology in India, the Maldives, and specifically Merhgarh circa 7000 BCE, with the most informative bricks ever discovered. However, other bricks are also involved in the evaluation, and there are three sets of sizes from differing regions and times in Indian development to take into consideration; these are amazingly accurate, and all connect metrologically to each other. There are hundreds of thousands of correlating examples from which mean values were derived by others, so we cannot argue with results. This is confirmation by repetition— the scientific method.

The next chapter confirms the calculations via the weights systems, which involves a return to the biblical descriptions of Solomon's Temple. This chapter reveals so many correlations and interrelationships that we cannot imagine readers doubting the evaluations and hence confirmation of the stated measurement units. We follow this with a discussion revolving around Sundaland as a possible source for the measures, with the penultimate chapter being a description of the measuring of Earth—in 9070 BCE! Here we describe the method probably employed, and once more a specific star is key to the dating. As the people of Merhgarh who made bricks complying with this Earth measurement came from Sundaland, confirmed via dental morphology, this appears to be an inevitable conclusion. It was here that knowledge of the size of Earth first emerged. We are then left with a very short concluding chapter and references.

In all, there are nineteen chapters and, again, over five hundred pages of detailed information, most of which is new and has not been in print previously. We feel that even though the argument and analysis and therefore conclusions contradict conventional thinking, they are correct. Every effort has been made to fault the arguments, but these attempts have failed, and as far as we can determine, the results of the evaluations are accurate.

Conclusion

Both *Deluge* and *Measurements of the Gods* were twenty-five years in the making. The principal researcher and author initially became interested in the origins of the British imperial system and rejected as unsound the belief that our measurements developed from Roman measuring systems—a theory trotted out in history books, in those odd volumes that managed to mention the subject.

It was John Michell's work that initially set the research on its path; although admittedly we did not accept it until we had accrued quite a body of supporting evidence. These two books confirm beyond a shadow of a doubt that Michell's evaluation of the ancient accepted circumference of Earth, a measurement that stood until the French metric system was adopted, was correct. Our research into the flood story revealed that the Bible used different measures to those evaluated by Michell. However, eventually a definitive set of measures emerged from this tale, and it was here that elements of time began to emerge as being highly significant. After a great deal of research and many years, it emerged that counts of time played an essential role in these matters, an idea confirmed by Indian writings. The work had taken a very different direction to any we had dreamt of at its outset. Much of that which is seen today as being of religious origin is ultimately related to calendar counts derived from observational astronomy or what we can legitimately term science.

This lengthy, frequently tedious and frustrating, but absolutely fascinating journey eventually came to an end, and the culmination of that long trek is the two books described here, which together detail the project *Megalith, Masonry, Myth and Measure.*

TEN

The Electric Jesus

THE HEALING JOURNEY OF A CONTEMPORARY GNOSTIC

JONATHAN TALAT PHILLIPS

Gnosis:
The Not-So-Secret History of Jesus

In December 1945, during the tail end of the most devastating war in human history, a peasant named Mohammed Ali of the al-Samman clan stumbled upon an earthenware jar near limestone caves in the deserts of Upper Egypt. He feared an evil *djin* (genie) resided inside, but hoping for lost riches, he still opened the jar. To his disappointment, twelve ragged leather-bound codices fell onto the ground. He didn't realize these 1,200 weathered pages contained a priceless treasure with dozens of lost Christian gospels that had been hidden away for 1,600 years. Mohammed carried them home to his mother, who kept herself warm throughout the night by feeding pages of what we now call the Nag Hammadi library to her fireplace.

These fifty-two texts, with titles like the Gospel of Thomas, the Secret Book of James, the Gospel of Mary, the Origin of the World, the Gospel of Philip, the Secret Book of John, and the Sophia of Jesus, showed that Christianity from the first through the fourth centuries was much more varied than previously thought, comprised of diverse sects claiming "secret knowledge" of heavenly realms. Modern scholars now label these texts as gnostic, since they lay out an initiatory process for candidates to overcome the "forgetfulness, drunkenness, blindness, and sleep" of the illusory world in order to access *gnosis*, direct experience or personal revelation of a divine reality.

The Nag Hammadi library supported the popular theory that Christianity stemmed from the ancient mystery school traditions of the Mediterranean, which featured dying and resurrecting godmen. In Egypt, they worshipped Horus; in Greece, Dionysus; in Syria, Adonis; in Asia Minor, Attis; in Persia (and later Rome), Mithras; and in Israel, Jesus (historically the most recent). The similarities among these hierophants were uncanny. Several of them, according to the legends, were born on December 25 around the winter solstice to a virgin in humble surroundings (a cave or a manger) with a star in the Eastern sky. Some grew up to be spiritual masters with twelve disciples (Horus, Mithras, Jesus), performing miracles, giving baptisms and communions. They all died (Dionysus dismembered by Titans, Attis and Adonis eaten by wild boars, and Horus, Mithras, and Jesus crucified) before experiencing a miraculous resurrection.

In *The Jesus Mysteries,* authors Timothy Freke and Peter Gandy discuss how the Vatican sits atop a destroyed Mithraic temple.

Where today the gathered faithful revere their Lord Jesus Christ, the ancients worshipped another godman who, like Jesus, had been miraculously born on December 25 before three shepherds. In this ancient sanctuary Pagan congregations once glorified a Pagan redeemer who, like Jesus, was said to have ascended to heaven and to have promised to come again at the end of time to judge the quick and the dead. On the same spot where the Pope celebrates the Catholic mass, Pagan priests also celebrated a symbolic meal of bread and wine in memory of their savor who, just like Jesus had declared: "He who will not eat of my body and drink of my blood, so that he will be made one with me and I with him, the same shall not know salvation."[1]

Freke and Gandy argue adamantly that there never was a historical Jesus who walked the sands of Israel, but rather he is a composite of the earlier godmen. But perhaps that's too hard of a line to draw, since mythical figures are often based on real people—think of Benjamin Franklin and George Washington, for example.

As the Egyptian god of daytime, Horus battled his jackal-headed enemy Set (as in sunset), the bringer of night, in a cosmic battle of light and dark. Jesus played a similar role as Horus in being "the light of the world" surrounded by twelve disciples who represented the twelve months of the year, and the twelve signs of the zodiac. The sun enters each zodiac sign at 30 degrees (30 times 12 equals 360); thus, these "Suns of God" embarked on their ministry at the age of thirty. The classic zodiac cross bisects the twelve astrological signs within a circle. The sun hangs "crucified" in the center as it passes through the precession of the equinoxes, something the mystery schools followed closely as each new sign marked the next world age.

Given the astrological significance of the cross, wisdom traditions often depicted the crucifixion in their writing and art. A notorious second-to-third-century European talisman reveals a human figure that looks like Jesus on the cross (with a crescent moon and seven stars above him), but the inscription reads "Orpheus becomes a Bacchoi." Orpheus was a prophet in the Dionysian mysteries, and Bacchio refers to an enlightened disciple who had undergone the final stages of initiation. Around the same time as the talisman had been crafted, a Roman graffiti artist sketched on a pillar the image of a crucified donkey, which symbolized the initiates' death to their animalistic nature and ascension to the higher self. The first portrayal of Jesus on a cross wouldn't appear until two hundred years later.

Rather than rejoicing in their similarities, "literalist" Christian leaders—those who had not experienced the secret gnosis (direct knowledge) of the highest mysteries—created dams and divisions between the diverse spiritual streams that originally flowed from the same mystical source. As Freke and Gandy explain, the parallels between Mithras and Jesus threatened the emerging "literalist church." Roman bishops such as Justin Martyr, Tertullian, and Irenaeus made the ridiculous claim that the devil had engaged in "diabolical mimicry," "plagiarizing by anticipation" the story of Jesus before it had actually happened in order to mislead the weak-minded.

The Golden Bough's Sir James George Frazer noted a similar contention between Attis, the mystery god from Asia Minor, and Jesus. "In point of fact it appears from the testimony of an anonymous Christian, who wrote in the fourth century of our era, that Christians and pagans alike were struck by the remarkable coincidence between the death and resurrection of their respective deities, and that the coincidence formed a theme of bitter controversy between the adherents of the rival religions, the pagans contending that the resurrection of Christ was a spurious imitation of the resurrection of Attis, and the Christians asserting with equal warmth that the resurrection of Attis was a diabolical counterfeit of Christ."[2]

Literalist Christians refused to accept that the rites of the mystery schools form the central narrative of the New Testament. But the similarities are too plentiful to ignore. Jesus encounters a baptism (spiritual cleansing), a Eucharist (communion), an anointing (Christ means "the anointed one"), and the death and resurrection ritual. These mystical rites provided a rare alchemical education, unifying spiritual energies (*pneuma,* as the early Christians called it) for candidates. In the words of the Gospel of Philip, one of the so-called gnostic texts, "The Lord did everything in a mystery, a baptism and a chrism, and a eucharist and a redemption and a bridal chamber. . . . he said, 'I came to make the things below like the things above, and the things outside like the things inside. I came to unite them in the place.'"

The word *mystery* appears twenty-seven times in the New Testament with Paul telling fellow Christians, "Let a man regard us in this manner, as servants of Christ and stewards of God." Jesus speaks of clandestine teachings for those in the inner circles when he says to his disciples, "You have been given the secret of God's imperial rule; but to those outside everything is presented in parables" (Matthew 4:11).

As an energy healer, I found myself especially drawn to how early Christians used pneuma for personal transformation. Jesus baptizes with "fire and spirit," heals with "power," and transmits wisdom to his disciples through the "bubbling spring" drawn from a higher source. The purpose of these schools was to create *pneumatics,* people full of spiritual energy. In the Gospel of Thomas, Jesus announces to his disciples, "Whoever drinks from my mouth will become like me; I myself shall become that person, and the hidden things will be revealed to him."

Even common Christian terms reveal clues to this ancient transformational process. I studied the original Greek word for sin, *harmatia,* which turned out to be an archery term meaning "missing the mark." It lacked the guilt and shame pastors used to control their flocks and simply indicated when seekers strayed from their path and needed to get back on course. Similarly, the Hebrew word *satan* (adversary) highlighted the ego/personality attachment the soul needed to overcome to reach higher states of consciousness.

Repent (*metanoia*) meant to "change one's mind" or "have a shift in consciousness," which can occur when absorbing higher frequencies from someone closely connected to source-energy, like Jesus. Most surprisingly, Christ was not our Lord and savior but rather our *soter,* meaning "healer," "bestower of health," or "one who makes whole." Staying connected to universal spirit, Jesus travels through the rift of separation consciousness to heal us and bring us back to our celestial home. "I am the one who comes from what is whole" (Gospel of Thomas). When we finally release our attachments to the material realm, we become redeemed; we experience *apolytrosis,* meaning "released."

Of course, I couldn't help wonder what happened to the original meanings of these words, as well as the numerous gnostic churches that had proliferated in the Middle East. When the Romans destroyed Jerusalem and its Second Temple in 70 CE, after the Jewish revolt, they left one-third of the population dead and the Christian mysteries fractured into pieces. Members joined the mass exodus out of the country. Those who hadn't been exposed to the inner mysteries started up literalist churches. The remaining gnostics called these rigid sects "imitation churches" as they did not teach the secret gnosis of the Christ within.

According to the Apocalypse of Peter, literalist church fathers were "waterless canals" bereft of consciousness-expanding pneuma who arrogantly claimed to be the sole gatekeepers of heaven. "Some who do not understand mystery speak of things which they do not understand, but they will boast that the mystery of truth is theirs alone." These "empty" churches sprouted up across the Roman Empire. In a sad touch of historical irony, their leaders, like the infamous Irenaeus, the bishop of Lyon, became heretic hunters attacking those who still carried the inner teachings of their religion. "We were hated and persecuted, not only by those who are ignorant, but also by those who think they are advancing the name of Christ, since they were unknowingly empty, not knowing who they are" (the Second Treatise of the Great Seth).

As the number of Christians multiplied in Roman lands, power-hungry Constantine switched the state religion to co-opt this growing movement, uniting Rome under "one God, one religion" and, incidentally, one emperor. In 325, he oversaw the Council of Nicaea, where the church fathers reduced the vast library of Christian written knowledge to a few documents that we now call the New Testament.

In 391, Emperor Theodosius passed an edict to close all "pagan" temples and burn their books. Christian hordes set out on murderous rampages across the empire, smashing all traces of the mystery traditions from which their own religion had blossomed. They killed off the last of the gnostic circles, including their libraries, churches, scrolls, and, most importantly, the flame of gnosis that had been carefully passed down throughout the ages. By 410 CE, the Roman Empire had nearly torn itself apart, and the Visigoths strolled in to finish the job. Only eighty-five years after the Council of Nicaea, the Dark Ages had begun.

While poring over the lost gnostic texts of the Nag Hammadi library, I was surprised how many of them focused on reframing the Garden of Eden story. These tales, like the Secret Book of John, explained the human origin story quite differently than Genesis. They described a complicated cosmology that began with a single being (or parent), who was ineffable, eternal, immeasurable light, and created an image or reflection of itself, Barbelo, which in turn begot a multitude of heavenly planes (aeons) that were part of a wider divine realm (the pleroma).

Christ was not just a man but a distinct aeon or larger divine being in the pleroma. Those who fully realized the mysteries became one with Christ, carrying this high vibrational force inside them. Bedazzled by the cosmic palace, Sophia, the aeon of wisdom, created her own world without consent from the über-parent or her male counterpart. This experiment went awry, and Sophia separated from the pleroma, creating a sinister Frankenstein ruler called the Demiurge (craftsman or maker), who manufactured our "counterfeit" material world.

This was the Old Testament God, who gnostics called Yaldabaoth, Samael (God of the blind), and Saklas (a fool), as he believed himself to be the only god in the universe, ignorant of the pleroma and the omnipresent light of the parent. Breathing life into Adam (and unknowingly the divine spirit of Sophia), the Demiurge ruled over humans with his demonic bully friends, the archons. The angelic realms of the pleroma embarked on a rescue mission for both Sophia and Adam and Eve. Like an undercover agent, Jesus snuck behind enemy lines into the Garden of Eden, inviting the first humans to eat of the tree of knowledge ("the Epinoia of pure light") to "awaken them out of the depth of sleep" and their "fallen state."

The gnostics' description of archons immediately intrigued an activist side in me. These devilish autocrats seemed representative of the oppressive empires that dominated Western history books. Today's Halliburtons and Bechtels, neocons and Exxons, seemed to follow a long shadowy lineage of hierarchical powers profiting from human suffering while expanding their empires. Maybe the gnostics understood that we needed mystical agents of transformation smuggling in celestial light to liberate lost souls on the planet.

And the Christ story seemed to be the perfect place to help free us from worldly bondage. I don't think it's an overstatement to say that millions of people living today have been wounded or misled by literalist Christianity, robbed of their own divine spark. For more than a millennia, the Judeo-Christian tradition has supplied the underlying operating platform for our whole society—our languages, laws, mores, work ethic, sexuality, even our way of perceiving time (with the Gregorian calendar)—shaping our worldview, whether we realize it or not.

Integrating this tradition could prove a powerful tool in coming to terms with ourselves, and our history. And that doesn't necessarily mean plodding through obscure gnostic texts, making sense of strange Demiurge names. The mysteries lie right there in the New Testament for those with "eyes to see" and "ears to hear." But we need an upgrade of the Protestant revolution, one that incorporates the gnosis of Christ consciousness. Imagine already established churches, the ones on your block, enhancing their services with meditation, prayer, breathwork, energy healing, body movement, possibly even late-night dancing, and, among the more radicalized churches, the ingesting of psychoactive sacraments in a safe and protected space. Why build entirely new systems for connecting us to pneuma when the institutions have already been created, whether Methodist, Lutheran, or Baptist? But these "waterless" religions would have to give up their addiction to dominating worshippers, address the evolution of the spirit, and infuse the essence of the mysteries into their hollow edifices.

Many of the popular Eastern disciplines of today have us turning away from the world around us, meditating on our navel. But Christ wasn't only a yogi; he was a mystical activist, carrying his message to those who most needed it. In this time of great transition, our ailing planet needs spiritual warriors, ones capable of standing up to the

Western materialist machine, so we can create sustainable societies that care for their citizens, harmonize with the cycles of nature, and receive and honor the vast healing light that quietly connects us all.

Notes

1. Timothy Freke and Peter Gandy, *The Jesus Mysteries* (New York: Three Rivers Press, 1999).
2. Sir James George Frazer, *The Golden Bough* (New York: Macmillan, 1992), chapter 37.

ELEVEN

Mithras and Jesus

TWO SIDES OF THE SAME COIN

FLAVIO BARBIERO

In 384 CE, Vettius Agorius Praetextatus, the last "papa" (acronym of the words *pater patrum* or father's father) of the so-called cult of Mithras died in Rome. His name and his religious and political appointments are found written in the basement of St. Peter's Basilica, together with the names of a long list of other Roman senators, spanning a period from 305 to 390. The one thing that they have in common is that they all are paters of Mithras. As many as nine among them have the supreme title of pater patrum, clear evidence that it was here, inside the Vatican, that the supreme leader of the Mithraic organization resided, at the side of the most sacred basilica of Christianity, erected by Constantine the Great in 320 CE. For at least seventy years, the supreme leaders of two religions that were always supposed to be competitors, if not sworn enemies, lived peacefully and in perfect harmony side by side. It was the same Praetextatus, as prefect of the town, who, in 367, defended Damasus against his opponents and confirmed him as bishop of Rome.

Praetextatus often declared that he would willingly be baptized if the see of St. Peter was offered to him. Following his death, however, the opposite happened. The title of pater patrum fell (today we would say by default) upon Damasus's successor, the bishop Siricius, who was the first, in the Church's history, to assume the title of papa (pope). Together with it he also took upon himself a long series of other prerogatives, titles, symbols, objects, and possessions, which passed en masse from Mithraism to Christianity.

We can only undertand this handover from the Mithraic pope to the Christian one in the light of what had happened in 383 CE, the year before. In that year, the senate almost unanimously voted for the abolition of paganism and all its symbols in Rome and throughout the Western empire. This vote has always puzzled the historians because, in their opinion, the majority of the senators were pagans and represented the last stronghold of paganism against the irresistible advance of Christianity. This opinion, however, is utterly in disagreement with what during those same years the bishop of Milan, Ambrose, used to declare, that the Christians had the majority in the senate. Who is right, Ambrose or modern historians?

The bishop of Milan was the member of a great senatorial family and closely followed Roman events, so it is unlikely that he could be wrong on a matter of that kind. On the other hand, we cannot ignore the historians because written and archaeological evidence confirm that the majority of the Roman senators were at that time paters of the Sol Invictus Mithras (the Invincible Sun Mithras), and therefore, according to common opinion, definitely pagans. What nobody seems to have understood, however, is that the two cults or religions, Mithraism and Christianity, were all but compatible. And there is no lack of historical evidence supporting that.

The most significant of many possible examples is Emperor Constantine the Great. He was an affiliate of Sol Invictus Mithras and never disowned it, not even when he openly embraced Christianity and declared himself to be "God's servant" and a sort of "universal" bishop. His biographer Eusebius hails him as the new Moses, but Constantine was baptized only on his deathbed, and he never stopped minting coins with Mithraic symbols on one side and Christian on the opposite; he even erected in Constantinople a colossal statue of himself wrapped up in Mithraic symbols.

As for the Roman senators, several contemporary sources, starting from St. Jerome, affirm that most of their wives and daughters were Christian. An extant example is St. Ambrose, himself a pagan and the son of a Mithraic pagan (the prefect of Gaul Ambrose), according to historians, although there is no doubt that his family was Christian and lived in a profoundly Christian environment. From his childhood, indeed, Ambrose loved to play the part of a bishop, and in the year 353, at St. Peter's, his sister Marcellina, still a young girl, received the veil of the consecrated virgins from Pope Liberius in person. Formally, however, he remained a pagan until he was designated bishop of Milan. He was actually baptized only fifteen days before being consecrated bishop. The fact is that in that period, Christians destined for a public career were baptized only at the point of death, or else when, for one reason or another, they decided to embrace the ecclesiastic career. This was normal practice. The senator Nectarius, who was designated bishop of Antioch by the council of Constantinople in 381, was forced to postpone the consecration ceremony because first he had to arrange his own baptism.

After the abolition of paganism, all Roman senators became Christian overnight, starting with Symmachus who went down in history for his stern defense of "pagan" traditions in front of Emperor Valentinian. A few years later, in fact, Emperor Theodosius, the most fanatic persecutor of heretics and pagans, appointed him as a consul, the highest position in the Roman bureaucracy.

How is it possible, one might ask, that people could follow two different religions at the same time? This is the essential point. There is an enormous and incredible misunderstanding (that in some way might be deliberate) about the so-called cult of the Sol Invictus Mithras, which is always presented as a religion that rose parallel with Christianity and was in competition with it. Some historians go so far as to maintain that this religion was so popular and deeply rooted in Roman society that it very nearly won the race with Christianity.

Yet there is absolute evidence that the so-called cult of Mithras in Rome was not a religion but an esoteric organization with several levels of initiation, which from the oriental religion had borrowed only the name and a few exterior symbols. For what concerns contents, scope, and operative procedures, however, the Roman Mithras had nothing in common with the Persian god.

The Roman Mithraic institution can in no way be defined as a religion devoted to the worship of the sun, no more than modern Freemasonry can be defined a religion devoted to the worship of the Great Architect of the Universe. The comparison with modern Freemasonry is quite appropriate and very helpful for understanding what kind of organization we are talking about. Actually, the two institutions are quite similar in their essential characteristic. Freemasonry's adepts are not requested to profess any particular creed but only to believe in the existence of a supreme being, however defined. This entity is represented in all masonic temples as the sun, inserted in a triangle, and with a name—Great Architect of the Universe—that is the same given by the Pythagoreans to the sun. In these temples ceremonies of various kind and rituals are performed that never have a religious character. Religion is explicitly banned from the masonic temples, but every adept is free to follow whatever creed he likes in his private life.

A link between the Mithraic and the Masonic institutions is far from improbable, as there are profound similarities in the architecture and decoration of the respective temples, symbols, rituals, and so on; but it's a theme outside the scope of this article. The comparison has been made only for the purpose of stressing the point that Mithraism was not a religion dedicated to the worship of a specific divinity but a secret association of mutual assistance, whose members were free, in their public life, to worship whatever god they liked.

And yet all the adepts of Mithras apparently shared a common attitude toward religion. This is a well-known fact. It is the same Praetextatus who exposes in an exhaustive way the philosophy of his organization in the book *Saturnalia,* written by Macrobius around

430 CE (well after the abolition of paganism). In a long conversation with other great Mithraic senators, like Symmachus and Flavianus, Praetextatus affirms that all the different gods of the pagan religion are only different manifestations (or even different names) of a unique supreme entity, represented by the sun. This syncretistic vision has been defined, with full reason, as monotheistic paganism.

Most historians agree that the followers of Mithras were monotheists; what they fail to underline is the fact that their particular syncretistic vision allowed them to infiltrate and get hold of the cult (and revenues) of all pagan divinities. In fact, all Mithraic grottos harbored (exactly as the masonic temples of today) a host of pagan gods like Saturn, Athena, Venus, Hercules, and so on, and the adepts of Mithras in their public life were priests at the service not only of the sun (who was worshipped in public temples, which had nothing to do with the Mithraic grottos) but also of all the other Roman gods.

In fact, all the senators who figure in the inscriptions at the base of St. Peters' Basilica, alongside the titles of *vir clarissimus* (senator), pater, or pater patrum in the cult of Sol Invictus Mithras, also held a long series of other religious positions: *sacerdos, hierophanta, archibucolus* of Brontes or of Hecate, Isis, and Liberius; *maior augur, quindecimvir sacris faciundis,* and even pontifex of various pagan cults. They were also in charge of the college of the vestal virgins and of the sacred fire of Vesta. In the senate, there was no manifestation of cult connected to the pagan tradition that was not celebrated by a senator adhering to the Sol Invictus Mithras. That same senator most of the time was backed by a Christian family.

So, what were they, pagan or Christian? The available evidence on this point is ambiguous. Also the character of Mithras himself, as he is depicted by Christian writers, is absolutely ambiguous. A long series of analogies exists between him and Jesus. Mithras was born on December 25 in a stable to a virgin, surrounded by shepherds who brought gifts. He was venerated on the day of the sun (Sunday). He bore a halo around his head. He celebrated a last supper with his faithful followers before returning to his father. He was said not to have died but to have ascended to heaven from where he would return in the last days to raise the dead and judge them, sending the good to paradise and the evil to hell. He guaranteed his followers immortality after baptism.

Furthermore, the followers of Mithras believed in the immortality of the soul, the last judgment, and the resurrection of the dead at the end of the world. They celebrated the atoning death of a savior who had risen on a Sunday. They celebrated a ceremony corresponding to the Catholic Mass, during which they consumed consecrated bread and wine in memory of the last supper of Mithras, and during the ceremony they used hymns, bells, candles, and holy water. Indeed, they shared with Christians a long series of other beliefs and ritual practices, to the point that they were practically indistinguishable from each other in the eyes of the pagans and also of many Christians.

The existence of a connection between Christianity and the sun cult from the earliest times is recognized by the church fathers, too. Tertullian writes that the pagans ". . . believe that the Christian God is the Sun, because it is a well-known fact that we pray turning towards the rising Sun, and that on the Sun's day we give ourselves to jubilation" (Tertullian, *Ad Nationes* 1, 13). He attempts to justify this substantial commonality in the eyes of the Christian faithful, attributing it to Satan's plagiarism of the most sacred rites and beliefs of the Christian religion.

Constantine believed that Jesus Christ and Sol Invictus Mithras were both aspects of the same superior divinity. He was certainly not the only one to have this conviction. Neoplatonism contended that the religion of the sun represented a "bridge" between paganism and Christianity. Jesus was often called by the name Sol Justitiae (Sun of Justice) and was represented by statues that were similar to the young Apollo. Clement of Alexandria describes Jesus driving the chariot of the sun across the sky, and a mosaic of the fourth century shows him on the chariot while he ascends to heaven, represented by the sun. On some coins of the fourth century, the Christian banner at the top reads Sol Invictus. A large part of the Roman population believed that Christianity and the worship of the sun were closely connected, if not the same.

For a very long time, the Romans kept on worshipping both the sun and Christ. On 410, Pope Innocentius authorized the resumption of ceremonies in honor of the sun, hoping with that to save Rome from the Visigoths. And in 460, Pope Leo the Great wrote: "most Christians, before entering the Basilica of St. Peter turn towards the sun and bow in its honour." The bishop of Troy openly continued to profess his worship of the sun even during his episcopate. Another important example in this sense is that of Synesius of Cyrene, a disciple of the famous Neoplatonic philosopher Apathias, who was killed by the mob in Alexandria in 415. Synesius, not yet baptized, was elected bishop of Ptolemais and metropolitan bishop of Cyrenaica, but he accepted the position only on condition that he did not have to retract his Neoplatonic ideas or renounce his worship of the sun.

In the light of all of this, how should we consider the position of Mithraists toward Christianity? Competitors or cooperators? Friends or enemies? Perhaps the best indication is given by the coins minted by Emperor Constantine until 320 CE, with Christian symbols on one side, Mithraic symbols on the other.

Were Jesus and Mithras two faces of the same coin?

The Origins of Mithraism and Christianity

In order to explain the strict relationship between Christianity and Mithraism, we have to go back to their origins.

Christianity, as we know it, by universal recognition, is a creation of St. Paul, the Pharisee who was sent to Rome around 61 CE, where he founded the first Christian community of the capital. The religion imposed by Paul in Rome was quite different from that preached by Jesus in Palestine and put into practice by James the Just, who was subsequently the leader of the Christian community of Jerusalem. Jesus' preaching was in line with the way of living and thinking of the sect known as the Essenes. The doctrinal contents of Christianity as it emerged in Rome at the end of the first century are, instead, extraordinarily close to those of the sect of the Pharisees, to which Paul belonged.

Paul was executed probably in 67 by Nero, together with most of his followers. The Roman Christian community was virtually wiped out by Nero's persecution. We do not have the slightest information about what happened in this community during the following thirty years; a very disturbing blackout of news because something very important happened in Rome at that period. In fact, some of the most eminent citizens of the capital were converted, like the consul Flavius Clemens, cousin of Emperor Domitian; in addition, the Roman Church assumed a monarchic structure and imposed its leadership on all the Christian communities of the empire, which had to adjust their structure and their doctrine accordingly. This is proved by a long letter of Pope Clemens to the Corinthians, written toward the end of Domitian's reign, where his leadership is clearly stated.

This means that during the years of the blackout, somebody who had access to the imperial house had revived the Roman Christian community to such a point that it could impose its authority upon all the other Christian communities. And it was "somebody" who perfectly knew the doctrine and thinking of Paul, 100 percent Pharisaic.

The Mithraic organization also was born in that same period and in that same environment. Given the scarcity of written documents on the subject, the origin and the spread of the cult of Mithras are known to us almost exclusively from archaeological evidence (remains of mithraea, dedicatory inscriptions, iconography and statues of the god, reliefs, paintings, and mosaics) that survived in large quantities throughout the Roman Empire. These archaeological testimonies prove conclusively that, apart from their common name, there was no relationship at all between the Roman cult of Mithras and the oriental religion from which it is supposed to derive. In the whole of the Persian world, in fact, there is nothing that can be compared to a Roman mithraeum.

Almost all the Mithraic monuments can be dated with relative precision and bear dedicatory inscriptions. As a result, the times and the circumstances of the spread of the Sol Invictus Mithras (these three names are indissolubly linked in all inscriptions, so there is no doubt that they refer to the same and only institution) are known to us with reasonable certainty. Also known are the names, professions, and responsibilities of a large number of people connected to it.

The first mithraeum discovered was set up in Rome at the time of Domitian, and there are precise indications that it was attended by people close to the imperial family, in particular Jewish freedmen. The mithraeum, in fact, was dedicated by a certain Titus Flavius Iginus Ephebianus, a freedman of emperor Titus Flavius, and therefore almost certainly a romanized Jew. From Rome, the Mithraic organization spread all over the western empire during the following century.

There is a third event, which happened in that same period, connected somehow to the imperial family and to the Jewish environment, to which no particular attention was ever given by the historians: the arrival in Rome of an important group of persons, fifteen Jewish high priests with their families and relatives. They belonged to a priestly class that had ruled Jerusalem for half a millennium, since the return from the Babylonian exile, when twenty-four priestly lines had stipulated a covenant among them and created a secret organization with the scope of securing the families' fortunes through the exclusive ownership of the Temple and the exclusive administration of the priesthood.

The Roman domination of Judea had been marked by passionate tensions on the religious level, which had provoked a series of revolts, the last of which, in 66 CE, was fatal for the Jewish nation and for the priestly family. With the destruction of Jerusalem by Titus Flavius in 70 CE, the Temple, the instrument of the family's power, was razed to the ground, never to be rebuilt, and priests were killed by the thousands.

There were survivors, of course, in particular a group of fifteen high priests, who had sided with the Romans, surrendering to Titus the treasure of the Temple. For that reason, they kept their properties and were given Roman citizenship. They then followed Titus to Rome, where they apparently disappeared from the stage of history, never again to play a visible role—apart from Josephus Flavius, the one who undoubtedly was the leader of that group.

Josephus was a priest who belonged to the first of the twenty-four priestly family lines. At the time of the revolt against Rome, he had played a leading role in the events that tormented Palestine. Sent by the Jerusalem Sanhedrin to be governor of Galilee, he had been the first to fight against the legions of the Roman general Titus Flavius Vespasianus, who had been ordered by Nero to quell the revolt. Barricaded inside the fortress of Jotapata, he bravely withstood the Roman troops' siege. When the city finally capitulated, he surrendered, asking to be granted a personal audience with Vespasian (The Jewish War, III, 8,9; in full, The Jewish War refers to *Flavius Josephus's Books of the History of the Jewish War against the Romans,* written around 75 CE). Their meeting led to an upturn in the fortunes of Vespasian, as well as in those of Josephus: the former was shortly to become emperor of Rome, while the latter not only had his life spared but not long afterward he was "adopted" into the emperor's family and assumed the name Flavius. He then received Roman citizenship, a patrician villa in Rome, a life income, and an enormous estate. The prize of his treason.

The priests of this group had one thing in common: They were all traitors of their people and therefore certainly banished from the Jewish community. But they all belonged to a millenarian family line, bound together by the secret organization created by Ezra and possessing a unique specialization and experience in running a religion and a country through it. The scattered remnants of the Roman Christian community offered them a wonderful opportunity to profit from their millennial experience.

We don't know anything about their activity in Rome, but we have clear hints of it through the writings of Josephus Flavius. After a few years, he started to write down the history of the events of which he had been a protagonist, with the aim, apparently, of justifying his betrayal and that of his companions. It was God's will, he claims, who called him to build a spiritual temple, instead of the material one destroyed by Titus. These words certainly were not addressed to Jewish ears but to Christian ones. Most historians are skeptical about the fact that Josephus was a Christian, and yet the evidence in his writings is compelling. In a famous passage (the so called Testimonium Flavianum) in his book *Jewish Antiquities,* he reveals his acceptance of two fundamental points: the resurrection of Jesus and his identification with the messiah of the prophecies, which are necessary and sufficient conditions for a Jew of that time to be considered a Christian. The Christian sympathies of Josephus also clearly emanate from other passages of the same work, where he speaks with great admiration of John the Baptist as well as of James, the brother of Jesus.

Josephus Flavius and St. Paul

The arguments used by Josephus Flavius to justify his own betrayal and that of his brethren seem to echo the words of St. Paul. The two seem to be perfectly in agreement with regard to their attitude toward the Roman world. Paul, for example, considered it his task to free the church of Jesus from the narrowness of Judaism and from the land of Judaea and to make it universal, linking it to Rome. They are also in agreement on other significant points: For example, both of them declare their belief in the doctrines of the Pharisees, which were those that were wholly received by the Roman church.

There are sufficient historical indications to lead us to consider it certain that the two knew each other and were linked by a strong friendship. In the Acts of the Apostles, we read that after reaching Jerusalem, Paul was brought before the high priests and the Sanhedrin to be judged (Acts 22:30). He defended himself:

> "Brethren, I am a Pharisee, the son of a Pharisee: of the hope and resurrection of the dead I am called in question." And when he had so

said, there arose a dissension between the Pharisees and the Sadducees: and the multitude was divided. For the Sadducees say that there is no resurrection, neither angel, nor spirit: but the Pharisees confess both. And there arose a great cry: and the scribes that were of the Pharisees' part arose, and strove, saying, "We find no evil in this man: but if a spirit or an angel hath spoken to him, let us not fight against God." And when there arose a great dissension, the chief captain, fearing lest Paul should have been pulled in pieces by them, commanded the soldiers to go down, and to take him by force from among them.

Josephus was a high-ranking priest, he was in Jerusalem at that time, and he certainly was present at that assembly. He had joined the sect of the Pharisees at the age of nineteen, and so he must have been among those priests who stood up to defend Paul. The apostle was then handed over to the Roman governor, Felix, who kept him under arrest for some time until he was sent to Rome, together with some other prisoners (Acts 27:1) to be judged by the emperor, to whom, as a Roman citizen, Paul had appealed. In Rome, he spent two years in prison (Acts 28:39) before being set free in 63 or 64 CE.

In his autobiography (Life, 3.13), Josephus says:

Between the age of twenty-six and twenty-seven I embarked on a journey to Rome, for the following reason. During the period when he was governor of Judaea, Felix had sent some priests to Rome to justify themselves before the emperor; I knew them to be excellent people, who had been arrested on insignificant charges. As I desired to devise a plan to save them, . . . I journeyed to Rome.

Somehow, Josephus succeeded in reaching Rome, where he made friends with Aliturus, a Jewish mime who was appreciated by Nero. Thanks to Aliturus, he was introduced to Poppaea, the wife of the emperor, and through her agency, he succeeded in freeing the priests (Life, 3.16).

The correspondence of dates, facts, and people involved is so perfect that it is difficult to avoid the conclusion that Josephus went to Rome, at his own personal risk and expense, specifically to free Paul and his companions, and that it was due to his intervention that the apostle was released. This presupposes that the relationship between the two was much closer than that of a simple occasional acquaintance. Thus, Josephus must have known much more about Christianity than is evident from his works, and his knowledge came directly from the teaching of Paul, of whom, in all likelihood, he was a disciple.

When Josepus returned to Rome in 70 CE, his master had been executed, together with most of the Christians he had converted. His fatherland had been annihilated; the Temple, destroyed; the priestly family, exterminated; his reputation, tarnished by the stain of treachery. He must have been animated by very strong desires for redemption and revenge. Besides, he probably felt responsible for the destinies of the humiliated remnants of one of the greatest families in the world—the fifteen high priests who shared his same condition. There is information about a meeting presided over by Josephus Flavius, unquestionably the strongest and most important character in that group of people, during the course of which the priests examined the situation of the their family and decided on a strategy to improve its fortunes. Josephus lucidly conceived a plan that, in those circumstances, would have appeared to anybody else to be the utmost folly. This man, sitting amid the smoking ruins of what had been his fatherland, surrounded by a few humiliated, disconsolate survivors rejected by their fellow countrymen, aspired to no less than conquering that enormous, powerful empire that had defeated him and establishing his descendants and those of the men around him as the ruling class of that empire.

The first step in that strategy was taking control of the newborn Christian religion and transforming it into a solid basis of power for the priestly family. Having come to Rome in the entourage of Titus, and thus strong in the emperor's protection and well supplied from an economic point of view, these priests could not have encountered great problems in taking over the leadership of the tiny group of Christians who had survived Nero's persecution, legitimated as they were by the relationship of Josephus Flavius with Paul.

Only six years had passed since he sought Paul's freedom from Roman imprisonment. The apostle of the nations must have died at least three years before. Josephus must have felt a moral obligation to continue the deeds of his ancient master whose doctrine he knew perfectly, and sensing its potential for propagation in the Roman world, he dedicated himself and his organization of priests to its practical implementation. Once he had created a strong Christian community in the capital, it could not have been difficult for the priests to impose its authority on the other Christian communities scattered around the empire—first of all, on those who had been created or catechized by Paul himself.

Josephus Flavius and the Sol Invictus Mithras

Josephus Flavius knew all too well that no religion has a future unless it is an integral part of a system of political power. This concept that religion and political power should live together in symbiosis, mutually sustaining each other, was innate in the DNA, so to speak, of the priests of Judah. It is unimaginable that he could think that the new religion would spread throughout the empire independently, or even in contrast to political power. His first aim was, therefore, seizing power. Thanks not only to the millennial experience of his family, but also to his own experience of life, Josephus knew all too well that political power, especially in an elephantine organism such as the Roman Empire, was based on military power, and military power was based on economic power, and economic power on the ability to influence and control the financial leverage of the country. He must have envisaged that the priestly family would sooner or later take control of these levers. Then the empire would be in his hands, and the new religion would be the main instrument to maintain control of it.

What was Josephus's plan to achieve this ambitious project? He didn't have to invent anything; the model was there: the secret organization created by Ezra a few centuries earlier, which had assured power and prosperity to the priestly families for half a millennium. He only had to make a few changes to disguise this institution in the pagan world as a mystery religion, dedicated to the Greek sun god Helios, a name with undoubted assonance with El Elyon, the Jewish god. He was represented as invincible, the Sol Invictus, to spur the morale of his adepts, and at his side was put, as an inseparable companion, a solar divinity of that same Mesopotamia from where the Jews had originated—Mithras, the sun's envoy on Earth to redeem humanity. And all around them, in the mithraea, were the statues of various divinities: Athena, Hercules, Venus, and so on. This arrangement was a clear reference to God the father and his envoy on Earth, Jesus, surrounded by attributes of wisdom, strength, beauty, and so on—well understood by the Christians but still perfectly pagan to a pagan's eye.

This organization didn't have any religious purpose: its scope was to preserve union between the priestly families and assure their security and wealth, through mutual support and a common strategy, aimed at infiltrating all the positions of power in Roman society.

It was secret. In spite of the fact that it lasted for three centuries and it had thousands of members, most of them very cultured men, there isn't a single word written by a member about what was going on during the meetings of the Mithraic institution, what decisions were taken, and so on. This means that absolute secrecy was always maintained about the works that were held in a mithraeum.

The access was evidently reserved for the descendants of priestly families, at least at the operative level, from the third grade up (occasionally people of different origin could be accepted in the first two grades, as in the case of Emperor Commodus). This system of recruitment is perfectly in line with the historical and archaeological evidence. Even at the peak of its power and diffusion, the Sol Invictus Mithras appears to be an elitist institution, with a very limited number of members. Most mithraea were very small in size and could not harbor more than twenty people. It was definitely not a mass religion but an organization to which only the top leaders of the army and of the imperial bureaucracy were admitted. Yet, we don't know anything about the enlisting policy of the Sol Invictus Mithras. Did it recruit its members among the high ranks of Roman society, or was the opposite true—that it was the members of this organization who "infiltrated" all the positions of power of that society? Historical evidence favors the hypothesis that membership in the institution was reserved on a ethnic basis. Access to it, at least at the operative level, was most likely reserved for descendants of the group of the Jewish priests who came to Rome after the destruction of Jerusalem.

The Sol Invictus Mithras
Conquers the Roman Empire

Written sources and the archaeological testimonies give evidence that from Domitian on, Rome always remained the most important center of the Sol Invictus Mithras institution, which had become firmly entrenched at the very heart of the imperial administration, both in the palace and among the Praetorian guard. From Rome, the organization soon spread to nearby Ostia, the port with the hightest volume of trading in the world, as goods and foodstuffs from every part of the empire arrived to delight the insatiable appetite of the capital. In the course of the second and third centuries, almost forty mithraea were built there, clear evidence that the members of the institution had taken control of trading activities, source of incomparable incomes and economic power.

Subsequently, it spread to the rest of the empire. The first mithraea to arise outside the Roman circle were built, shortly before 110 CE, in Pannonia, at Poetovium, the main customs center of the region, then in the military garrison of Carnuntum, and soon after in all the Danubian provinces (Rhaetia, Noricum, Pannonia, Mesia, and Dacia). The followers of the cult of Mithras included the customs officers, who collected a tax on every kind of transport dispatched from Italy toward central

Europe and vice versa; the imperial functionaries controlled transport, the post, the administration of finance and mines, and, last, the military troops of the garrisons scattered along the border. Almost in the same period as in the Danubian region, the cult of Mithras started to appear in the basin of the Rhine, at Bonn and Treves. This was followed by Britannia, Spain, and North Africa, where mithraea appeared in the early decades of the second century, always associated with administrative centers and military garrisons.

Archaeological evidence, therefore, conclusively demonstrates that throughout the second century CE, the members of Sol Invictus Mithras occupied the main positions in the public administration, becoming the dominant class in the outlying provinces of the empire—especially in central and northern Europe. We have seen that members of Sol Invictus Mithras had also infiltrated the pagan religion, taking control of the cult of the main divinities, starting with the sun.

The winning move, however, which made success of the Mithraic institution irresistible, was seizing control of the army. Josephus Flavius knew, from direct experience, that the army could become the arbiter of the imperial throne. Whoever controlled the army controlled the empire. The main aim fixed by him for the Mithraic organization, therefore, must have been infiltrating the army and taking control of it.

Soon, mithraea sprang up in all the places where Roman garrisons were stationed. Within a century, the cult of Mithras had succeeded in controlling all the Roman legions stationed in the provinces and along the borders, at a point that the worship of Sol Invictus Mithras is often considered by historians to be the "religion" typical of Roman soldiers.

Even before the army, however, the attention of Sol Invictus had been concentrated on the Praetorian guard, the emperor's personal guard. It is not by chance that the second known dedicatory inscription of a Mithraic character regards a commander of the Praetorium, and that the concentration of mithraea was particularly high in the area surrounding the Praetorian barracks. The infiltration of this body must have started under the Flavian emperors. They could count on the unconditional loyalty of many Jewish freedmen who owed them everything—their lives, their safety, and their well-being. The Roman emperors were somewhat reluctant to entrust their personal safety to officers who came from the ranks of the Roman senate, their main political adversary, and so the ranks of their personal guard were mainly filled with freedmen and members of the equestrian class. This must have favored the Sol Invictus, which made the Praetorium its unchallenged fief from the beginning of the second century on.

Once it achieved control of the Praetorium and the army, the Sol Invictus Mithras was able to put its hands also on the imperial office. This actually happened on 193 CE, when Septimius Severus was proclaimed emperor by the army. Born in Leptis Magna, in North Africa, to an equestrian family of high-ranking bureaucrats, he was certainly an affiliate of the Mithraic organization, having married Julia Domna, sister of Bassianus, a high priest of Sol Invictus. From then on, the imperial office was the prerogative of the Sol Invictus Mithras, as all emperors were proclaimed and/or removed by the army or by the praetorian guard.

As far as we can judge with hindsight, the final objective of the strategy devised by Josephus Flavius was the complete substitution of the ruling class of the Roman Empire with members of Sol Invictus Mithras. This result was achieved in less than two centuries, thanks to the policy enforced by the Mitharaic emperors. The backbone of the Roman imperial administration was formed by new families of unknown origin who had emerged at the end of the first century and the beginning of the second; they were antagonistic to the senatorial aristocracy and traditionally opposed to the imperial power. They formed the so-called equestrian order, which soon became the undisputed fiefdom of the Sol Invictus Mithras. For sure, most of the families of the fifteen Jewish priests of Josephus Flavius's entourage—rich, well connected and enjoying the imperial favor—belonged to this order.

The Sol Invictus emperors all belonged to the equestrian order and governed in open opposition to the senate—humiliating it, depriving it of its prerogatives and wealth, and striking it physically with the exile and execution of a great number of its high-profile members. At the same time, they started introducing equestrian families into the senate. This policy had been initiated by Septimius Severus and developed by Gallienus (who, we must remember, was also the author of the first Edict of Tolerance toward Christianity), who established by decree that all those who had held the position of provincial governors or prefects of the praetorian guard (both appointments reserved for the equestrian order) would enter by right into the senatorial ranks. This right was later extended to other categories of functionary, great bureaucrats and high-ranking army officers (all members of the Mithraic institution). As a result, within a few decades, virtually the whole equestrian class passed into the ranks of the senate, outnumbering the families of the original Italic and Roman aristocracy.

In the meantime, the spread of Christianity throughout the empire proceeded at a steady pace. Wherever the representatives of Mithras arrived, a Christian community immediately sprang up. By the end of the second century, there were already at least four bishop's sees in Britannia, sixteen in Gaul, sixteen in Spain, and one in practically every big city in North Africa and the Middle East. In 261, Christianity was recognized as lawful religion by the Mithraic Gallienus and was proclaimed the official religion of the empire by the Mithraic Constantine at the beginning of the fourth century, although it was still in a minority in Roman society. It was then gradually enforced on the population of the empire, with a series of measures that culminated at the end of the fourth century with the abolition of the pagan religions and the mass "conversion" of the Roman senate.

The final situation regarding the ruling class of the Western Empire was the following: the ancient nobility of pagan origin had virtually disappeared, and the new great nobility, which identified itself with the senatorial class of the landowners, was made up by former members of the Sol Invictus Mitras. On the religious level, paganism had been eliminated, and Christianity had become the religion of all the inhabitants of the empire; it was controlled by ecclesiastical hierarchies, coming entirely from the senatorial class, endowed with immense landed properties and quasi-royal powers within their sees.

The priestly families had become the absolute master of that same empire that had destroyed Israel and the Temple of Jerusalem. All its high offices, both civil and religious, and all its wealth were in their hands, and supreme power had been entrusted in perpetuity, by divine right, to the most illustrious of the priestly tribes, the Gens Flavia (starting with Constantine, all Roman emperors bore the name of Flavius), in all likelihood descendants of Josephus Flavius.

Three centuries earlier, Josephus had written with pride: "My family is not obscure, on the contrary, it is of priestly descent: as in all peoples there is a different foundation of the nobility, so with us the excellence of the line is confirmed by its belonging to the priestly order" (Life, 1.1)

By the end of the fourth century, his descendants had every right to apply those same words to the Roman Empire. At that point the institution of the Sol Invictus Mithras was no more necessary to boost the fortunes of the priestly family, and it was disposed of. It had been the instrument of the most successful conspiracy in history.

TWELVE

Star Beings in Stone?

A ROCK ART SITE
IN CENTRAL SOUTH AFRICA

GARY A. DAVID

Under the South African Sun

At the southern tip of Africa, equidistant from the Indian Ocean and the Atlantic, lies a high plateau known as the Great Karoo. This arid savannah aptly called the thornveld is dotted with camel thorn and umbrella trees. South of the fabled Kalahari Desert, the harsh region is still hot enough in summer for temperatures to reach well over 100 degrees Fahrenheit.

The late summer monsoon rains drawn from the Indian Ocean sometimes collect in saltpans spread across the barren plains—then quickly dry up. Rainfall in the northern part of the Great Karoo averages only about eight inches annually. Thunderstorms are violent but patchy, with ribbons of rain sometimes evaporating before reaching the ground—much like on the deserts of the American Southwest. However, the rainfall here was once sufficient to support a rich diversity of wildlife: giraffe, zebra, wildebeest, hartebeest, eland, springbok, buffalo, and ostrich. Along riparian areas rhino, hippo, and elephant roamed. Predator species included lion, leopard, hyena, and wild dog.

This unforgiving territory is the ancestral homeland of the San, sometimes known as Bushmen, and the Khoi, the latter formerly called the Hottentots. In fact, the word *karoo* is a San word that means "land of great thirst." Diffusionist archaeologist Cyril A. Hromnik, who was born in Slovakia, educated at Syracuse University, and lives in Cape town, South Africa, claims that the word *karu* is actually a Tamil term (Dravidian of southern India) meaning "arid country."[1] Hromnik further believes that the Khoi (Hottentots), whom he calls the Quena, are descendants of Indian fathers and South African San mothers.[2] The San were basically hunter-gatherers, whereas the later Khoi were pastoralists, herding sheep and cattle. The San and their famous click language were introduced to Western popular culture by the humorous movie *The Gods Must Be Crazy* and the more recent Disney film *A Far Off Place*.

On the distant horizon flat-topped hills (koppies) of sandstone and shale also resemble the mesas of my home territory in the southwestern United States. Dark dolerite outcroppings strewn with mineral-stained, igneous boulders were perfect for carving petroglyphs, or, as they call them in South Africa, rock engravings.

In September of 2009, I had the opportunity to travel there to assist my friend and colleague Rob Milne with his rock art research.[3] He and I, along with his wife, Slava, visited a site called Driekopseiland, an Afrikaans name meaning "three hills island." It is located on a working farm along the Riet River near the city of Kimberley in Northern Cape Province. Little did I expect to encounter images in stone that resembled the star beings carved by the ancient Hopi Indians of Arizona.

We arrived on the vernal equinox (September 22) at about 5 a.m., when Orion was just reaching its meridian. Getting out of the car to open the farm gates, I saw both Crux (the Southern Cross) and the brilliant Canopus for the first time in my life—the second brightest star in the night sky after Sirius. The San, by the way, consider Sirius to be the grandmother of Canopus. A few rabbits and a steenbok (antelope) darted across the dirt road, as we made our way to the site in the predawn chill. (Later in

Figure 12.1. The author Rob Miln, and San guide, Adam. Photo by Bronislava Milne.

the day, we saw a warthog dash across the road and a troop of mongooses scampering about and chattering. Surely a cobra must have been nearby.)

The Riet (Reed) River, a tributary of the mighty Orange River that flows into the Atlantic, is lined with nonindigenous eucalyptus trees and reeds over fifteen feet high.* Driekopseiland contains over 3,500 engravings pecked or chiseled into a glaciated andesite "pavement" that parallels the river. The main part of this blue-gray slab is cut by natural fractures, thin and straight, that divide the horizontal rock expanse into various sections or panels. The whole area is at least 150 yards long and 75 yards wide (see color plate 6).

According to archaeologist David Morris, whom we later met at McGregor Museum in Kimberley and who autographed his new book for us (see note 8), over 90 percent of the petroglyphs are geometric, abstract, or nonrepresentational: grids, meanders, dots, hatches, zigzags, concentric circles, ovals, spirals, star shapes, sunbursts, nested figures, and calendar wheels. Every foot or so we came across some bewildering design deeply

---

*As I wrote in my book *Eye of the Phoenix,* the reed is a universal symbol of civilization, high culture, education, writing, and even celestial significance. For instance, the Hopi refer to the Milky Way by the term *songwuka,* literally "big reed." They have a legend of coming up through a great reed from the previous Third World to the present Fourth Wold. This perhaps suggests an interstellar journey along the galactic axis.

carved into a plane of stone so smooth it almost looked polished. Ranging in size from a few inches to a few feet, these perplexing petroglyphs were rarely superimposed—that is, one carved on top of the other.

We even found a great number of Celtic crosses, which are equilateral crosses inside circles. South African scholar Brenda Sullivan comments on their meaning:

> This symbol has many names. It has been called the five-fold bond, the tree of life enclosed within the circle of eternity, and more commonly, the Celtic cross. Well, the Celts may claim pride of name, but this most ancient symbol has been associated with the isangomas [medicine people] of Africa for millennia, and is still one of Africa's most powerful signs of protection and communication with the Creator through the Shades.[4]

On a panel downstream from the main section of the site, we also found petroglyphs that represented a number of animals: eland, elephant, rhino, baboon, anteater, and warthog. We encountered a few human-shaped engravings cut into the horizontal surface as well, which in some cases was as flat as a paved roadway.

Because rock art is difficult to date, the time frame of these images frozen in stone is anybody's educated guess. Estimates range widely—from between the tenth millennium BCE and the end of the first millennium CE.

Figure 12.2. Dawn along the Riet River, South Africa. The dam (seen in the background) was built upstream from the petroglyphs in the 1920s.

Figure 12.3. Foreground: profile of creature with headdress framed by natural triangular fractures

Figure 12.4. Celtic crosses (upper left), sunburst, abstracts. Photo by Bronislava Milne.

Figure 12.5. Lunar calendar: 13 lines inside inner circle and 28 lines in outer circle

Figure 12.6. Cupules forming space-capsule cone (?); ingot shape (upper left) is one of a group.

Figure 12.7. Geometric petroglyphs at Driekopseiland. Photo by Bronislava Milne.

Whenever the Driekopseiland glyphs were incised, they certainly took a long time to make. In other words, these labor-intensive markings were no idle doodling to while away a hot afternoon. Andesite is a fairly hard mineral and is rated 6 on the Mohs scale. Granite is a bit harder at 6.5 and quartz is only 7. Diamond is the hardest mineral and rates 10 on the scale. Mined for thousands of years not far from here, the holy "Stones of the Sun" were most likely used to carve this hard rock. In 1866, these valuable gems were discovered downstream from the confluence of the Orange and Vaal rivers, and hordes of miners flooded the area. Kimberley, of course, is now home to the world-famous De Beers Corporation, whose "Big Hole" and museum Rob, Slava, and I later visited.

But what is the meaning of these enigmatic dream symbols carved into the bedrock? David Lewis-Williams, cognitive archaeologist and specialist in South African rock art, says that these engravings were not merely representations of the natural world or abstractions of inner space rendered on static stone. Unlike the modern artist's canvas, they were instead "windows on other worlds"—veils between the physical world and the spirit world. Like the interactive screens of a sacred video game, the petroglyphs were in fact "reservoirs of potency" that came alive the moment the San people trance-danced*[5] in front of them.[6]

Lewis-Williams is also the major proponent of the theory that the geometrics found at Driekopseiland were a depiction of the entoptics created by the optic nerve in the initial stages of an altered state. The shaman experienced these varied abstract shapes via intense drumming and dancing, sometimes in conjunction with hallucinogens. Just rub your eyes hard to get a mild sense of this phenomenon.

---

*The trance dance is a curing ritual whereby spirits are contacted. Resembling the Native American Ghost Dance of the late-nineteenth century, it is performed by dancing in a ring, using hyperventilation in order to create a state of transcendent exhaustion. "The !Kung [San] medicine man gradually works himself up into a state of trembling and sweating. When he approaches trance, he feels a rising sensation which he ascribes to the 'boiling' of his medicine (n/om); as he enters deep trance, he falls to the ground, sometimes executing a somersault."

Even the academic Professor Morris admits to the sacrosanct function of the engravings. "As a powerful portal between spiritual realms, a point of breakthrough perhaps second to none in the area, Driekopseiland would have been the kind of place where !Khwa was appeased, where protections were sought, so that 'the rain comes down gently.'"[7]

Like the Pueblo people of the American Southwest, the San distinguish between (1) "male rain," or lightning, fierce winds, and thunderstorms that pummel Earth, causing floods, and (2) "female rain," or gentle rains that slowly soak into Earth.[8] Morris believes that the ancient people who made these carvings conceptualized the river as the mythic water snake* named !Khwa, a figure prominent in San mythology.

> The regular emergence and submergence of images from the waters of the Gama-!ab [San term for Riet River] seems to us a crucial element in the power of the engravings and, arguably, a key to their meaning. Like the body of a large beast living in the depths of the river, the rock surfaces appear to rise from one medium to another, glistening, striated and engraved. Using a related analogue, the artist Walter Battiss spoke of "great whales lying in the mud" of Driekops Eiland, their backs "decorated with innumerable designs."[10]

Arching its engraved back, the giant snake breaks the surface of the water—then plunges back into the stream. This vertical undulation has cosmological significance due to the fact that "to go under water" is a San trance metaphor for death or to die.

Likewise, the Hopi describe a subterranean water serpent known as Pálulukang, which lives in springs, waterholes, or rivers and controls thunderstorms and floods (see plate 7). Hopi cosmology also identifies the underworld with a pluvial afterlife where departed spirits reside.

The late epigrapher Barry Fell had interpreted some of the more

---

*The San used to call out to the mythical Water Snake: "Your breast gurgles because it is full of water. The stars love you—therefore the gemstone gleams on your head." Was this gemstone a diamond?[9]

*Figure 12.8. Phallic engravings with cupules next to river
(dark area to the left)*

abstract symbols at Driekopeiland as Libyan inscriptions written in Ogam script, one translation of which is as follows: "Under constant attack we have quit this place to occupy a safe stronghold." Brenda Sullivan amplifies Fell's rendition: "'People suffering. A time of death and suffering. People were forced to abandon the place, and seek protection elsewhere'—either because they were attacked, or because of violent storms and flooding."[11]

Although I am not psychic, as I sat in the midday sun at this site, a vague sense of malaise and subliminal tension pervaded the atmosphere. Even my South African friend Rob admitted he would not camp overnight there, due not to the dangerous wildlife but because of the evil spirits that potentially inhabit the place even today. Maybe we were simply experiencing, to quote the South African author Laurens van der Post, "the ghosts of Africa which, as we all knew, walked not at midnight but noon."[12]

Some of the most puzzling engravings that we found depicted

humanoids with some sort of bizarre paraphernalia. What Rob has dubbed "the spaceman" is located adjacent to "the flying saucer" and "the rocket." The protrusion from this figure's helmet is somewhat similar to the cone-shaped nose on a Hopi kachina, or spirit messenger (see plates 8 and 9; and plate 10).

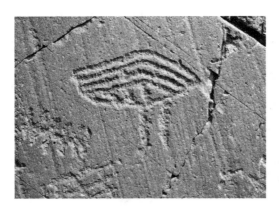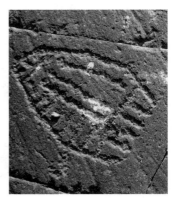

Figure 12.9. Left: Petroglyph of flying saucer ascending (?).
Right: Petroglyph of cone-shaped rocket (?).

The intimacy that many African tribes have with the celestial realm is presently confirmed by a world-renowned Zulu *sangoma* (medicine man) and high *sanusi* (uplifter of the people), whose name is Vusamazulu Credo Mutwa. Unlike most academics, who seem to put up barriers between peoples and compartmentalize them for study, Baba Mutwa continuously shows us the enduring but dynamic connections between continents. For instance, he sees direct parallels between Native American and African tribes.

> There is not a single nation among Native American peoples whom I visited in my journeys to the United States that does not have cultural and linguistic links with Africa. Among the Hopi Indians of the American Southwest, I found a custom where masked people, who are called *Kachinas,* come at certain times during the year and conduct sacred ceremonies and bless the people. In the African country known as Zambia, there is a group of people who practice what

is called *Mackishee*. People wearing elaborate masks, which refer to certain spirits, visit villages at times and listen to confessions of the villagers' sins. These "spirits" bless the people for the coming period of time and go on their way again.[13]

Credo Mutwa claims that creatures from a star in Orion once lived in prehuman times on Earth and built a huge subterranean metropolis in the heart of Africa.

Before human beings were created on this planet, there had existed a very wise race of people known as the Imanyukela. These people had come from the constellation known to white people as Orion, and they had inhabited our earth for thousands and thousands of years. And that before they had left our earth to return once more to the sacred Spider constellation, they made a great evacuation under the earth, beneath the Ruwensory [Rwenzori] Mountains—the Mountains of the Moon. And deep in the bowels of Mother Earth, the Imanyukela built a city of copper buildings. A city with a wall of silver all around it. A city built at the huge mountain of pure crystal. The mountain of knowledge. The mountain from which all knowledge on earth comes. And a mountain to which all knowledge on earth ultimately returns.[14]

The Hopi also have a female spider figure named Kokyangwuhti, who usually assists people in their quests and was present during the origin of humankind. The Hopi, incidentally, acknowledge four races of people. Spider Grandmother gathered four colors of mud—black, white, yellow, and red—and mixed them with her saliva to create these four races, each with its own basic language. Humans were, by the way, created in the image of the sky god Sótuknang (see plate 10). In addition, the Hopi have many legends of what they call "flying shields."

Rob Milne believes that the depiction of the eight legs would be superfluous, because the spider is stationary. Credo Mutwa claims that Orion is the spider constellation.

10-25 mm

Trapdoor burrow

Figure 12.10. Left: Driekopseiland "spaceman" engraving next to trapdoor spider and burrow. Right: The trapdoor spider, a nocturnal arachnid.

One petroglyph that Rob showed me ostensibly looked like a sun symbol, with rays emanating from the circle. Then I flashed on another icon of a very different sort and thought, "no, that can't be it," and put it in the back of my mind.

There are seven rays in each hemisphere of the circle, corresponding to the pulsars (see figure 12.11, left). At the upper right is a circle that contains two lines, corresponding to the hydrogen molecule on the plaque. The outer circle may contain thirty-three rays, but it is impossible to tell because the rock surface is flaked to the immediate right of the circle.

Later, I got a picture of NASA's Pioneer plaque and compared it with the engraving with a radial pattern (see figure 12.11, right). The six-inch-by-nine-inch gold-anodized aluminum plaque shows the position of the sun with respect to the center of the galaxy and nearby pulsars. Carl Sagan and Frank Drake created it in an attempt to communicate with extraterrestrial life somewhere in the far reaches of outer space. Launched in 1972, the Pioneer 10 and the Pioneer 11 were the first spacecraft designed to leave the solar system, and both carry duplicates of the plaque. It displays the then nine planets, including Pluto, which, by the way, was discovered at Lowell Observatory in Arizona. It also shows the Pioneer spacecraft's planet of origin, its trajectory past Mars and Jupiter, and its slingshot past Saturn, outward from our helio-

heart. The radial pattern consists of fourteen lines made up of long binary numbers that represent the periods of the pulsars. The horizontal line that extends past the humans represents the sun's relative distance to the center of the galaxy. A silhouette of the spacecraft in scale is juxtaposed to the humans so that relative size can be determined. The two circles at the top represent the fundamental state of the hydrogen atom, which acts as a universal clock. The regular decrease in the frequency of the pulsars will enable extraterrestrials to determine the time elapsed since each spacecraft was launched. In about two million years, the plaque should arrive at Aldebaran, sixty-eight light-years away. Let's hope that whatever intelligence retrieving this message in a bottle is not reading an elegy to an extinct civilization.

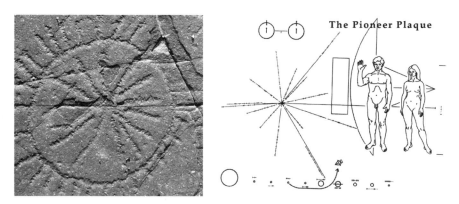

Figure 12.11. Left: Petroglyph with radial pattern. Photo is rotated so the natural rock fracture bisecting the circle is horizontal. Right: NASA's Pioneer plaque.

Did the people who made this South African rock engraving, perhaps thousands of years ago, actually "remote view" the future and glimpse this image we created in the late twentieth century, which is now bound for the stars? Were they in contact with an intelligence that knew about the Pioneer plaque from their journeys through space-time and wanted to convey its significance to indigenous tribes? Or is this all just a big coincidence?

Countless hours were spent carving sacred symbols into obdurate stone. These inner visions of the spirit world had been received from both cathartic trance states and quiescent deep meditation. The veil between the physical and nonphysical universes was extremely thin, and in many cases, the interaction between the two occurred right at the rock surface, which appeared as a translucent and permeable membrane.

Beyond the two worlds merging like dual circles of the *vesica piscis* are myriad realities, world upon world. Some of these are stars with revolving planets inhabited by entities whose technologies may be millions of years ahead of ours. Other worlds are purely interdimensional, with completely different laws of physics and ontological paradigms. As postmodernists thousands of years removed from San sensibilities, we must in the end admit that we are nothing but Horatios confronting this "wondrous strange." At the end of the nineteenth century, one San informant reported: "We do not utter a star man's name."[13]

Notes

1. Maré Mouton, "South Africa Is Denied Its Rich Cultural History," *Village Life* 15, December 2005–January 2006: 21.

2. "Were Indians the First Colonists in SA?" Electronic Mail & Guardian, October 7, 1997, www.montaguguanocave.co.za/docs/cave-article.pdf.

3. See Rob Milne's excellent book *Anecdotes of the Anglo-Boer War* (Johannesburg, South Africa: Covos Day Books, 2000). For photos and explanations of South African rock art, see his website: www.robmilne.com. Also, read his description of an Orion Correlation and engraving site near Lydenburg in Mpumalanga ("rising sun") Province of South Africa, which was published in appendix 1, Gary A. David, *Eye of the Phoenix* (Adventures Unlimited Press, 2008). Rob's comprehensive book on South African archaeoastronomy titled *Beyond Orion* is forthcoming.

4. Brenda Sullivan, *Spirit of the Rocks* (Cape Town/Pretoria/Johannesburg, South Africa: Human & Rousseau, 1995), p. 13. For information on the Celtic cross as ancient navigational instrument and architectural tool, see Crichton E M Miller's excellent book *The Golden Thread of Time* (Rugby, Warwickshire, U.K.: Pendulum Publishing, 2001).

5. J. David Lewis-Williams, *A Cosmos In Stone: Interpreting Religion and Society*

Through Rock Art (Walnut Creek, California: Altamira Press, 2002), 59.

6. David Lewis-Williams and Geoffrey Blundell, *Fragile Heritage: A Rock Art Fieldguide* (Johannesburg, South Africa: Witwatersrand University Press, 1998), 24–25.

7. David Morris, "Introducing a new interpretation of Driekopseiland," www .driekopseiland.itgo.com/about.html.

8. Lewis-Williams and Blundell, *Fragile Heritage,* op. cit., 21.

9. "/Xam [San] astronomical references in G R von Wielligh's Boesman-Stories," www.psychohistorian.org/astronomy.

10. John Parkington, David Morris, and Neil Rusch, *Karoo Rock Engravings: Marking Places in the Landscape* (Cape Town, South Africa: Southern Cross Ventures, August 2008), 78.

11. Barry Fell, "Ogam Inscriptions from North and South Africa," and Brenda (Sullivan) Wintgen, Ph.D., "Ntethological Analysis of Ogam Script from Driekopseiland Translated and Published by Professor Barry Fell," both articles from the Epigraphic Society Occasional Publications, vol. 6, no. 116, 1979.

12. Laurens van der Post, *The Lost World of the Kalahari* (Middlesex, England: Penguin Books, 1968), 37.

13. Vusamazulu Credo Mutwa, *Zulu Shaman: Dreams, Prophecies, and Mysteries,* edited by Stephen Larsen, original title *Song of the Stars* (Rochester, Vermont: Destiny Books, 2003, 1996), 157.

14. "Vusa'mazulu Credo Mutwa—Biography 03: Mysteries of Africa," http://credo-mutwa.com/about/biography-03.

15. "Story: We do not utter a star man's name," Lucy Lloyd /Xam Notebooks, December 1878, The Digital Bleek & Lloyd, http://lloydbleekcollection.cs.uct .ac.za/data/stories/826/index.htm.

THIRTEEN

Serpent of the North

THE OVERLOOK MOUNTAIN–DRACO
CONSTELLATION CORRELATION

GLENN M. KREISBERG

The stone constructions discussed in this article represent the discovery of a petroform, that is a purposeful arrangement in rock or stone that may be geometric, animal, or human in shape. Covering an area of several acres on a southeastern-facing slope of Overlook Mountain in Woodstock, New York, a grouping of very large, carefully constructed lithic formations, when connected together and taken as whole, appear to create a serpent or snake figure or effigy. The large stone constructions, consisting of six very large stone cairns along with two snake effigies or serpent walls, are surrounded by a few dozen, much smaller stone cairns arranged in clusters and rows. Native American seasonal habitation sites have been documented nearby dating to 4000 years BCE and the site, in recent years, was visited by a Native American tribal preservation officer who, along with many other individuals who have visited the site, felt great awe, wonder, and deep respect for the ancient stone symbols present at the site. If the petroform is confirmed as authentic and constructed in antiquity, it can be inferred that the site was at one time (and still should be) considered sacred. Additionally, because of the close correlation between the two representations, it is proposed that the snake symbol petroform created by the large lithic structure on Overlook Mountain may represent the star constellation Draco (the dragon).

History and Description of the Site

Overlook Mountain has long been an iconic image, looming above the Hudson River Valley, acting as sentry to the easternmost woodland slopes of the Catskill Mountains in upstate New York. Drawn to those slopes for thousands of years, humans have worked and roamed there as prehistoric hunter-gatherers, early agrarians, colonial lumber cutters and hide tanners, early American glass blowers and quarrymen, and twentieth-century utopians, hikers, and hunters. With such a long and varied past, it's safe to say Overlook Mountain can be recognized as

Figure 13.1. Overlook Mountain

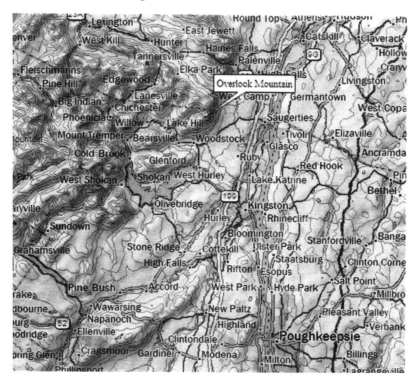

a serial-use area: an area used by many different groups of people, for many different purposes and reasons, for thousands of years.

Beyond that, Overlook Mountain has inspired, enlightened, and invoked. From the practical to the artistic and spiritual, the mountain has been the source and subject of countless paintings, drawings, illustrations, meditations, poetry, and books, all seeking in some way to capture, experience, and ultimately document the essence and nature of the tangible as well as intangible aspects the mountain possesses.

There is little doubt an aspect of paramount importance to the early indigenous dwellers of Overlook Mountain and the lands surrounding, whose connection to the natural world was both intimate and profound compared to this day and age, would have been the relationship and connection between the mountain and the sky.

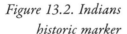

Figure 13.2. Indians historic marker

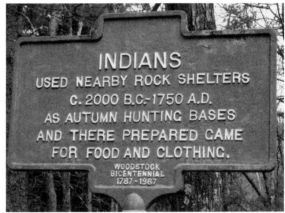

My interest in the history of Overlook Mountain began in 2004 when a cell tower was proposed for the California Quarry, a historic bluestone quarry on the lower slopes of the mountain, which operated from the 1830s to the 1890s. During that period, the California Quarry, along with other, smaller, surrounding quarries, contributed greatly to early American industry and commerce in the region. While researching the quarry property, I was introduced to the many stone mounds that were present on the 196-acre quarry property and nearby adjacent parcels. Early property deeds for the area show "ancient stone

Figure 13.3.
Bluestone quarry
historic marker

NEW YORK

BLUESTONE QUARRY
THE CALIFORNIA QUARRY, ON
OVERLOOK MOUNTAIN, NORTH,
WAS ONE OF THE LARGEST OF
THESE INDUSTRIES, WHICH
FLOURISHED, 1839–1900.

STATE EDUCATION
DEPARTMENT 1935

monuments" present from the first land grants, patents, and subdivisions recorded.

In all, nearly five dozen cairns have been identified on the southeastern slopes of Overlook Mountain between an elevation of 1,100 and 1,500 feet. Most of the cairns are well formed and show deliberate construction techniques and practices, such as dry stacking and the use of retaining walls. In some cases, it appears quartzite and hematite

Figure 13.4. Overlook Mountain cairn

"donation" stones, which are not structural in nature, were left on the piles.

The construction of the cell tower caused the destruction of five of the nearly sixty stone cairns present in the vicinity. In 2006 as part of the cell tower application review process, Sherry White, tribal preservation officer of the Stockbridge Munsee Community Band of Mohican, visited the cairns and expressed the belief that the larger of the structures could be a memorial or burial cairn. Having toured the entire site, it was her belief the Overlook Mountain cairn complex can likely be seen as a sacred precinct where local groups constructed memorial or burial cairns over successive generations, but it may also be part of more widely spread spiritual, ritualistic, and ceremonial practices and beliefs. Due to the presence of cultural resources of historic (and perhaps prehistoric) significance at the site, a National Register of Historic Places application for the California Quarry property was prepared, submitted, and is currently in review and pending with the New York State Office of Parks, Recreation and Historic Preservation.

In 2008, members of the New England Antiquities Research

Figure 13.5. Overlook Mountain great cairn

Association (NEARA) visited the site along with researchers from the New York State Museum in Albany. Museum GIS (geographic information systems) specialist Susan Winchell-Sweeney conducted a GPS site survey documenting the quantity and location of the remaining stone constructions. In all, six very large or great cairns (up to 100 feet in length), forty-six small cairns (up to 10 feet in length), two walls (90 feet long) in the shape of snakes, and two springs were identified and their size and location data recorded.

After receiving the plotted site data image from Winchell-Sweeney in late 2008 (see figure 13.6), I initially made little of the distribution, concentration, or configuration of the several dozen plotted points. There did seem to be deliberate groupings and clusters of the smaller cairns, while the great cairns appeared to be spread about more randomly. But nothing really jumped out at me. It wasn't until about a year later (late 2009), that I revisited the data image with the intention of connecting the dots.

Figure 13.6. GPS site survey

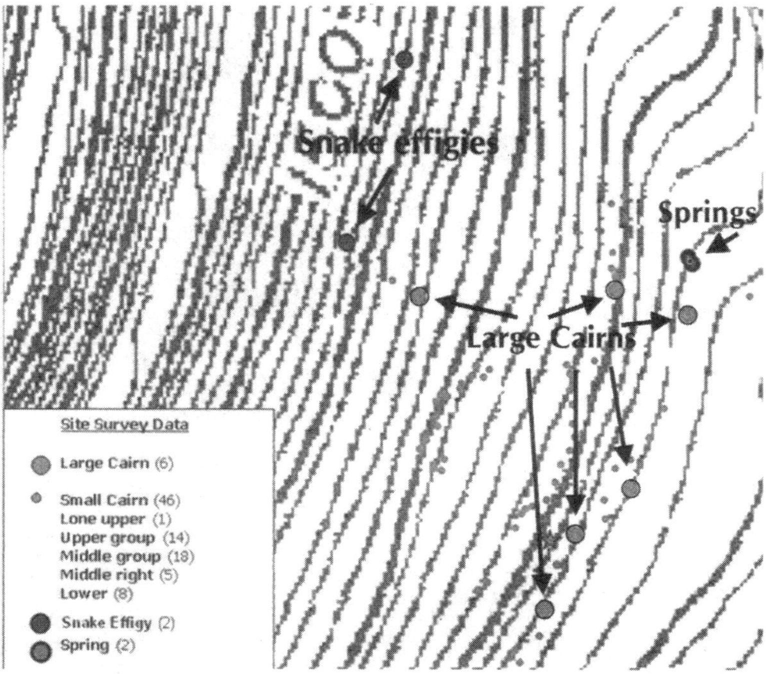

Snake effigies

Springs

Large Cairns

Site Survey Data

● Large Cairn (6)

● Small Cairn (46)
  Lone upper (1)
  Upper group (14)
  Middle group (18)
  Middle right (5)
  Lower (8)

● Snake Effigy (2)
● Spring (2)

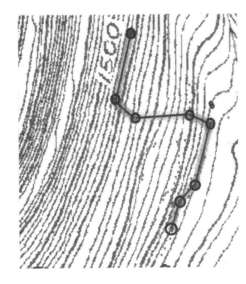

Figure 13.7. Image of the plotted GPS data points of the eight large lithic constructions

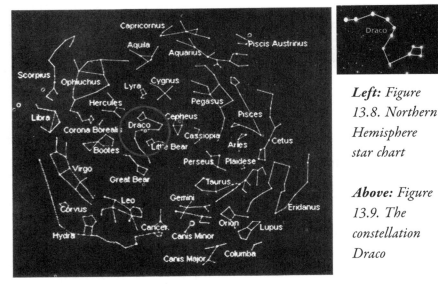

Left: *Figure 13.8. Northern Hemisphere star chart*

Above: *Figure 13.9. The constellation Draco*

My good friend and fellow NEARA member David Holden, who had first introduced me to the cairns, had suggested that perhaps connecting the points could reveal a pattern, which he believed, on a hunch, could depict the Pleiades star cluster. Somewhat skeptical, I decided to conduct the exercise of tracing the dots onto a piece of paper and comparing them to a star chart of the northern constellations. Winchell-Sweeney's data revealed there were eight large stone constructions

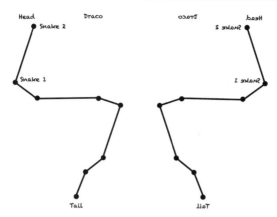

Figures 13.10a and 13.10b. Figure 13.10a shows the original tracing of the cairn configuration, and 13.10b shows the flipped or mirrored version.

seemingly randomly scattered about the mountain-side site, six great cairns, and two snake effigy walls, each separate construction from fifty to one hundred feet in length. I decided to start by tracing the point of those eight locations on a piece of paper. I then connected the dots with straight lines in the only obvious and logical manner possible.

By comparing the tracing to the constellations we see only one match that comes close. The constellation Draco, known as the serpent or snake constellation, is a close match in shape, configuration, and layout to the positions of the stone mound constructions laid out on the ground. In fact, by mirroring the image of the cairn configuration, we see what appears to be an image of the constellation Draco reflected from the sky.

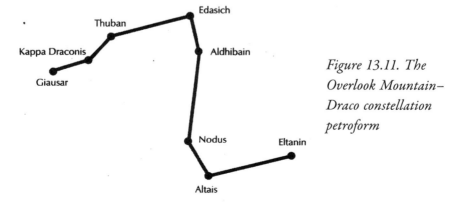

Figure 13.11. The Overlook Mountain–Draco constellation petroform

It should be pointed out that the eight points used to create the snake figure were not "cherry picked" but were distinguished from the rest of the cairns by size and the fact that the large construction (50 to 100 feet in size) appears to be randomly placed as opposed to the smaller cairns (6 to 10 feet in size), which appear in organized rows and clusters. Sorting artifacts by features such as size and relative position is, I believe, a standard method of classification and in this case provides the basis for determining the stone mounds that constitute the petroform on Overlook Mountain.

Comparative and Descriptive Analysis

Draco is the eighth largest constellation, occupying over one thousand square degrees in the sky as it winds from the Pointers of Ursa Minor nearly to Vega in Lyra. Yet it has no bright stars. Gamma Draconis, or Eltanin, the brightest star of Draco, has a magnitude of 2.2 and is one of three or four stars that typically represent the head of the serpent. It is famous for being the star observed by the eighteenth-century English astronomer James Bradley when he was trying to detect parallax and so calculate the distance. Since the star Eltanin is considered the brightest star in the constellation, it is most likely to be seen as the star representing the head of the serpent on the Overlook representation, which appears to be consistent between the two representations. The spacing and angle between the stars of the two representations, while close, is not an exact match, and the angle between Altais and Eltanin would also suggest that Eltanin is the single "head" star in the Overlook Mountain representation of Draco, as opposed to Rastaban.

The total number of stars that represent the constellation Draco can vary from 9 to 14 depending on the culture on which the representation is based. The constellation Draco has 7 stars that are less than 10 parsecs (32 light-years) from the sun, has 3 stars brighter than 3.00 magnitude, and 6 that are currently known to have planets. The total number of stars represented in the Overlook Mountain–Draco constellation depiction is 8.

I thought it might be interesting to compare the magnitude or apparent brightness of the stars that comprise Draco to the size of the cairns on the ground to determine if there is any correlation between size and brightness. The chart below lists the eight brightest stars in the Draco constellation and their apparent magnitudes. In the same chart is a list of the corresponding great cairns and their respective sizes.

Star	Magnitude (Lower numbers are brighter)	Great Cairn	Size (ft)
Giausar	4.1	GC6	50
Kappa Draconis	3.88	GC5	50
Thuban	3.64	GC4	90
Edasich	3.22	GC3	60
Aldhibain	2.73	GC2	60
Nodus	5.7	GC1	60
Altais	4.7	Snake Effigy II	90
Eltanin (Head)	2.42	Snake Effigy I	90

A description of the individual component constructions that constitute the Overlook Mountain petroform follows, beginning with the two snake effigy walls located at the highest elevation (1,420 feet) of the eight locations involved. The easternmost of these two walls would serve as the head of the larger, component serpent (Draco?) petroform. The two slightly curving stonewalls, each approximately 90 feet long, end at a large glacial erratic, which serves as a head to each individual effigy form. It would appear the area around where the figure's mouth would be located on the glacial erratic has been worked to accentuate

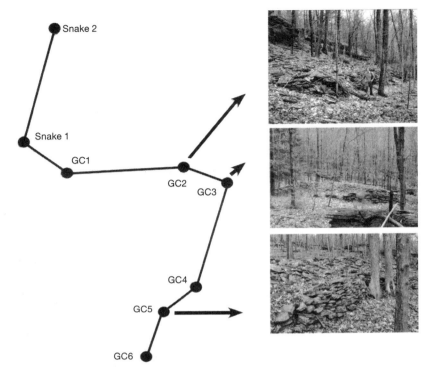

Figure 13.12. An image showing the location of the cairns described in the table on page 1932. The arrows from GC2, GC3, and GC5 point toward the actual photograph of these three great cairns.

the appearance of the mouth. The two walls, whose tails point toward one another, are located approximately 100 yards apart and are visible to and from each other when foliage is lacking, if one knows where to look. In fact it was determined during a recent winter visit to the site that each of the large constructions is visible from the next nearest petroform component. The six great cairns making up the remaining, lower portion of the petroform (between 1,140 and 1,300 feet in elevation) range from approximately 60 to 90 feet in length and are elongated and oval or crescent shaped. The three largest of the great cairns are curved or horn shaped and employ the use of retaining walls on the downward slope to allow the high piling up of the stones within, in some place to a height of 12 feet.

Native Stone Constructions

According to Edward Lenik in his book *Picture Rock: American Indian Rock Art in the Northeast Woodlands,* "Snakes or serpents are ancient symbols and appear in rock art sites across North America. They are considered to be creatures of great power and craftiness. Among Algonquian speaking peoples, they may have represented evil and darkness or the energy of life or regeneration, or served as vehicles of transition for the soul of the deceased to the spirit world." Could the Overlook Mountain petroform function as a guardian of the pathway souls follow to the heavens? Lenik also associates the Algonquin mythical thunderbird as a guardian of humans against the Great Serpent of the underworld. If the thunderbird is seen as the symbol of the protection of life, could the Serpent represent protection of the pathway of the dead?

Accounts of Native American stone constructions associated with definite astronomical attributes are not unique. Research in *Manitou: The Sacred Landscape of New England's Native Civilization,* by James Mavor and Byron Dix, went a long way toward proving that the Native culture of Northeast America built with stone and that many of these constructions were associated with astronomical alignments and observations. This should not be surprising as examples of this apparently geographically diverse cultural practice are well documented throughout the Americas, and in fact worldwide.

Examples of stone serpent effigy mounds (a wavy continuous line with snakelike configurations) exist and have been documented. An apparent stone serpent effigy has been found in Boyd County, Kentucky. Brisbin (1976) was the first to describe this serpent effigy. Sanders's (1991) article includes a nice drawing of the site and notes that it is "unique for its much larger size, well-defined serpent outline, strikingly bifurcated tail, and associated stone ring, which may represent an egg" (not dissimilar to the Ohio Serpent Mound). This effigy is said to have a solar alignment in the configuration of the head and tail. Brisbin notes also that the sandstone forming the serpent was quarried locally and that "in the head and coil portion, the stones are regularly piled to a height of 12 feet, but in the area of the body, they are stacked about 4 feet high and 5 feet wide until they thin out in the tail." Sanders gives a little more up-to-date information on the site. It is owned by Ashland Oil, and the company has established a 90-meter buffer between the mound and a nontoxic landfill, which serves an Ashland Oil refinery. The head of the serpent has been damaged by both pits excavated into the rock by unknown individuals and by the construction of a radio tower access road.

Additionally, specific examples of Native American petroforms matching the constellations exist as well. In his paper "'Star-Beings' and Stones: Origins and Legends," researcher Herman Bender argues convincingly for a petroform in Wisconsin, known as the Kolterman petroform effigy, consisting of stone "stickman" formations constructed on the ground, which create human figures known as star beings. The effigy figures are said to be associated with the Native American thunderbird tradition and mirror on the ground the constellations Libra and Scorpio as they appear in the night sky.

Further research led to Professor Harry Holstein, of Jacksonville State University in Alabama, who has discovered apparent serpent effigy stone walls associated with archaeological sites he's excavated in Alabama and Georgia.

When researching Earth surface constructions that specifically reflect the constellation Draco, I discovered there are examples from around the world, including the temples at Ankor Wat, in Cambodia, documented by Graham Hancock. It also turns out the well-documented Great Serpent Mound in Ohio, already mentioned as a serpent effigy, also conforms to the constellation Draco. Also, a site discovered and documented by Lee Pennington in Fort Mountain, Georgia, is said to represent the serpent constellation. Lastly, I discovered that author and researcher Phillip Callihan documented that the positions of the famous Irish round towers are configured to reflect the the northern constellation, including Draco.

That all these sites are believed to be configured to represent the circumpolar constellation Draco is fascinating.

In the case of the Overlook Mountain petroform, the comparison to the star group known as Draco cannot help but be made. I have consulted with astronomer Kenneth Leonard, who published "Calendric Keystone (?) The Skidi Pawnee Chart of the Heavens: A New Interpretation" and have confirmed the constellation Draco would be visible rising above the summit of Overlook Mountain directly to the north before it reached its zenith overhead during daylight hours. And further confirming the assertion, using Starry Night Pro computer modeling astronomy software demonstrates that Draco rose above the mountain on February 1, 2700 BCE (when Thuban was the pole star), just before sunrise. And, the serpent constellation has continued to rise over Overlook Mountain, throughout the night for thousands of years since, occupying a position perpetually spinning around the fixed celestial North Pole.

This is significant because to early sky watchers living in the Hudson Valley, occupying lands stretching for miles to the south, east, and west, Overlook Mountain would have been the place to look toward to see the serpent of the north rising, night after night, to fulfill its duties, protecting and making "precession proof" the heavens. This is important because by "precession proof" I mean no matter where the celestial pole drifted over time (due to precession), the dutiful dragon would always appear wrapped around that point diligently spinning about the celestial pole, marking its location for those watching. We must remember that no star ever marks the exact celestial pole, which is the point in space where Earth's axis points and which also draws a slow circle in the heavens (over 24,000 years) due to the apparent wobble of precession. What we consider the north star now, Polaris, is merely the star that closest marks the exact, true celestial pole. This star changes over time due to precession—more on this later.

Besides the connection to the sky, the connection of this mountain to the serpent is also undeniable, and I don't see this likely a

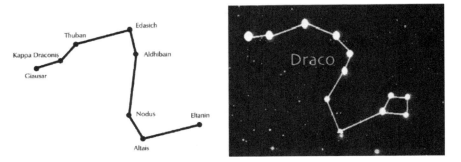

Figure 13.13. Comparing and matching the stars to the petroform

coincidence since Overlook Mountain has the highest population of eastern rattlesnakes in New York state according to the Department of Environmental Conservation. It is estimated, based on the wear marks on the bedrock at the den entrances, that some of the rattler habitats have existed for centuries—at least. I think this is significant given the reverence the snake was accorded by the indigenous people and helps complete the picture of the sacred nature of the mountain in the culture of the Native population.

Serpent Mound Connection

Documented images of snakes and serpents are not uncommon in the Northeastern woodlands and elsewhere, and at least one significant Native American example is claimed to have a connection specifically with the constellation Draco. It is said the Serpent Mound of Ohio may have been designed in accordance with the pattern of stars composing the constellation Draco. The star pattern of the constellation Draco fits with fair precision to the Serpent Mound. The fact that the body of Serpent Mound follows the pattern of Draco may support various theses. Putnam's 1865 refurbishment of the earthwork was correctly accomplished, and a comparison to Romain's or Fletcher and Cameron's maps from the 1980s show how the margins of the serpent align with great accuracy to a large portion of Draco.

Some researchers date the Ohio Serpent Mound earthwork to around five thousand years ago, based on the position of the constellation Draco, through the backward motion of precession, when the star Thuban, also known as Alpha Draconis, was the pole star. Alignment of the effigy to the pole star at that position also shows how true north may have been found. This was not known until 1987 because lodestone and modern compasses give incorrect readings at the site. Most scholars date the Serpent Mound to the Adena culture, which flourished from 1000 to 200 BCE. Though little details are known regarding the religious beliefs and rituals of the Adena, many believe that the Serpent Mound sat at the center of their religious rituals and may have even served as a pathway for practitioners to walk, chanting hymns and thanking their gods for the continued fertility of the land and praying for its continuance.

It has been documented that trading territories and routes of the Adena culture extended along the southeastern shores of the Great Lakes, as well as the Hudson, Ohio, and St. Lawrence rivers. So, it is likely some of the religious and ritualistic aspects of the Adena culture diffused to the tribes of those regions and vice versa.

Draco and Mythology

From antiquity, Draco has long been known as the serpent or snake constellation. For a period in human history, the star Thuban in Draco marked the north point in the sky, as Polaris does now. This is a significant fact, which I'll take a closer look at later in this article.

Ophiolatreia, the worship of the serpent, next to the adoration of the phallus, is one of the most remarkable and, at first sight, unaccountable forms of religion the world has ever known. Until its true source can be determined and understood, its nature will remain as mysterious as its universality. It is difficult to reconcile humanity's worship of a creature that is generally found repulsive. Yet, there is hardly a country of the ancient world where it cannot be traced, pervading every known system of mythology and leaving proofs of its existence and extent in the shape of monuments, temples, and earthworks of the most elaborate and curious character.

Babylon, Persia, India, Ceylon (Sri Lanka), China, Japan, Burma, Java, Arabia, Syria, Asia Minor, Egypt, Ethiopia, Greece, Italy, Northern and Western Europe, Mexico, Peru, America—all yield abundant testimony to the same effect and point to the common origin of "pagan" systems wherever found. Whether the worship was the result of fear or respect is a question that naturally enough presents itself, and in seeking to answer it, we're confronted with the fact that in some places, such as Egypt, the symbol was that of a good deity, while in India, Scandinavia, and Mexico, it was that of an evil one—a paradox that no doubt speaks to the struggle between good and evil in humans and a duality pervasive in their nature and the nature of the universe.

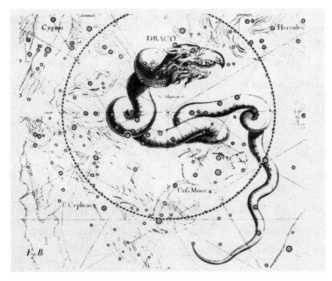

Figure 13.14. Draco in mythology is most commonly depicted as a coiled snake.

Snakes, dragons, and other similar creatures often played a role in creation myths. In these stories, the gods would often battle such creatures for control of Earth. When defeated, the serpents were flung up into the skies. To the Babylonians, Draco was Tiamat, a dragon killed by the sun god in the creation of the world. To the Greeks, Draco guarded the golden apples of the sun in a magical garden.

In many early cultures, the serpent and the sun were strongly connected in their belief systems. Native American oral tradition relates

Figure 13.15. Left: Serpent wall/snake effigy. One of two that are part of the Overlook Mountain Petroform. Right: Serpent effigy crafted in rock outcropping on the author's driveway.

how at one time people worshipped reptiles but were later compelled to recognize the sun, the moon, and other heavenly bodies as the only object of veneration. It's said the old gods were secretly entombed in earthworks built to symbolize and represent the heavenly bodies.

Serpents are a common feature in the art of the Late Prehistoric Period (900 CE to 1650 CE). As already mentioned, many Native Americans of the Eastern Woodlands in North America believed the great serpent was a powerful spirit of the underworld. Serpent mounds and snake effigies may be a representation of these beliefs and hold a connection to the cosmos through the constellation Draco.

In *Reachable Stars: Patterns in the Ethnoastronomy of Eastern North America,* author George Lankford's volume focuses on the ancient North Americans and the ways they identified, patterned, ordered, and used the stars to enhance their culture and illuminate their traditions. They knew them as regions that could be visited by human spirits, and so the lights for them were not distant points of light, but "reachable stars." Guided by the night sky and its constellations, they created oral traditions, or myths, that contained their wisdom and which they used to pass on to succeeding generations their particular worldview. However, they did not all tell the same stories or see the same patterns. Lankford uses that fact—patterns of agreement and disagreement—to discover prehistoric relationships between

Native American groups. In his research, Lankford devoted an entire chapter to the serpent in the stars, seen usually by the Natives as the Scorpio or Draco constellations.

The great constellation of Draco was seen and revered by most of the civilized cultures and tribes of the Northern Hemisphere. The Nordics shaped their great boats in the form of Draco the cosmic dragon. The Native Americans named their tribes after it, and performed many dances to represent celestial movements. The Irish Druids made good use of the symbol on their monuments. During the time that Draco's star Thuban was the pole star, it may have appeared to ancient sky watchers that Earth revolved around Draco. E. Valentia Straiton writes about the mythology entwined with the serpent and the tree of life.

> A symbol of sacred knowledge in antiquity was a tree, ever guarded by a serpent, the serpent or dragon of wisdom. The serpent of Hercules was said to guard the golden apples that hung from the pole, the tree of life, in the midst of the garden of Hesperides. The serpent that guarded the golden fruit . . . and the serpent of the Garden of Eden . . . are the same.

Kennersley Lewis also wrote of the connections between sacred trees, the serpent, and the acquisition of knowledge.

> [T]he nuptial tree, round which coils the serpent, is connected with time and with life as a necessary condition; and with knowledge—the knowledge of a scientific priesthood, inheriting records and traditions hoary, perhaps, with the snows of a glacial epoch.

From these quotes we see that serpent worship was at the heart of humans' earliest religious beliefs. But the concepts involved were far from primitive. Consider the mythological serpent as a representation of the constellation Draco and the tree of life as the pole or axis on which Earth spins. Through the association of the serpent and the tree, and the position of the stars relative to Earth's axis (precession), the importance placed on the certainty of this relationship by the ancients becomes clearer, as well as why any disturbance in that relationship, metaphorically and perhaps literally, could portend a major imbalance in the energy and natural cycles of the universe, with the results nearly always disastrous.

Thuban, the Once and Future Pole Star

As mentioned already, due to the precession of the equinox, Thuban, the third star from the tail of Draco, was the star closest to the North Pole, according to the naked eye, from 3942 BCE, when it moved farther north than Theta Boötis, until 1793 BCE, when it was superceded by Kappa Draconis. It was closest to the pole in 2787 BCE, when it was less than 2.5 arc minutes away from the pole. This was at the height of the Egyptian dynastic era, and a shaft in the Great Pyramid at Giza points to Thuban as it was the pole star at the time the pyramid was constructed. Thuban remained within 1 degree of true north for nearly 200 years afterward and even 900 years after its closest approach was just 5 degrees off the pole. Thuban was considered the pole star until about 1900 BCE, when the much brighter Kochab began to approach the pole as well.

Slowly drifting away from the pole over the last 4,800 years, Thuban now appears in the night sky at a declination of 64 degrees 20 minutes 45.6 seconds, RA 14h 04m 33.58s. After moving nearly 47 degrees off the pole by 10,000 CE, Thuban will then gradually move back toward the north celestial pole. In 20,346 CE, it will once again be the pole star.

Conclusions and Further Inquiry

It can be said the configuration and layout of large stone constructions on Overlook Mountain, consisting of six large stone cairns and two serpentine walls, when taken as a whole constitute a component petroform that resembles a serpent. Specifically, in form and composition, the Overlook

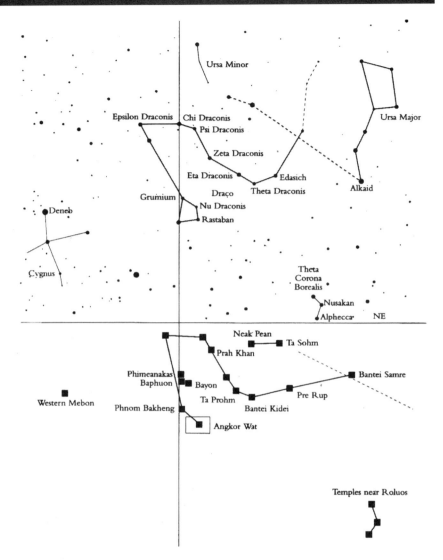

Figure 13.17. Sky charts showing the pole star position over the course of time.

Mountain petroform bears a striking similarity to the star constellation Draco. If the Overlook petroform is not an intentional construction depicting the serpent constellation (Draco) that has risen over the mountain over the course of time for many centuries, it is a remarkable coincidence. Either way, it appears the presence of the cairn and serpent wall constructions are evidence of significant cultural activity and resources.

Careful archaeological and geological inspection and analysis of the cairns and serpent walls could help provide answers as to the age and purpose of those constructions. Studying the settled and compacted soil, particles, and pebbles between stones of one cairn and comparing them to others could help determine which of the structures is the oldest or the most recent. That, as well as comparing lichen colony growth rates, from stones on the outer surface of the structures to those on the interior, could help shed light on when the stones were first placed in the cairns and walls. Identifying when could help determine the context within which they were built and the purpose for which they once served, if any.

It's reasonable to wonder: Were a people and culture present at the Overlook Mountain site that created ritual and ceremonial constructions of stone, exploiting and manipulating the natural environment and materials found there, to express certain aspects of their belief system? Were landscapes routinely identified and modified appropriately to create relationships between the land and the sky, to venerate and preserve symbols and events associated with celestial observation? Many examples of this have been identified, reported, and documented in the Northeast and elsewhere.

Could this be more evidence of a diffusion of the Adena, mound-building culture into the Northeast region? After all, these are mounds we are talking about, albeit mounds made of stone in the Northeast. But then again, stone would have been one of the only materials available in this region for constructing mounds. Mounds made of stone instead of earth makes sense if there is no earth to use, yet mounds are what you wish to build. And, should we consider conversely that the megalithic mound-building concept and culture of the Adena may have spread from the Northeast to the Midwest, having first arrived on our eastern shores from Europe, in an early wave of migration? Until the full picture is known, this idea should not be ruled out.

As has been suggested with the Serpent mound in Ohio, is the Overlook Mountain serpent petroform a representation on the ground, which is connected to the constellation Draco in the night sky? The crucial question of whether Draco currently or in the past appears in the night sky above the Overlook Mountain has been answered: it has and does. Now, how does it match up and align with the position of the large cairns and effigies as laid out on the ground? Are the orientation—that is the direction, position, layout, and configuration—consistent with, matching, or close to the position of the constellation in the sky above? Is there an actual, visual line up and alignment based on that orientation, and when does that occur? And, perhaps most critically, considering precession of the equinox, what was the position of Draco above the site, going back hundreds or thousands of years? These are the relevant questions that remain to be answered about the site.

Evidence for the veneration of the four directions—north, east, south, and west—by the Native tribes of America is well documented, dating back to before the time of first European contact and as witnessed by many of the first Europeans to arrive. In many Native ceremonial practices, offerings are made to the four directions, relating each to a season and many times a relative. To this group, the pre-European Native civilization of Northeast America, there was no more sacred and important knowledge than in which direction to face to make such offerings. Keeping track of and preserving that knowledge would have been an important task with both practical as well as ritual aspects, and every opportunity and advantage would have been taken to do so. Knowing the true location of celestial north and tracking it over time would have been the key to accounting for the celestial motion caused by precession, and this may have been the single greatest undertaking of the "big thinker" of those ancient days.

Until further evidence is found, speaking to the identity and motives of the Catskills stone mound builders, it is hard to make a stronger case for a correlation between the ground constructions on Overlook Mountain and the stars above. However, further research into finding out how the constellations were identified by Native American northeasterners, particularly the Algonquin-speaking tribes, and whether the existence and knowledge of the serpent constellation was present in Northeast tribal mythology, or if they identified what ancient Europeans called Draco as a serpentlike creature as well. Such evidence could considerably strengthen the argument for a correlation existing; a correlation, between Earth and sky, between the lithic constructions on Overlook Mountain and the serpent constellation in the stars above, marking the position of the eternal, celestial north. Documenting and confirming this correlation, this serpentine connection between the real and mythical, the grounded and the godly, humanity and heaven would surely attest to the truly sacred nature of the site and provide a crucial clue to this unfolding mystery—one most deserving of further investigation and serious, scholarly attention.

References

Bender, Herman. "Star Being and Stones: Origins and Legends." In *Indian Stories, Indian Histories: Nova Americana in English*. Edited by Fedora Giordano and Enrico Comba. Turin: Editore, 2004.

Brisbin, L. G. "The Stone Serpent Mound in Kentucky and Other Monuments." *West Virginia Archaeologist* 25 (1976): 26–36.

Broadhurst, Paul, and Hamish Miller. *The Sun and the Serpent*. Pendragon Press, 1990.

Deal, Michael. "Early Woodland: Northeastern Middlesex Tradition." Lecture notes, week seven, anthropology 3291, 2001; www.ucs.mun.ca/~mdeal/Anth3291/notes7.htm.

Hamilton, Ross. *The Mystery of the Serpent Mound*. New York: Random House, 2001.

Hirshfeld, Alan. *Parallax: The Race to Measure the Cosmos*. New York: Henry Holt, 2001.

Kreisberg, Glenn. "The California Quarry and Nearby Stone Cairns of Woodstock, NY." *NEARA Journal* 41, no. 1 (summer 2007).

Lankford, George E. *Reachable Stars: Patterns in the Ethnoastronomy of Eastern North America*. Tuscaloosa: University of Alabama Press, 2007.

Lenik, Edward. *Picture Rocks: American Indian Rock Art in the Northeast Woodlands*. Lebanon, N.H.: University Press of New England, 2002.

Leonard, Kenneth C., Jr. "Calendric Keystone (?) The Skidi Pawnee Chart of the

Heavens: A New Interpretation." *Archaeoastronomy: The Journal of Astronomy in Culture* 10 (1988–87): 76.

Mavor, James W., Jr., and Byron E. Dix. *Manitou: The Sacred Landscape of New England's Native Civilization.* Rochester, Vt.: Inner Traditions/Bear & Co., 1989.

Muller, Norman. "Stone Mound Investigations as of 2009." *NEARA Journal* 43, no. 1 (summer 2009).

Oldham, C. F. *The Sun and the Serpent: A Contribution to the History of Serpent-Worship.* London: Archibald Constable & Co., 1905.

Ridpath, Ian, and Wil Tirion. *Stars and Planets Guide.* Princeton, N.J.: Princeton University Press, 2007.

Ritchie, W. A., and D. W. Dragoo. "The Eastern Dispersal of Adena." *American Antiquity* 25 (1959): 43–50.

Sanders, S. L. "The Stone Serpent Mound of Boyd County, Kentucky: An Investigation of a Stone Effigy Structure." *Midcontinental Journal of Archaeology* 16, no. 2 (1991): 272–84.

Steinbring, Jack. "The Tie Creek Boulder Site." In *Ten Thousand Years: Archaeology in Manitoba.* Commemorating Manitoba's Centennial 1870–1970. Edited by Walter M. Hlady. Winnipeg: Manitoba Archaeology Society, 1970.

Straiton, E. Valentia. *Celestial Ship of the North.* Kila, Mont.: Kessinger Publishing, 1992.

Winchell-Sweeney, Susan. *Lewis Hollow GIS Site Survey.* Albany, N.Y: New York State Museum, November 2008.

Woodward, Susan L., and Jerry N. McDonald. *Indian Mounds of the Middle Ohio Valley.* Blacksburg, Va.: McDonald & Woodward, 1986.

FOURTEEN

Secrets of the Serapeum at Saqqara

PARTS 1 AND 2

ANTOINE GIGAL

Part I

In this article I'm going to take you to Saqqara, a site on the Giza Plateau that is 6 km from north to south and about 2 km wide (29° 58' 51"N by 31° 07' 14"E, for those who want to look at the satellite views) and is southwest of Cairo, near ancient Memphis. I'm not going to talk about the famous Step Pyramid of Djoser (3rd dynasty, 2630 BC officially) built by his grand vizier, Imhotep, or of one of many mastaba; no, not this time. Instead I'll let you discover one of the most mysterious places in Giza and the whole of Egypt, the Serapeum, these strange catacombs.

Look at the view from above. The entrance to the Serapeum is almost in a straight line well above the small pyramid of Userkaf and slightly on a diagonal above the great Step Pyramid of Djoser (see figure 14.1, and see plates 11 and 12). Figure 14.1 from 1957 clearly shows the entrance; but today, the ground in this area is so dug over, excavated by archaeologists' concessions, that it is difficult to see where the entrance is.

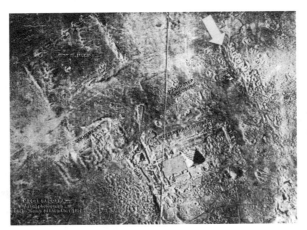

Figure 14.1.
Satellite view

Some people, like Dr. Aidan Dodson, a professor of archaeology at the University of Bristol, do not hesitate to regard the Serapeum (in Greek Serapeion, formerly Sinopeion) as the most important monument in the history of Egyptology. This extraordinary subterranean site was rediscovered first by the indefatigable Greek geographer Strabo, who traveled in Egypt around 24 CE, accompanying his friend, the Roman prefect Aelius Gallus, all along the Nile. It was he who alerted us in his writings to the sandstorms that can dangerously take you by surprise at the entrance to the site, concealed between two dunes, and bury you before you even find the door. He also mentioned the Avenue of the Sphinxes in particular, which made a 2.7-kilometer-long path through the dunes toward the Serapeum. This was a very important clue that made it possible much later to rediscover the site, which had disappeared from view, completely covered by sand.

Figure 14.2. The Greek geographer
Strabo(57 BCE–25 CE)

Then a great Italian traveler, Giovanni Gemelli Careri, seems to have seen or at least approached it in 1693. He spoke of "a subterranean labyrinth" that he saw "not far from the pyramids." But we think he saw other catacombs, not the Serapeum itself, or rather one of its extensions, because he spoke of corridors running "for miles like a city under the ground." He added that the Egyptians he had met called this place the labyrinth, not to be confused with the famous aboveground labyrinth at Hawara in the Fayum area.

 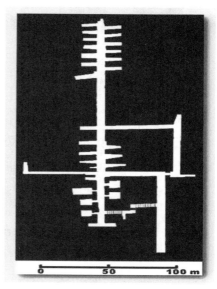

Figure 14.3. Left: The great Italian traveler Giovanni Gemelli Careri who inspired Jules Verne and who went to Egypt in 1693. Right: Plan of part of the Serapeum.

At roughly the same date, Paul Lucas, a French merchant who bought up antiquities on behalf of Louis XIV, found and visited the site and spoke of galleries already collapsed. I think Benoit de Maillet, consul of France in Cairo from 1692 to 1708, also saw this place, but it was very difficult at the time, when nobody could read hieroglyphs, to identify and understand it. Up until now, it's been a great puzzle to researchers, perhaps even more so than the Great Pyramid itself. Also

Figure 14.4. Benoit de Maillet, French consul in Cairo in 1738

the place is closed to the public, and you need a special permit to enter. By visiting this site through this article, you'll enter a world of high strangeness; you can judge for yourself (see plates 13 and 14).

Note in passing how the French became interested in Egypt, well before Napoleon. If anyone has given its letters of nobility to the Serapeum, it is our dear Auguste Mariette (1821–1881) who discovered the complex on November 1, 1850. If only a few years earlier, Napoleon had searched frantically for the Serapeum, without success, it is because something special must be there. In fact, Mariette's discovery, made almost by accident at first, changed his life, and after this, he decided to devote himself to Egyptology. The discovery must have been of great significance to inspire such a vocation—another clue to the importance of the site.

In fact, Mariette had been sent to Cairo in the first place for a quite different reason: He was commissioned on behalf of the Louvre to find and collect Syrian and Coptic manuscripts from the patriarchs of the monasteries still in existence. Only problem was his mission soon became difficult because the English were in the process of snapping up everything. Competition was fierce. It was even said that the English achieved their ends by getting the monks drunk: They then snatched the manuscripts from their precious archives, something that the honest and refined Mariette could never do. And then when you are surrounded by Egyptian monuments half visible above the sand and the excavations have just started, it is not very appealing to attend to other things such as texts that are by definition on quite different subjects.

Mariette had read the Greek Strabo, who described some of the Egyptian buildings firsthand. His description of the Avenue of the Sphinxes at Saqqara and the mysterious Serapeum, to which access was virtually impossible, had aroused Mariette's interest. So he decided to take a look in the dune-covered northern part of Saqqara. This was the right move because he soon came across a small sphinx half buried in the sand, a prelude to the famous avenue leading to the famous Serapeum. Given the competition, there was no time to lose. And so, as he loved to recount: "On 1 November 1850, during one of the most beautiful sunrises I've ever seen in Egypt, with a group of thirty men working under my orders near this sphinx," about a hundred of these small sphinxes on each side of an avenue began to take shape. As the days went by, a classic *dromos,* a sacred way leading to an important place, formed before his very eyes.

He soon came to what he described as a courtyard of the ruins of a small temple. There he found the famous statue of the seated scribe who is now in the Louvre and a statue of the god Bes, whose name means "to be initiated, to be born" and whose ugliness was believed to repel evil forces. Eventually, on November 12, 1851, a year later because of the tons of sand to be moved, he found lower down the real entrance to the catacombs of the Serapeum. If you look closely at pictures of the site as it is now, the place is still totally buried below the level of the dunes. Mariette had to use explosives to break through the rock of the sealed entrance. He then entered a long gallery containing niches with votive stelae and twenty-four side rooms, like alcoves, each containing a huge dark granite sarcophagus. These sarcophagi were nowhere near human scale, as to reach the top one has to climb a ladder of at least eight full steps; I checked it myself. In addition, each sarcophagus, carved from a single block of granite, measures 4 meters long, 2.30 meters wide, and 3 meters 30 centimeters tall and weighs about 80 tons, proof of a remarkable feat of technology (see plates 16 and 17).

Figure 14.5. Look at the enormous size of the sarcophagus.

We are told that these sarcophagi are the tombs of mummified sacred Apis bulls of the Twenty-sixth Dynasty (664–525 BCE) up to the Ptolemaic period. These huge sarcophagi are therefore supposed to have been receptacles for the mummified bodies of bulls that in real life would not have been much more than 1 meter 60 centimeters high over all and would have weighed as an adult about a ton at the most. The least one can say is that these granite sarcophagi were oversized compared to their supposed content. Strange, isn't it? I will come back to this. We are also told that the granite sarcophagi are empty (it's true, I was able to check on the spot). Supposedly their contents were looted in antiquity. They were thus found as they are now; that is to say empty, with no signs of any mummified bulls. Keep that in mind. Marietta also found that most of the lids had been moved.

He continued the excavations, and the following year he found other galleries, dating from Ramses II (1279–1212 BCE, Nineteenth

Figure 14.6. Look at the height of the sarcophagus cover.

Dynasty) and thus even older. This time they did in fact contain twenty-eight Apis mummies, but in small caves and in wooden sarcophagi that matched the actual size of a mummified bull. Moreover, the bull mummies were always embalmed in the kneeling position like sphinxes, which took up even less space. The wooden sarcophagus of Apis XIV dating to the forty-fourth year of the reign of Ramses II has come down to us intact. We know from later texts (votive stelae did not exist at the time) that during the sixty-seven-year reign of Ramses II, seven Apis bulls were embalmed. Mariette then found a third network of rooms containing other smaller burials, dating from the time of Amenhotep III (1387–1350 BCE, Eighteenth Dynasty). The only wooden sarcophagi still intact were those of the Apis VII and the Apis IX discovered with *ushabtis* (funerary figures), canopic jars, and amulets. So the only record we have is of a few bull mummies enclosed in wooden sarcophagi and several stone sarcophagi of normal size. But nothing about the twenty-four huge sarcophagi of granite.

At this point, a lot of questions raise their heads, but before I go into them any deeper, let's look at something else: Why this worship of bulls? The word *Serapeum* comes from Serapis, a composite god Sokar-Osiris-Apis created on purpose by the late Pharaoh Ptolemy I Soter (305–282 BCE after the Thirty-first Dynasty). The pharaoh had a major problem to solve: he had to reconcile and unify two different cultures mingling in Egypt, Egyptian and Greek. Thus, the new cult of Serapis was created, combining the ancient Egyptian cult of the Apis bull with the ancient Greek cults of Zeus, Hades, Asclepius, and Dionysus, trying to bring them all together into this composite god who represented fertility and the powers of the underworld.

Yes, but before that? The cult of Apis was certainly in existence a very long time before. According to Manetho, who I have already spoken of a lot, it went back to the Second Dynasty. But for me and many other Egyptologists and researchers, it is much older still, because many objects from the earliest times that show the importance of the bull in connection with the heavens have been found, for example the palette from the predynastic period of Naqada (4000–3000 BCE).

So why the deified bulls? To the ancient Egyptians, the bull Apis contained the divine manifestation of the god Ptah and later of Osiris. The Apis bull was thus the actual receptacle selected by the soul of Ptah to come and incarnate on Earth. When Osiris later absorbed the identity of Ptah, he symbolized life in death, that is to say, resurrection. The Osiris living in the underworld is also the Osiris of fertile vegetation, he who has conquered evil and death. All these associations between similar gods through the centuries, common in Egypt, actually have a very important meaning, a significance that sometimes contains more than one secret. Thus the Babylonian god Ea was called Serapsi, that is to say King of the Depths, which also relates to our Egyptian Serapis.

But back to the god Ptah, the former Atum, demiurge, creator of the world, the one who shapes, who builds, the Divine Architect of heaven and earth, the possessor of creative fire. On the Shabaka Stone it is said that Ptah "brought the world into existence." The equivalent of Ptah for the Greeks was Hephaistos and for the Romans, Vulcan, also identified with Zeus. Ptah is represented standing upright wrapped in the shroud of mummification, like Osiris, which to me clearly indicates that he resides in the underworld. He does not have the freedom of movement that one has on the surface of Earth. He is a prisoner of a place and a form that was not his in the beginning.

The fact that he is wearing a blue cap (which the blacksmiths adopted later on) shows that he is invisible when on the surface of Earth (see plate 15). In ancient Egypt, the color blue indicated things and beings that were invisible. Thus Ra was originally depicted in blue, as was Amon. It is the blue of heaven, associated with the creative breath of the life. Ptah has mastered all the secrets of manipulation, which gives him the power to dominate and shape all matter. A chthonic god, he reigns over the minerals in the depths of Earth. Another important link, he is also associated with Ta Tenen, the island rising out of the submerged land (which brings us back to the Great Flood, or to several of them). In any case, he is a god who was present when the first land appeared above the waters—and who perhaps in order to manifest on Earth has to enclose himself in a form, so why not choose the form of the bull Apis?

His consort was Sekhmet the powerful, great in magic, the feared and untameable lion. She was the guardian of the threshold, protector of the gods, the warrior that Ra did not hesitate to send to punish the people on earth who no longer wanted any contact with the heavens and were cutting themselves off from the divine. Some texts even give the impression that she had a part in unleashing the Flood. Then in the Greek tradition, let us not forget that there is the disturbing story of the nymph transformed into the cow Io by Zeus (associated with Ptah) and who, after an epic journey, ends up arriving in Egypt, where Zeus (Ptah) gives her back her human form and where she gives birth to Epaphus (the Egyptian Apis) and spreads the cult of Isis. The Egyptians associated Io with Hathor, and according to some researchers, Epaphus-Apis became king of Egypt and founded Memphis and was venerated as the god Apis. Strange, aren't they, all these interconnections? In any case, from this story we also learn that Zeus was willing to turn himself into a bull at times. So here we have a divine being, Ptah, linked with the underworld, linked with the creation of the world or its re-creation needed after the Flood, and his consort Sekhmet, who also has a link with the Flood.

But what further explanation is there for the Apis bull and the sarcophagi in the Serapeum? Let's look at what we know from the texts. This descent of a god into a body of animal flesh on Earth gave rise to all sorts of very strict rules.

The choice of the bull used for the physical manifestation of the god was far from being left to chance. Judge for yourself: the bull had to be black with a white belly, have a white triangular mark on its forehead, an eagle with spread wings on its back, a crescent moon on its side, a scarab-shaped mark under its tongue, and a tail with long hairs parted in two. So it was a bull that was predestined for the role.

Herodotus even tells us that the Apis is "a calf from a cow that cannot bear any more offspring. The belief of the Egyptians is that a flash of lightning descends upon the cow and makes it receive Apis." Priests scoured the whole country to find such a calf. Once he was found, he was carried down the Nile to Memphis by boat, housed in a magnificent golden cabin. There followed a great celebration because it meant that the living god had come to incarnate in the country; it was a tremendous honor and great joy.

A seven-day feast was held to mark his entry into the temple of Serapis, after which he had an easy life, with tasty delicacies and priests in his service, a harem herd available, music, jewelery to adorn him, and great popularity each time he was led out in grand style for festivities among the cheering people. He was so handsome that Plutarch wrote, strange as it may seem to us today, that "Apis is a beautiful image of the soul of Osiris."

There were further reasons for his popularity. Indeed, it was said that every child who felt the breath of the Apis then had the ability to predict the future.

Thus people crowded round him. In fact, Apis himself was consulted as an oracle.

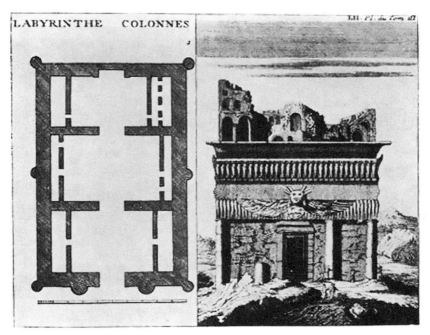

LABYRINTHE   COLONNES

Figure 14.7. A drawing by Paul Lucas, the great collector of antiquities for Louis XIV who traveled to Saqqara in 1700. The upper part gives a good idea of what lies beneath inside the Serapeum.

If he accepted the food you handed him, if he extended a particular leg for instance—everything was matter for interpretation. He was also revered because in the afterlife, anyone who was under his protection had control over the four winds. He was also apotropaic, meaning he was supposed to divert bad fortune. And as soon as one Apis died, the search for another one began.

Also, according to my research, the Apis is linked to what is called the sign of Tanit. Tanit, of Phoenician origin, was a moon goddess of fertility, birth, and of the city of Carthage. Her shrine is at Serepta (still close to the word *Serapis*) in southern Phoenicia, where she is associated with the goddess Astarte (Ishtar). And brace yourself, in Egyptian Tanith equals Ta Nit, which is to say the land of Neith. The goddess Neith was another warrior, who also watched over the mummy of Osiris; thus she is a goddess who fights and is connected with the

Figure 14.8. One of several blocked-up entrances

underworld and resurrection. There's always this tangle of deities in different areas and different eras.

But if you look at the whole picture, it's always about the same thing! And everything takes us back to Egypt. To help you understand why the Apis was related to the sign of Tanit, first look at Apis as he was usually represented, gilded with the solar disc between his horns; then look at the sign of Tanit—the bull seen from the front represents the crescent moon (the horns), the sun (the disc that he was always adorned with), and the pyramid (his triangular snout). According to the Phoenicians, the whole thing was represented by a person raising his arms in prayer to the heavens. I should add that in the secret language of the Egyptian priests, the symbol of the sun meant look at what is fixed (the divine), and the symbol of the moon meant look at what is changeable, mutable (the incarnation). So we are faced with the notion of the animal being the very representation of prayer to the heavens, of the link with the divine, of the ladder to the sky. What other animal could serve so well as a link with the gods?

In addition, the design forms an ankh cross with the central line split in two at the base, which some believe could be the ankh sign of life in its very distant original form. A bull, then, as the symbol of life linked with the sky, linked with resurrection, and, better still, with ascension. We're just beginning to glimpse why so many important people have been interested in the Apis and the Serapeum. The rites surrounding the Apis were considerable. There was even a rite of baptism practiced in Rome much later, when the cult of Apis gained much success. This ritual was very similar to the Christian one.

What's even more significant, the word *bull* is pronounced ka, exactly like another ka, the one that, according to the ancient Egyptians, represented a person's double and held his or her creative energy. Each living being had its own ka, and the Egyptians said in the texts that to die is to pass into your ka. It is no coincidence that everything is a deliberate game in Egyptian writing. The ka was represented in hieroglyphics by two arms raised to the sky, a symbol seen also in the hieroglyph of the bull. So in the symbolic role given to this animal, the Egyptian priests revealed a favored pathway to the divine and a means to reach eternity.

Conclusion to Part I

We are thus faced with a place that speaks of resurrection, ascension, and eternity, and one that is hiding more than a few secrets. To help you understand even better the interest certain people have taken in this place, let me tell you that Mariette's first reports—the detailed discovery of each sarcophagus, each grave, each new underground passage, all through several years—have completely disappeared. Everything significant on the Giza plateau tends either to disappear or, if it can't be moved, to be closed to the public.

Among other things, all along the outer walls of the Serapeum there are dozens of openings more or less effectively sealed up, some with electric wires coming out of nowhere, overlooking places that one cannot visit, not even with special permission. On the inside, these

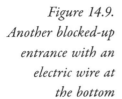

*Figure 14.9.
Another blocked-up
entrance with an
electric wire at
the bottom*

*Figure 14.10.
Close-up of the black
electric wire*

places are walled off, hidden behind heavy wooden panels and inaccessible. Since it was discovered some years ago that the workmen repairing the corridors of the Serapeum were exposed to breathing in excessive doses of radon (28.83mSv per year instead of the maximum of 10mSv per year), the site has been closed to the public. However, I've seen the whole air circulation system, and everything has been working wonderfully well for quite a while.

So I think the Serapeum will soon be reopened to the public, after the long period of repair it has undergone. On the other hand, it is clear that whole sections of it are not on the site map. We also know that in certain places where the corridors have fallen in, it is still obvious that they carry on farther and that the huge granite sarcophagi are impossible to move or to transport. Someone has already tried it with a big team and heavy equipment, and the sarcophagus, slightly smaller than the others, is sitting right in the middle of the return corridor, abandoned there because it could not be dragged any farther. We know also that these sarcophagi are proof of an incredible technology, and one wonders how they could have been brought here in these narrow underground passageways where cranes cannot go.

I discuss this again in detail, but first I must tell you about the mysterious Imhotep, architect of the pyramid of Djoser, and about Prince Khasekhemwy, a son of Ramses II who was one of the greatest priests and magi of all Egypt, and about Aesculapius and the snake. Only then will you begin to glimpse what might have happened in this incredible place. And if you can, do go and take a look at everything to do with the Apis bull in the Louvre or the British Museum.

Part 2

So, I've just been telling you about the incredible discovery made by Mariette on November 1, 1850, of the entrance to the Serapeum, this mysterious place at Saqqara on the Giza Plateau, with its complex network of underground tunnels containing a number of sarcophagi. These sarcophagi raise many questions, as their existence represents a technological feat that cannot be explained in today's terms. I have also talked about the religious rituals that were carried out around this place devoted to the Apis bull, which according to the ancient Egyptians represented the form in which the manifestation of the god Ptah/Osiris chose to incarnate and which symbolized resurrection, the link with heaven, a pathway to eternity.

Before returning to the challenge of the sarcophagi, I will focus on an essential topic that usually fails to be addressed in discussions about the Serapeum: Imhotep/Asclepius. Remember the statue of Bes that Mariette found at the beginning of his exploration of the entrance to the Serapeum? Note that this being, revered for its oracles at Abydos, was also known to be a magician of dreams; that is he inspired dreams that could then be interpreted. Egyptians often placed a statue of Bes in their bedroom. At the time, dreams were seen as an important means of therapy; a fact that is essential for understanding the meaning of the Serapeum. In ancient times, dreams were associated with healing and medicine.

Remember that we are near the Step Pyramid of Pharaoh Djoser at Saqqara, built by the legendary Imhotep some time before 2660 CE. Imhotep, whose name means "the one who comes in peace," was not only chief minister of Djoser, the architect of the kingdom (the first in Egypt according to many scholars), high priest of Heliopolis and grand magus, and chief of all the priests in northern Egypt, but also a great doctor (probably the first also) with his school of medicine and his temple next to the Serapeum. More than 2,200 years before the birth of Hippocrates in Greece, still known as the father of our medicine, Imhotep in Egypt knew how to diagnose and treat over two hundred diseases, using anatomical terms and practicing surgery.

We can find hints of this in the famous Edwin Smith Papyrus. The great Egyptologist James Henry Breasted says of Imhotep: "In priestly wisdom, in magic, in the formulation of wise proverbs; in medicine and architecture; this remarkable figure of Zoser's reign left so notable a reputation that his name is not forgotten to this day." In the canon of Turin, Imhotep is designated as the son of Ptah. Apart from Amenhotep, he is the only mortal or hybrid Egyptian who managed to attain the full position of a god. The Greeks who settled in Egypt equated the Egyptian Imhotep with their god Asclepius, the god of medicine, and called Imhotep's school of medicine the Asklepieion. It is quite possible that both Asclepius and Imhotep are one and the same person.

But first, who was this Asclepius? Nothing less than the son of Apollo, the ancient texts tell us, and of the nymph Koronis-Arsinoe. (Note in passing, the city of Fayoum in the confines of the Giza Plateau is called Arsinoe.) Yet another demigod? In any case, we are told that his cult, which had already existed on the island of Kos for a very long time, was introduced to Rome in 290 BCE during an outbreak of plague. His temple was erected on an island in the Tiber, and later it was confused with Serapis. You read correctly, Serapis. So, maybe the cult of Serapis is a later disguised version of a cult to Imhotep-Asclepius! But what else is said about Asclepius? That he was raised by the centaur Chiron (the last centaur on Earth according to the ancient Greeks—now that's an "animal" that would fit quite well into our large sarcophagi) in an underground cave and was taught by him everything about medicine and more besides, because Asclepius was not content just to heal but he also raised the dead. The god Zeus in his heaven, disturbed by Asclepius's enthusiasm for immortalizing earthlings and thus upsetting the natural order of things, finally struck him with a thunderbolt. Does this not remind you of how the cow receives a flash of lightning before conceiving the Apis bull? The fact is that Ptah is often connected with Zeus and with lightning.

Figure 14.11. Left: Asclepius. Right: The caduceus.

Asclepius appeared in dreams to the priests and revealed to them the remedies for their patients, or else the patients received them in a dream and were cured. He was shown with a rod with a snake coiled round it, the symbol of medicine (not to be confused with the caduceus of Mercury, with two snakes symbolizing commerce and communication). Asclepius had three boys and six girls, including Hygeia, Panacea, and Meditina. Meditina is of particular interest, as you'll see a little further on, for she was said to be a snake bearer. When Zeus struck

Asclepius, he was transformed into the constellation Ophiuchus, which means snake bearer, also called Serpentarius—strange, isn't it? Ancient Egyptians taught that the gods when they died were transformed into a constellation or a star. And as you'll see, the snake plays a major role in the Serapeum. It is important to emphasize that our Hippocrates (the father of medicine, from whom we derive the oath our doctors take) is recognized as a descendant of Asclepius on his paternal side. Even if it is to him we owe the words *chronic, endemic, epidemic, convalescence, paroxysm,* and so on, and though Western medicine claims him as parent, in reality his concept of medicine was very different from ours. Dr. Houdant for example says that "the Hippocratic treatment is much more of a meditation on death." In fact, Hippocratic medicine was a carbon copy of that of Asclepius and was practiced in temples that had certain features in common. They had to have a temple-sanatorium at ground level and subterranean caves with an underground spring. That is what we also have with the Serapeum of Saqqara. In Athens, you can still see the sanctuary of Asclepius today on the southern flank of the Acropolis, beneath the Parthenon, with its grotto and its spring. This grotto has since been taken over by the Orthodox Church.

It is important for me to explain how Asclepius and his descendant Hippocrates treated their patients because they probably worked in the same way as Imhotep in the vicinity of the Serapeum. Besides their treatments with plant compounds and apart from dealing with fractures and surgery, the heart of their medicine primarily consisted of making their patients drink the water from underground springs and bathe in it, because for them it was obvious that the water carried in it the healing powers of the spirits of Earth. After that, they only dealt with those who had the courage and determination to undergo the treatment. Patients had to fast and make repeated ablutions in the sacred precincts of what was called the Abaton; that is to say, in the temple, the caves, and the underground passages, which no one else was allowed to enter. Then the patients were made to sleep in the group dormitories of the Abaton so that they would dream. There were specific

Figure 14.12. Asclepius and his daughter Hygeia

rituals for encouraging dreaming; the deepest wisdom of Mother Earth was supposed to send the patient dreams revealing the reasons for his or her illness and how to treat it. The next day, the patient told his or her dream to the priests who would then prescribe a treatment. It was also said that the first image that came into the dreamer's mind would become a guardian spirit and would never leave him or her.

The lesson to be drawn from this study of dreams was very sophisticated. They did not give a generalized interpretation of the dreams; they considered that a dream symbol gave rise to a different meaning depending on the person. Each person was considered to have his or her own dream language, and detailed work was done on the images and emotions of the patient. But Asclepius did not work only with the priests of his cult; he was assisted by—guess what?—a horde of snakes. Nonvenomous snakes slithered all over the floor of the dormitories during the night and were believed to be divinities who mediated between Asclepius and the patient. Because of the way snakes shed their skins, they were a symbol of rebirth and resurrection. (Incidentally, I can tell you that the word *life* in Chaldean is the same as for snake, and in Arabic, it's the same except for one letter.) Among the ancient Egyptians, the uraeus—the divine cobra on the headdress or forehead of the pharaoh—represented the life force with all its power, as it was supposed to strike with lightning any enemy or any negative principle. However, they did not confuse this snake of highly positive qualities with the other—the serpent Apophis who brought chaos and negativity.

Figure 14.13. Hippocrates treating a patient

As a rule, the snake had the reputation of being invigorating and of bringing eternal youth and immortality. Why? Snake venom has powerful properties. Asclepius had a reputation for knowing how to administer doses of poison and antidote, including snake venom, with such skill that he was able to bring the dead back to life. He was known in antiquity to be a master of resurrection thanks to his snakes. We now understand better why he was transformed into the constellation of Ophiuchus, the serpent bearer. We can also understand better why the symbol of medicine is a rod with an entwined snake. In the small Imhotep museum that has just opened next to the Serapeum and displays objects and statues from in and around the Serapeum, what do we find? Snakes in all forms. The feet of a statue of Imhotep posed on beautiful painted snakes, carved cobras that covered the enclosure walls around the pyramid of Djoser, friezes of snakes in bas-relief found above the Serapeum, and so on—snakes everywhere (see plate 19).

And what was Imhotep's genealogy? His mother Kheredu-ankh was a mortal raised to the rank of semidivine (like the mother of Asclepius) as she claimed that her father was the god Banebdjedet, a ram god of fertility that the Greeks later named Pan.

This very strange ram curiously had four heads, two facing backward, two facing forward. It was said that within it was incorporated the essence of the world in four forms representing the four spirits or souls (ba) of the four masters of the world Ra-Shu-Geb-Osiris (perhaps at a time when these four deities were embodied together in a ram?). In any case, in Edfu, Banebdjedet was celebrated as one of the great ancestors. And at Mendes (Tell el Rub'a), there were found sarcophagi (of normal size) containing mummified sacred rams. His wife was the fish goddess Het-Merit. In ancient Egypt, fish represent the transformation of the gods. Don't you find that all this fits the same theme of metamorphoses and transformations, of gods producing different frequencies and manifestations? In short, there's a lot of similarity with Asclepius. Let's not forget that the ancient Greeks already disagreed about Asclepius, saying he was much older than the official dating was willing to say (even then). Linguists argue that the true meaning of the

Figure 14.14.
Banebdjedet

name *Asklepios* etymologically is "the hero of the mound." Now all the sacred history of Egypt is based on a primitive mound raised above the waters.

Finally, might not Asclepius and Imhotep be the same person? Do they not seem alike because of their semidivine origins, their concept of medicine, and the almost miraculous power that they had over health, transformation and even resurrection? In both cases, there is the use of a temple sanatorium (at Saqqara archaeologists know there was one next to the Serapeum like that of Alexandria) and of an underground network, all related to snakes. According to the Egyptian historian Ahmed Osman, the Serapeum was maintained and served by volunteer monks, who watched over the patients in the complex. "The followers of the cult of Serapis were supposed to be granted the right to eternal life without the need of mummification if they showed devotion to the deity and went through an initiation ritual that included baptism with water." Is it not this same immortality that one is supposed to gain in Catholicism through baptism?

On the other hand, we have a cult of metamorphosis, that of the sacred bull Apis as Ptah/Zeus/Jupiter honored among the ancient Egyptians, Greeks, and Romans. There are a large number of ancient writings on the many transformations of Zeus/Jupiter into a bull; for example, the whole story of Io (her other name is Europa), who is transformed into a cow by Zeus, then arrives in Egypt, recovers human form, and gives birth to Apis, who propagated the cult of Isis, founded Memphis, and was worshipped as a god-pharaoh, as I mentioned in the first part of this article. Io was said to correspond to the goddess Hathor, which would be very consistent. On the other hand, many Egyptologists equate Imhotep with Thoth-Tehuti. The cult of Thoth resulted in a cult of the ibis, his preferred form of transformation, and there are catacombs filled with the mummies of this bird beside the Serapeum of Saqqara as well as in Abydos.

It is time to say something about one of the greatest magicians of all Egypt. More than a thousand years after his death, he was still

Figure 14.15.
Auguste Mariette

considered a hero by the Greeks and the Egyptians. He is the Prince Khaemweset (1290–1224 BCE), son of the pharaoh Ramses II. Why was this prince so dedicated to the Serapeum during his life? When Mariette had to use explosives to get through a large rock blocking the first gallery of the Serapeum, and in the rubble found a mummy with a golden mask with human features, he deduced that it could only be Prince Khaemwaset. Certainly, his seal was everywhere on the objects and jewelery found with the mummy. However, a significant doubt remained. First, Mariette could have been influenced at the time by late stories attributing to the prince a desire to be buried with the bulls. Furthermore, certain things just didn't hold together. Some Egyptologists think this mummy could very well be that of an unknown man buried in a crypt above the vault. Apparently, the wall of the crypt collapsed under the impact of the blast. For others, much better informed in my opinion, this mummy, even though it had an anthropomorphic shape and gold funerary mask with human features, in fact contained the remains of a bull that had been given human shape, with jewelery and amulets bearing the name of Khaemwaset.

Why is there still a doubt? Well, simply because the mummy has vanished. Yes. As usual, the really significant objects cannot be found. It is even more unfortunate because Mariette's detailed reports on the Serapeum have also disappeared, strangely enough. The fact is that Prince Khaemwaset did not only contribute to the enlargement of the underground labyrinth and oversee seven Apis burials in the Serapeum, but he showed a genuine devotion to this place. Why? Why did the fourth son of the pharaoh Ramses II undertake throughout his life to restore the teachings of the great ancestors, those who had arrived first in the land of Egypt? The prince was working to reestablish those aspects of the tradition that were the most sophisticated, the most secret, and the most magical. Why did he, as we are told, at the end of his life live almost all the time in the underground Serapeum?

First of all, who was he? After a period of military honors—he was known to have been present at the famous Battle of Kadesh—he became a priest and then governor of Memphis and Grand Sem Priest of Ptah worship in Memphis. He was president of all the craftsmen. He is often called the first Egyptologist in history because he carried out an unprecedented campaign to restore the ancient monuments of his country, such as the Pyramid of Unas and a dozen pyramids and important monuments of previous dynasties. His passion for his country's past made him inscribe on a statue, "I love so much antiquity and the nobility of the earliest times." Very learned, he also had a huge library of documents on sacred and magical subjects that aroused envy in the ancient world. He founded the library of the Ramesseum in Western Thebes, which contained only papyri about magic. He is said to be, among other things, the author of the "Papyrus that produces terror and respect," mentioned in the time of Ramses III.

This attitude of collecting, of gathering evidence and knowledge of the past, of respect and maintenance of the tradition, in itself marks Khaemwaset as a constant researcher of the hidden principle of divine intelligence and the human capacity to rediscover it. His approach corresponds to the spirit of the god Thoth-Tehuti, whom many experts now dare to think could be an ancestor of Imhotep, if they are not the same

Figure 14.16. Left: Prince Khaemwaset when young. Right: Prince Khaemwaset depicted on the wall of his tomb.

person. Much later, the Greeks claimed that Khaemwaset possessed the famous Emerald Tablet of Thoth-Tehuti-Hermes, and they always called him the King of Magicians. Remember that in the third century, Clement of Alexandria considered Egypt to be the Mother of all Mages. Khaemwaset was known for working against the Nubian magicians to prevent any foreign takeover of Egypt. He was a great magical protector of the existence of the country and of pharaoh. In short, the prince was passionate about the most secret mysteries (see plate 18).

What do we learn from this? That one of the projects that he held closest to his heart was to restore in his lifetime the practice of the Heb Sed Festival. This was a great ritual festival that originally was to be celebrated every thirty years of the pharaoh's reign so as to renew his accession. It was the celebration of the jubilee. In fact, the prince reintroduced the Heb Sed Festival in favor of his father Ramses II, who celebrated it fourteen times during his reign. Why? Well, because to initiates, Sed was in truth a great ritual of rejuvenation. No need to wonder at the incredibly long life in full fitness of his father Ramses II, the pharaoh who lived the longest. In the original form of the Heb Sed

Festival, the pharaoh had to run naked in the full sun and without food or drink, until sundown some say, around places that symbolized the different provinces of southern and northern Egypt. If he did not die of exhaustion, that meant that he was reinstated in office by the approval of the gods. After that came all sorts of secret rites enacted out of sight in the holy of holies of the temple, including invigorating rituals of rejuvenation. It is mentioned sometimes that the pharaoh had to spend a whole night wrapped in a bull's hide. If he could not stand the physical effort of running, if he was taken ill, it was said that it was time for him to join his ka; that is, move on to the next world.

As you see, being pharaoh was no easy job because the pharoahs carried the responsibility for the cohesive force of the world on their shoulders—at least the earliest pharaohs did—and they absolutely had to be equal to the task. They were the bearers of the positive force, of the harmony of life, and had to keep the upper hand at all times over the forces of chaos that threatened the positive development of events, of things, and of people in the country. So Prince Khaemwaset, a great expert on the Sed rituals, with uncommon powers and knowledge, passionate about medicine, rejuvenation, and resurrection, spent most of his time in the corridors of Serapeum following the example of Imhotep or of Asclepius. Why? Surely for something closely connected to his passionate research, don't you think? In 1991, a Japanese team from Waseda University discovered north of the Serapeum a building containing 2,500 items bearing the seal of Khaemwaset.

Conclusion to Part 2

For one thing, we have Apis bulls buried in small sarcophagi, usually made of wood, that do not take up much space because the bulls are mummified in the sphinx position. Three have survived intact from the time of Khaemwaset including the Apis XIV, witness to the continuing worship of the incarnation of the god Ptah in a bull. This cult, dedicated to the metamorphosis of a god who, as the ancient Egyptians believed, took physical form on Earth, thus lasted a very long time. Then there is an underground place that was used to treat, to heal, and even to restore people to life with the help of live snakes. And then we have twenty-four huge granite sarcophagi that look nothing like any others. Apart from their exceptional size, each receptacle has a lid that alone weighs twenty-seven tons and fits perfectly. A careful observer will also notice notches in the walls of the narrow niches where these sarcophagi are placed. These notches allow the 4-meter-long 30-centimeter-wide lid to be rotated sideways on its central axis and to remain in position on the edge of the sarcophagus. This indicates that the sarcophagi were used open as often as closed.

What was kept inside them? Was there any liquid? Were the sarcophagi used in the metamorphoses of the gods, in their possible changes of frequency, in medical treatments with snakes, in a rejuvenation process? Were they the receptacles for giants or were they used for the resurrection of the dead? We are told that they date from the Eighteenth Dynasty. Guess what, this dating is based solely on bits of Eighteenth Dynasty pottery found nearby. Who are they kidding? By that time, the art of stone carving was in rapid decline in Egypt. And there we have these containers of eighty tons that are found nowhere else in Egypt or in the world. Imagine the technological precision used to drill to perfection these enormous thick troughs of granite in one piece, with corners that are perfect inside and out, exactly parallel. It's just incredible, unequalled to this day, and represents an achievement way beyond the ordinary. In the words of the engineer Christopher Dunn, who went in 1995 to take measurements with properly calibrated instruments, "Nobody makes such things without having a very good reason for their design," and "the tools used to create [these objects] are so precise that they are incapable of producing anything other than perfect accuracy." We are far from the worker with a hammer trying to gouge out a lump of stone. The surfaces of these huge containers are perfectly smooth with precise and perfect edges, made from a solid block of granite of an unbelievable thickness. For many experts, this perfection is proof that a very advanced civilization lived in Egypt for a very long time ago.

These containers are completely smooth and devoid of any inscription, except for two partially inscribes ones. But when you look at one of the two inscribed containters, you see a wobbly and very inaccurate line and poorly drawn hieroglyphs in the design that was very common in the late period of false doors—a very clumsy effort. Now genuine inscriptions on sarcophagi are always perfectly accurate; the royal scribes and sculptors had a total mastery of writing and of their materials, even in bas-reliefs. Writing that was flawed would not have been allowed or tolerated on such objects. So at what point were these writings added—perhaps quite recently? Has someone tried to make us believe, misguidedly and without success, that these objects are not so old after all? And why try to disguise the glaring truth, namely that these objects were designed to be mysteriously smooth and without any inscription? Why would anyone want to turn them into ordinary items, when their dimensions speak for themselves?

Finally, last question: How were people in the old days able to transport these very heavy sarcophagi into these deep and narrow niches? In our time, as I described at the beginning, a serious attempt was made to carry one of them up to ground level but after a few meters, it had to be given up. So, is it not reasonable to think that these sarcophagi were actually already there, long before Khaemwaset, as vestiges of a remarkable technology? They were revered for the extraordinary purposes to which they had been put in the distant past—secret purposes that a few rare scholars, like Prince Khaemwaset, still jealously guard.

FIFTEEN

The Case for the Daemon

ANTHONY PEAKE

The woman had settled down to a quiet evening in, curled up with a book. She was engrossed in the story and at first was not sure what she had heard. It then repeated itself. It was a voice that was somehow inside her head and yet not part of her thought processes.

The voice was absolutely insistent. It had arrived from nowhere and was quite clear about its purpose. It told her that she had a medical problem but that she was not to worry because it was there to help her.

After a few weeks of these strange communications, some of which where precognitive, the woman, known as AB, decided that her only course of action was to go and see her doctor. The local doctor simply could not understand what was happening but assuming that the problem was psychological referred her to Dr. Ikechukwu Azuonye of the Mental Health Unit at London's Royal Free Hospital. In the winter of 1984, Dr. Azuonye diagnosed a straightforward case of hallucinatory psychosis. He prescribed a course of the antipsychotic drug thioridazine and expected that would be the end of it. How wrong he was.

Initially, the thioridazine seemed to work. Thinking the voice was simply a peculiar psychological interlude, AB and her husband went off on a holiday. However, while out of the country, the voice had found its way through the drug barrier and was more insistent than before. It pleaded with her to return to England as soon as possible, saying that she needed urgent medical treatment. Indeed it even told her an address that she should go to for help.

The voice was now becoming quite precise concerning AB's medical problem. It told her that it had two reasons for wanting her to have a scan: first, that she had a tumor in her brain and, second, that her brain stem was badly inflamed. She convinced her husband that they had to go and find the address the voice had told her. Much to her surprise, and concern, the address turned out to be the computerized tomography unit of a large London hospital.

This scared her so much that she went back to see Dr. Azuonye. The psychiatrist was, not surprisingly, reluctant at first to do as the voice requested. He knew that the woman had none of the symptoms associated with a brain tumor and for him to force the issue would reflect badly on his professional reputation—particularly if he divulged the source of the diagnosis. Against his better judgment, he agreed that he would write to the clinic and see what they said.

A few months later, and after many letters, the clinic agreed to do the scan. Much to the surprise of all concerned, with the clear exception of the voice, the scan clearly showed an unusual mass in the brain.

AB was called in to meet with a neurological consultant. The consultant explained that the mass was probably a meningioma tumor. As he said this, AB heard the voice agree with this diagnosis. However the voice was concerned that there had already been too much delay. It demanded that she be operated on straight away. Not only this, but the voice wanted the operation done at Queen's Square Hospital. This was because it knew that that particular hospital specialized in neurological diseases.

This time the hospital authorities agreed, but the operation was to take place at the Royal Free. The voice considered this and decided that it was acceptable. A few days later AB and, presumably, the voice itself were under full anaesthetic and being wheeled into an operating theater.

As AB came to after the operation, the first thing she was aware of was the voice. All the insistence had gone. It said, "I am pleased to have helped you. Good-bye."

When the surgeon came round to see her, she already knew that her life had been saved. He explained to her that he had removed a 6.4-cm (2.5-inch) tumor from her brain. He added that he was sure that, had it not been removed, she would have most certainly died.

Over the years, this case continued to fascinate Dr. Azuonye. By 1997, he had moved to Lambeth Healthcare NHS Trust and had mentioned the AB case many times to his associates. He found that the response was always either extremely positive or extremely negative, and with this in mind, he decided to submit an article describing the event to the *British Medical Journal*. He was pleased when he received a positive response, and the article appeared in the December edition.[1]

Many hypothetical suggestions have been made as to what took place in 1984, but none have been considered satisfactory. However, there is now a possible answer to the question of what was happening to AB.

Who or what was this voice and how did it know what was about to take place? How did it know that AB was dangerously ill? How did it know exactly what the cure could be? And how did it know who would be of the greatest help? Could it be that we all have a secret lodger in our brain—a being that has knowledge far greater than our own?

The central concept of my recent book *The Daemon: A Guide to Your Extraordinary Secret Self* is exactly this: that all conscious beings consist of not one but two semi-independent entities—one of which knows what will happen in the future. In this article, I wish to present the evidence for such an idea. I will first review the philosophical, historical, and theological background to such a belief, and then I will apply some astonishing evidence from modern neurology and consciousness studies that may show that such a belief may, in fact, be true.

The Evidence from Theology

Although early civilizations such as the ancient Egyptians had a form of duality that implied more than a simple soul-body dichotomy, it was the ancient Greeks who refined this into a coherent philosophy. For the Greeks, human duality was reflected in two beings: a lower, everyday self called an *eidolon* and an immortal, transcendental being called a *daemon*.

Through the fascincating etymology of the word *daemon* (or *daimone,* as it is sometimes written), a good deal is revealed about social and cultural history. The ancient Greek word was *daimön,* meaning deity or god. As such, the Greeks definition of the word was positive, or at least ambivalent. The Romans Latinized the Greek word, turning it into daemon. For the Romans, a daemon was an inner or attendant spirit that sometimes gave humble man a touch of genius (hence the phrase *the demon of creativity* that is still used by people who never seem to see how curious the statement is).

The word *eidolon* also has an interesting philological history. Originally, this word was used to describe an image or statue of a god. Eventually, it came to mean a copy of something divine; the copy looked like the original but lacked all its qualities. For the pagan sages, this perfectly described the part of the human duality trapped in the realm of darkness. This entity thus became known as the eidolon, which is the embodied self—the physical body and the personality, the person him- or herself. This lower self is mortal and is totally unaware, unless initiated into the mysteries, of its higher self. It is very much part of the world of darkness. It is a slave to emotion and all the other ills that beset the physical being. The daemon, on the other hand, is the immortal self. This daemon is always with the eidolon and, where possible, tries to assist and guide.

The idea of this daemon-eidolon duality fascinated the ancient Greeks, and soon a whole philosophy of universal structure was around this relationship. The earliest known writer on the subject was Empedocles. For him the daemon, although semi-imprisoned in the body, is a divine being exiled from its rightful place among the gods. It exists totally independently of its lower self, or eidolon, and has great knowledge and power.[2] However, our knowledge of this interesting belief really comes from the writings of Plato and his descriptions of the teachings of his master, the famed Socrates.

Plato reports that throughout his life his great teacher had assistance from a guide. Socrates called this discarnate voice his Divine Sign. From childhood, this voice had communicated to him its opinions on what he was doing or intended to do. According to Plato, this voice forbade Socrates from doing certain things and regularly gave prognostications on whether good or bad luck would follow a certain action. It is as if Socrates's Divine Sign was directly aware of the philosopher's potential future. Plato was at great pains to point out that many of these predictions were marked by extreme triviality—as if this spirit were tied very closely to the minutiae of Socrates's life. Socrates explained this in the following speech to the jury who were about to condemn him to death: "I have had a remarkable experience. In the past the prophetic voice to which I have become accustomed has always been my constant companion, opposing me even in quite trivial things if I was going to take the wrong course."[3]

In this final act of his life, Socrates was to find that his Divine Sign did not oppose him. It was as if his lifelong guide and mentor was resigned to the inevitable; Socrates had to die as decreed both by fate and the jury. The hemlock goblet could not be avoided. The voice remained silent.

However, the idea that all human beings have two independent elements did not remain silent. The theology proposed by Empedocles and refined by Socrates was to find many followers in the ancient Greek world and was to become a central tenant of the school of philosophy that was to become known as Stoicism.

Epictetus, the major Stoic philosopher, was quite fascinated by this duality. As with Socrates and Empedocles, nothing remains of his original writings. However, his pupil Arrian wrote down his teachings, recording them in two works: *Discourses* and *Encheiridian* (or manual). In these works, it is clear that he had taken the evidence of Socrates's

Divine Sign and the old belief of human duality and created a cogent philosophy. He wrote:

> God has placed at every man's side a guardian, the Daemon of each man, who is charged to watch over him; a Daemon that cannot sleep, nor be deceived. To what greater and more watchful guardian could have been committed to us? So, when you have shut the doors, and made darkness in the house, remember, never to say that you are alone; for you are not alone. But God is there, and your Daemon is there.[4]

Here we see the ongoing idea that this other entity, the daemon, is more than simply another facet of human nature. It is an independent being that watches over its lower self. That it has an ongoing consciousness is stated by the phrase that it cannot sleep. Indeed, the implication is that the daemon perceives even when the eidolon sleeps.

This belief, however, was not unique to Epictetus or even the Stoics. According to the noted historian of the late classical and early Christian period, Robin Lane Fox, the Romans had an ancient but popular belief that each person had his or her own attendant spirit who followed that person throughout his or her life. This being, termed the genius, was born with the individual and as such was honored, therefore, by each individual, on his or her birthday.[5]

For many of the early Christians, the idea of such a duality of spirit was a dangerous heresy, particularly as it clearly had pagan roots. In order to deal with this, the early Church Fathers applied simple semantics. They took the word *daemon* and consistently used it to designate a disincarnate spirit that has been spawned by the devil to tempt humanity away from the true God. Over time the letter *a* was dropped, and the word mutated into one we all know so well, demon. Job done.

Well, not exactly. There was another group of Christians who found a good deal of theological justification for the daemon-eidolon duality. These were the little known, and quite intriguing, gnostics.

According to the gnostics, the universe was under the influence of two conflicting forces; light and darkness. Human beings are in turn a reflection of this duality. Our soul is a spark that comes from the light. It is therefore part of the positive side. However our bodies are made up of matter. Matter is part of the darkness. As such, there is this ongoing conflict within the human condition. Human beings are imprisoned in this body of darkness but a part of them retains memories of their divine origin. The part rooted in the darkness equates to the eidolon. This being is made of matter and will cease to be when the body dies. However, the part that retains the memory is the daemon.

The central tenant of gnosticism was that an eidolon had to reach a state of *gnosis* (literally knowledge), and having done so, the eidolon could achieve union with the daemon and thereby move away from this corrupt world of matter. To do this, the eidolon would need to spend many years being initiated into the secrets of gnosticism.

However, there are times when the daemon chooses to make itself seen or heard by its eidolon without initiation. The eidolon in these circumstances will perceive the daemon to be some form of guardian angel or spirit guide. Indeed, Plato writes, "We should think of the most authoritative part of the soul as the Guardian Spirit given by God which lifts us to our heavenly home."[6]

The gnostic sages carried this belief forward in its entirety. Valentinus taught that a person receives gnosis from his or her guardian angel, but that in reality that being is simply that person's own higher self.[7] This implies that the angels that communicate between the world of light and the world of darkness are, in fact, not independent beings at all; they are daemons from this world. We are our own teachers!

This is all very interesting with regard to the history of religion and mysticism, but it really has no relevance to twenty-first-century psychology and neurology. Or does it?

The Evidence from Neurology

That human consciousness may be dual rather than unitary may fly in the face of common sense, but for those who study the brain, such an idea is not only possible but probable. A swift review of brain anatomy cannot but support such a proposition. The most immediate thing that strikes you when you observe a brain for the first time is that it is not, in fact, a brain at all. It is two, virtually identical brains, joined together by a mass known as the corpus callosum. Every structure in one side is mirrored in the other, with one, curious exception, the pineal gland. There are two of everything: two limbic systems, two temporal lobes, two amygdalas—the list goes on. The singularity of the pineal gland was noted in ancient times, and because of its unique position, it has been thought of as the location of the soul.

Neurologists have long been puzzled by this. Why should the brain be structured in this way? Indeed, the puzzle has deepened in that it has been shown that certain individuals continue as normal people even when one of the hemispheres is damaged or removed. Indeed, in the past fifty years or so, surgery has advanced to such an extent that the corpus callosum can be cut, and in doing so, the two hemispheres cease to have a line of communication. When this is done, these patients literally have split brains. They also end up with two independent centers of consciousness. The implication of this is both clear and mind-blowing: we have two independent beings sharing our perceptions.

It is generally the case that one side of the brain is dominant and one is passive. The dominant hemisphere (usually, but not always, the left) is rational, objective, and unemotional. The nondominant (right) is understood to be irrational, subjective, and emotional. However, this does not on its own imply two foci of consciousness, just simply two aspects of the same consciousness. The two elements are simply seen as aspects of a unitary consciousness with the left hemisphere being generally in control with the occasional eruption of emotion from the right. This is why in recent years there have been so many self-help books suggesting techniques by which people can attune to their intuitive right brain. But the reality is far more complex—and fascinating.

Usually, the two hemispheres work in tandem, with the left generating a constant stream of inner dialogue that gives us our sense of self.

Meanwhile, the right hemisphere is still actively involved in all cognitive processes, working away in the background. However, and here comes the surprise, the being known as I or me is generally completely unaware of what its silent partner is up to. Indeed, for most of the time, the I is completely unaware of its partner. Problems arise when the two fall out of phase. Suddenly I senses us. However, it is much more disturbing than that. The dominant hemisphere perceives its nondominant twin as an external presence, a being that is not self but other. To the experiencer, this sensed presence is not him- or herself at all but an outside being.

Michael Persinger of the Laurentian University in Sudbury, Canada, has spent many years studying this peculiar psychological effect. He even has a term for this perception. He calls it the *visitor experience.* Indeed, he has been able to reproduce the sensation under laboratory conditions. Persinger believes the experience shows a linear progression. At its weakest, the subject just feels that he or she is not alone; that there is something else in the room that he or she cannot see. However, at its strongest, the subject perceives an objectively existing being of tangible reality, a being that has great emotional significance to him or her. For some, this being may be an angel or even a god.

As the intensity increases, the manifestation may become even more immanent in the sensual world of the subject. Sensations such as weird buzzing sounds, tingling sensations, and, occasionally, a huge energy release from within subject's body.

What was significant to Persinger was that the brain of the subject, when measured with an encephalograph, showed activity in the temporal lobes. As the experience became more intense, the occipital lobes became activated. When this happened, there was a sudden externalization of the sensation: The sensed presence manifested itself as a visual being fully external to the subject. A common description is of a cowled figure with just a face and hand visible through the folds.

What is very interesting is that if the lower portion of the temporal lobes becomes activated at this time, then long dormant memories may spontaneously enter the subject's mind. The being will then communicate information that seems intensely personal. This may be interpreted as telepathy or omnipotent knowledge. However, there is more. According to Persinger, past-life memories can be evoked in a panoramic life rerun, similar to those reported during the phenomenon known as the near-death experience.

If this is the case, could it be that the other major element of the near-death experience—seeing a being in white—is really an external projection of the experiencer's nondominant consciousness? If so, it would certainly explain how this being shows such intimate knowledge of the dying person's past life.

Could it be that this being really is an independent focus of consciousness that has shared the life of its alter ego? Could the experiments of Persinger show that the daemon is a very real aspect of every human being's neurological makeup?

Cheating the Ferryman?

In my first book, *Is There Life after Death: The Extraordinary Science of What Happens When You Die,* I present evidence that, during the last few seconds of life, we all split into the two entities I term the daemon and the eidolon. Up until this moment, both entities have been united as one being and do perceive themselves as two separate entities. The daemon, suddenly discovering its true vocation, is aware that it is responsible for the experience called the past-life review. It begins the review, while at the same time manifesting itself as an image perceived by its eidolon as a figure. For some, this image will be the classic grim reaper figure, whereas to others, the daemon may be seen as a relative, religious figure, or even an animal—anything that fits the eidolon's preconceptions of who will be there to welcome him or her into the next life. The daemon then starts the past-life review using the memory stores of the temporal lobes. However, to be a reported near-death experience, actual death does not take place. The subject lives to tell the tale. Many of these survivors describe how their life flashed before their eyes. This may be because the daemon, suddenly becoming aware that death will be avoided this time, metaphorically presses the fast-forward button and aborts the process.

What happens in a real-death experience is that the daemon starts the past-life review without the need to fast-forward. The dying eidolon, in the last few seconds of its life, falls out of time and relives again its whole life in a minute-by-minute three-dimensional re-creation of a life that is indistinguishable from the real thing. However, there is one major difference: this time, the daemon is not only self-aware but remembers what happened last time. In this way, the daemon reproduces exactly the role as described by the gnostics, the Stoics, and pagan sages: It becomes a guardian angel looking after the life of its lower self, exactly as described by Socrates.

Can it be that most of us are living our lives in a three-dimensional illusion? Well, it would help to explain certain ongoing mysteries. Precognition suddenly does not defy scientific knowledge because it is simply a memory. Déjà vu can be seen for what it is—a jump in the playback mechanism or simply a flashback. And what about those weird hunches, synchronicities, and intuitions that seem to regularly enter our consciousness? Could they be just messages from our own higher self—our daemon?

Notes

1. Ikechukwu Obialo Azuonye, "A Difficult Case: Diagnosis Made by Hallucinatory Voices," *British Medical Journal* 315 (1997): 685–86.

2. W. K. C. Guthrie, *History of Greek Philosophy* (Cambridge, U.K.: Cambridge University Press, 1962), 318.

3. Apology 31d, Phaedrus 242 and Republic 496c.

4. Epictetus, *The Teachings of Epictetus* (Stanford, Calif.: Stanford University Libraries, 1992), 145.

5. Robin Lane Fox, *Pagans and Christians* (London: Penguin, 1986), 129.

6. Timothy Freke and Peter Gandy, *Wisdom of the Pagan Philosophers* (Boston: Journey Editions, 1998), 40.

7. Carl Jung, *The Gnostic Jung,* edited by R. A. Segal (London: Routledge, 1992).

SIXTEEN

The Intention Economy

FROM EGO TO WE GO

DANIEL PINCHBECK

While exploring shamanism and nonordinary states, I discovered the power of intention. According to the artist Ian Lungold, who lectured brilliantly about the Mayan calendar before his untimely death a few years ago, the Maya believe that your intention is as essential to your ability to navigate reality as your position in time and space. If you don't know your intention, or if you are operating with the wrong intentions, you are always lost and can only get more dissolute.

This idea becomes exquisitely clear during psychedelic journeys, when your state of mind gets intensified and projected kaleidoscopically all around you. As our contemporary world becomes more and more psyche-delic, we are receiving harsh lessons in the power of intention, on a vast scale. Over the last decades, the international financial elite manipulated the markets to create obscene rewards for themselves at the expense of poor and middle-class people across the world. Using devious derivatives, cunning CDOs (collaterized debt obligations), and other trickery, they siphoned off ever-larger portions of the surplus value created by the pro-ducers of real goods and services, contriving a debt-based economy that had to fall apart. Their own greed—such a meager, dull intent—has now blown up in their faces, annihilating, in slow motion, the corrupt system built to serve them.

Opportunities such as this one don't come along very often and should be seized once they appear. When the edifice of mainstream society suddenly collapses, as is happening now, it is a fantastic time for artists, visionaries, mad scientists, and seers to step forward and present a well-defined alternative. What is required, in my opinion, is not some moderate proposal or incremental change, but a complete shift in values and goals, making a polar reversal of our society's basic paradigm. If our consumer-based, materialism-driven model of society is dissolving, what can we offer in its place? Why not begin with the most elevated intentions? Why not offer the most imaginatively fabulous systemic redesign?

The fall of capitalism and the crisis of the biosphere could induce mass despair and misery, or they could impel the creative adaptation and conscious evolution of the human species. We could attain a new level of wisdom and build a compassionate global society, in which resources are shared equitably while we devote ourselves to protecting threatened species and repairing damaged ecosystems. Considering the lightning-like speed of global communication and new social technologies, this change could happen with extraordinary speed.

To a very great extent, the possibilities that we choose to realize in the future will be a result of our individual and collective intention. For instance, if we maintain a puritanical belief that work is somehow good in and of itself, then we will keep striving to create a society of full employment, even if those jobs become "green collar." A more radical viewpoint perceives most labor as something that could become essentially voluntary in the future. The proper use of technology could allow us to transition to a postscarcity leisure society, where the global populace spends its time growing food, building community, making art, making love, learning new skills, and deepening self-development through spiritual disciplines such as yoga, tantra, shamanism, and meditation.

One common perspective is that the West and Islam are engaged in an intractable conflict of civilizations, where the hatred and terrorism can only get worse. Another viewpoint could envision the Judeo-Christian culture of the West finding common ground and reconciling with the esoteric core, the metaphysical purity, of the Islamic faith. It seems—to me anyway—that we could find solutions to all of the seemingly intractable problems of our time once we are ready to apply a different mind-set to them. As Einstein and others have noted, we don't solve problems through the type of thinking that created them, rather they dissolve when we reach a different level of consciousness.

We have become so mired in our all-too-human world that we have lost touch with the other, elder forms of sentience all around us. Along with delegates to the UN, perhaps we could train cadres of diplomats to negotiate with the vegetal, fungal, and microbial entities that sustain life on Earth. The mycologist Paul Stamets proposes we create a symbiosis with mushrooms to detoxify ecosystems and improve human health. The herbalist Morgan Brent believes psychoactive flora like ayahuasca and peyote are "teacher plants," sentient emissaries from superintelligent nature, trying to help the human species find its niche in the greater community of life. When we pull back to study the hapless and shameful activity of our species across Earth, these ideas do not seem very farfetched.

In fact, the breakdown of our financial system has not altered the amount of tangible resources available on our planet. Rather than trying to rejigger an unjust debt-based system that artificially maintains inequitiy and scarcity, we could make a new start. We could develop a different intention for what we are supposed to be doing together on this swiftly rotating planet and institute new social and economic infrastructures to support that intent.

From Ego to We Go

When I was in my twenties, literature was my ruling passion, and my heroes were writers like F. Scott Fitzgerald, Jack Kerouac, Virginia Woolf, and Henry Miller. I longed to emulate the passionate intensity of their prose and the "negative capability" that infused their characters with recognizable life. When I passed through the crucible of my own transformational process, I lost interest in novels and discovered a new pantheon of intellectual heroes. These days, I find the same level of electrical engagement that I used to find in novels in the works of thinkers whose central theme is the evolution and possible extension of human consciousness. This varied group is made up of mystics, physicists, philosophers, cosmologists, and paleontologists—the roster includes Rudolf Steiner, Carl Jung, Edward Edinger, Jean Gebser, Teilhard de Chardin, F. David Peat, Sri Aurobindo, and Gerald Heard.

For me, personally, most contemporary fiction, like most current film, has an increasingly retrograde quality. In their efforts to make their audience identify with a particular drama or trauma or relationship saga, these products seem almost nostalgic. We live in a culture that continually seeks to entertain or at least distract us with an endless spew of personal narratives, whether paraded on low-brow talk shows or parsed in literary novels. If you step outside the cultural framing, you suddenly become aware of the mechanism that keeps us addicted to the spectacle— and, above all, hooked on ego. Our entire culture is dedicated to inciting and then placating the desires and fears of the individual ego—what the media critic Thomas de Zengotita calls "the flattered self."

Although they use different languages to define it, the various theorists on the evolution of the psyche all agree that the crux of our current crisis requires that we transcend the ego. They suggest that the stage of material progress and scientific discovery we attained in recent centuries is not the end of human development but the launching pad for another stage in our growth. However, this next stage differs from previous phases in one essential way: it requires a mutation in consciousness that can only be self-willed and self-directed. According to this paradigm, it is as if physical evolution has done billions of years of work on our behalf to get us to this point. Right now, it is our choice whether we would like to go forward or fall by the wayside like untold millions of other species who overadapted to one set of conditions and could not re-create themselves as their environment changed.

In his influential book, *Pain, Sex and Time,* the British polymath Gerald Heard defined three stages in human evolution: physical, technical, and psychical. "The first is unconscious—blind; the second is conscious, unreflective, aware of its need but not of itself, of how, not why; the third is interconscious, reflective, knowing not merely how to satisfy its needs but what they mean and the Whole means," wrote Heard, who believed we were on the cusp of switching from the technical to the psychical level of development. As we enter the psychic phase, we shift "from indirect to direct expansion of understanding, at this point man's own self-consciousness decides and can alone decide whether he will mutate, and the mutation is instantaneous." Originally published in 1939, Heard's book has just been reprinted in the United States; it was James Dean's favorite work and inspired Huston Smith to turn to religious studies.

Despite its antique provenance, *Pain, Sex and Time* remains "new news" for our time. Heard viewed the immense capacity of human beings to experience pain and suffering and the extraordinary excess of our sexual drive compared to our actual reproductive needs as signs of a tremendous surplus of evolutionary energy that can be repurposed for the extension and intensification of consciousness if we so choose. "Modern man's incessant sexuality is not bestial: rather it is a psychic hemorrhage," Heard wrote. "He bleeds himself constantly because he fears mental apoplexy if he can find no way of releasing his huge store of nervous energy." Heard foresaw the necessity of a new form of self-discipline, a training in concentrating psychic energy to develop extrasensory perception, as the proper way to channel the excess of nervous hypertension that would otherwise lead to our destruction. He thought that we would either evolve into a "supraindividual" condition, or the uncontrolled energies would force us back into "preindividuated" identifications, leading to nationalist wars, totalitarian fervors, and species burnout.

A sign I saw at last year's Burning Man put it succinctly: "From Ego to We Go." As the climate changes and our environment deteriorates, we are being subjected to tremendous evolutionary pressures that could push us beyond individuation into a deeply collaborative mind-set and a new threshold of psychic awareness. Seventy years after Heard's manifesto, whether or not we want to evolve as a species remains an open question. But the choice is in our hands.

Enlightenment Reason or Occult Conspiracy?

What holds our world together is not only the laws of physics but language, myth, and story. Our narratives create the framework in which our actions and our intentions have meaning, or at least some kind of order. It is very hard for us to live without any coherence at all. It may even be impossible, as our minds immediately begin to weave together some type of fable to support whatever it is we find ourselves doing.

Lately, I find myself switching back and forth between divergent models or myths of reality and seeking to integrate them. One of them is the story of progress and reason, the inheritance of the secular and scientific Enlightenment. The progressive believes that a flawed society can be improved by rational policy and political pressure. The world can be made better for more people, inequities reduced, and health care guaranteed. Although he has been strategic in his pronouncements, Barack Obama seems the model of a progressive reformer, promoting the type of sensible policies that led to the New Deal and the Great Society.

The other mythic structure that entices me is occult and conspiratorial. According to this story, there is a hidden agenda beneath the façade of chaotic events. This agenda is orchestrated by "them," a group of elite cabals and secret societies, an amalgam of Free Masons, Vatican priests, the descendants of the Nazi scientists brought to the United States after World War II, and so on. To approach this concealed dimension of world affairs, to separate accurate insights from disinformation, is extremely difficult and perhaps impossible. The quest involves long reading lists of small-press and self-published tomes and many hours on YouTube, watching lectures presented by anxious men in drab conferences. From such unreliable sources, one learns that much alien technology has already been recovered and reverse engineered, that a new world order of total social control is being orchestrated, that the ark of the covenant is a torsion field generator perhaps hidden in the Pentagon, that shape-shifting reptilians are controlling everything, and other tidbits.

Personally, I don't reject the possibility that there is an occult element in global affairs, a distorting factor that makes true understanding difficult to achieve. During my shamanic work, I encountered spiritual and demonic forces appearing as visions and voices but also causing effects that seemed to cross the barrier between the psychic and the physical. According to shamanic traditions, spirits operate across the entire field of our world. Rather than a fine-tuned conspiracy of elite cabals, the true story might be far more muddled, with various factions holding pieces of a puzzle, mired in outmoded rituals and incoherent beliefs, lacking shamanic skills. Many of those involved in these cabals may suffer from guilt and fear the consequences if their shadowy actions are revealed to the public.

Out on the esoteric edge of the cultural imagination, one finds an increasing convergence of thought streams. The works of Steven Greer, David Wilcock, and Richard Hoagland, as well as Nassim Haramein's DVD set *Crossing the Event Horizon* (available at theresonanceproject. org) all suggest that, beyond a certain threshold, technological advances may be linked not just to technical knowledge but to our level of consciousness, requiring higher awareness as well as purified intentions to function. As Haramein theorizes, the ark of the covenant might have been an actual device preserved from antediluvian civilizations, capable of generating extraordinary amounts of energy—enough to open a passage through the Red Sea but requiring an initiate on the level of Moses to operate it without causing mayhem. Many of these thinkers offer intriguing scenarios in which alchemical or extraterrestrial possibilities could manifest in tangible forms.

Can someone pursue Enlightenment ideals while simultaneously exploring occult conspiracies? If we avoid becoming obsessive or dismissive, it seems possible to hold contrasting myths or models of reality in our minds at the same time. We can study the Mayan calendar, extraterrestrials, and gnostic cosmology while fighting for social and environmental justice, campaigning for political reform, and so on. Whether or not our corrupt system can be changed, we could learn a great deal by joining any valiant effort made in that direction.

For Enlightenment thinkers, the sun symbolized the clear light of reason they adored. The clear light of reason may stream from the sun, but as the French philosopher Georges Bataille noted, if you turn your gaze upward to look at its source, you blind yourself. Those who stare at the sun for too long may go insane. The source of reason in itself produces unreason, blindness, and madness. Reason appears to have an innate contradiction at its center. Reason, by itself, may not be enough to get us out of our planetary plight. If spiritual forces operate within our world, then meaningful social change requires, along with political reform, initiatory processes and shamanic practices that could, perhaps, open our minds to new myths of reality.

Building a Scaffold for Social Change

For the most part, the mainstream media and federal government still treat the economic collapse as something that can be fixed so that economic growth can resume in a few years. Some commentators are beginning to realize that our meltdown represents a deeper and more permanent paradigm shift. The physical environment can no longer withstand the assaults of our industrial culture. We are experiencing a termination of capitalism as we have known it, a shutdown recently dubbed the "Great Disruption" by Thomas Friedman, in the *New York Times*. Until recently, a leading cheerleader for neoliberal globalization, Friedman has come to the late realization "that the whole growth model we created over the last 50 years is simply unsustainable economically and ecologically and that 2008 was when we hit the wall." The longer that the general population is allowed to remain in denial about what is happening, the more dire the probable consequences, such as widespread famine, civil unrest, and a disintegration of basic services.

The truth is that we need to make a deep and rapid change in our current social systems and in the underlying models and ideals of our society. It is highly unlikely that those who have been part of the power structure, whether within government or the mainstream media, possess the necessary will, vision, or inspiration to make this happen. Also, when we consider their self-serving support for a delusional model of infinite growth on a finite planet, ignoring all evidence to the contrary, our mainstream pundits and politicos have clearly forfeited any claim to authority and should never be trusted again.

Many elements of an alternative paradigm, a participatory model in which power is restored to local communities, have been developed over the last decades. One example is the transition town model in Britain, which serves as a foundation to help communities move toward resilience and self-reliance. Extraordinary initiatives are presented annually at the Bioneers Conference, and their website maintains an archive of these projects, from bioremediation to complementary currencies that could be rapidly scaled up if the collective will is mobilized. The nonprofit organization Pro Natura has developed an alfalfa leaf extract that can fulfill a person's annual nutritive needs for a negligible sum—and many other innovators and activists are holding crucial pieces of the new puzzle we need to assemble quickly.

What blocks real efforts at social transformation is the current level of human consciousness. The Italian political philosopher Antonio Negri has noted that the most important form of production in our postindustrial culture is the production of subjectivity. Our media and education systems have mechanically imprinted a certain level of awareness onto the masses, a passive, consumer consciousness. People have not been encouraged to think or to act for themselves. Now, their very survival may depend upon learning these unfamiliar skills.

Since I comprehended the full depth of the crisis heading our way, I have been working with friends and collaborators to envision and enact solutions. We saw the need for an alternative social network and media that could integrate many aspects of the new paradigm while providing a scaffold for a large-scale process of social transformation. Facebook and MySpace have shown the extraordinary power of social networks to reach an enormous audience, but they have mainly provided a place for people to display and distract themselves in new ways. Most popular social networks are designed to support the flattered self, constantly craving attention, and the main purpose of these networks is to make a profit for large corporations.

We recently launched Evolver, an independent social network built on open-source software that is designed to support collaboration between individuals and groups and to engage people in the process of transforming their own consciousness and their local communities. While we still use many of the standard social networking tools, we have shifted the focus to members' mission and projects. We have also created an internal rating system for members to vote on the initiatives presented by other members so that the best ideas in every area will rise to the top and gain more attention. We are currently facilitating a network of local groups, across the United States and eventually globally, that meet in person every month and engage in immediate actions to change their world. These groups are called Evolver Spores; you can check evolver.net to see if there is a spore in your area, or start your own.

Years ago, Barbara Marx Hubbard wrote, "If the positive innovations connect exponentially before the massive breakdowns reinforce one another, the system can repattern itself to a higher order of consciousness and freedom without the predicted economic, environmental, or social collapse." We are quickly approaching the critical threshold where breakdown or breakthrough becomes inevitable. I don't know if

Evolver will reach mass popularity as a tool to bring about this repatterning. Of course, I hope this is the case. In the guise of a for-profit company, we have sought to create something akin to a social utility. At a turbulent time when nobody knows what is going to happen next, it feels good, at least, to have launched something into the world that can help the process of transformation.

SEVENTEEN

2012 and Beyond

THE TORTUGUERO PROPHECY UNRAVELED

GEOFF STRAY

Before 2006, many anthropologists, archaeologists, and other Mayan scholars stated that there was nothing in the Mayan inscriptions about the end of the current 5,125-year era of the long count calendar. They often did this to dismiss the increasing discussion about 2012. But in April 2006, epigrapher Dave Stuart answered an enquiry on a specialist discussion group announcing that there is one known inscription from the classic era that mentions the end of the thirteenth *baktun*.[1] It is on Monument 6 from a little-known site called Tortuguero, in the state of Tabasco in Mexico. Many maps don't even show the site or vary in their positioning of it.

Tortuguero was discovered in 1915, but in 1978 and 1980, Berthold Riese, Ph.D., published studies on the inscriptions found there. The papers are in German. Since then, very little emerged until Sven Gronemeyer's master thesis of 2004—also in German.[2,3] An updated version was published in English in 2006.[4] A cement factory was built on top of the site in 1981, but a few ruins remain.

Tortuguero Monument 6

Tortuguero's most famous artifact is the Tortuguero box—a well-preserved, carved wooden box inscribed with glyphs that describe, among other things, the burial of the Tortuguero ruler, Bahlam Ajaw (Lord Jaguar). Monument 6 is broken into seven parts, four of which are in the Villahermosa Museum, not far from the Tortuguero site. Another part is in the Metropolitan Museum of New York, and two other fragments are thought to be in the hands of a private collector. The monument was originally a T-shaped stela, and one of the wings—the left one that starts the narrative—is missing. It is the other wing—the final part of the narrative—that refers to the end of the thirteenth baktun.

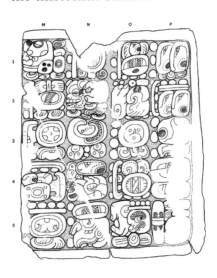

Figure 17.1. The right wing of Monument 6 from Tortuguero, which refers to the end of the thirteenth baktun. Drawing by Sven Gronemeyer.

Gronemeyer has split the translation of the monument into six sections. The first section concerns the birth and enthronement of Bahlam Ajaw. The second section concerns "star wars" (wars that were timed by the first appearance of Venus as evening or morning star) and decapitation of prisoners. The third section describes the war against the neighboring town Comalcalco and the consequent "harvest of white-flower souls." The fourth section describes unknown events, since some of the glyphs are damaged. The fifth section describes the ritual burning of a house, the setting up of images of Bahlam Ajaw, and a ruler-binding ritual.

This is the context of the final section that commences three glyphs before the right-hand side wing and continues through the wing. I have rendered Gronemeyer's translation of this section into English:

> 7 days 7 Uinals 0 Tuns and 8 Katuns, previously it happened. On 8 Chuen 9 Mak, it was completed for rebirthing [or nascent becoming], the pibnaah of Ahkal K'uk. It was 2 days, 9 Uinals, 3 Tuns, 8 Katuns, and 3 Baktuns before the thirteenth Baktun is completed on 4 Ahau 3 Kankin. Then it will happen—darkness, and Bolon-Yokte will descend to the [?].

The monument was set up in 669 CE to commemorate a building known as a *pibnaah,* which was built around 160 years earlier in 510 CE. A pibnaah is often translated as a steam bath or sweat lodge, and this is how Gronemeyer has translated it. The construction of the pibnaah is directly forward referenced to the end of the thirteen-baktun era in 2012 with its predicted event—darkness accompanied by the descent of the god Bolon-Yokte. But the prophecy cannot be completed due to damage to the glyphs.

The first question this prompts is: Who is Bolon-Yokte?[5] The name *Bolon-Yokte* translates to the god of nine strides or the god of numerous strides, since *bolon* means both nine and many. Sometimes the god is referred to as B'olon Yookte' K'u or B'olon Okte' K'uh, where K'uh means deity. He has also been called Ah Bolon Yocte of Nine Paths in the postconquest books of Chilam Balam. The god has an association with the underworld, conflict, war, dangerous transition times, social unrest, eclipses, and natural disasters like earthquakes.[6] He appears at the end of baktuns; he assisted at the creation of the current world and will be present at the next creation in 2012. Other translations of the name are God of Nine Steps, the Nine-Footed God, and Jaguar-Foot-Tree, because the word *bolon* or *balan* (nine) was used by the Maya as a pun for *balam* (jaguar). The god was seen alternatively as nine individuals or as a collective god.

The Pibnaah and the Kiva

There are at least two examples of a pibnaah or steam bath at Chichén Itzá. These sweat lodges are still used by the Maya today and are called *tuj,* or sometimes *chitin* or *kun* (oven). The Aztecs also used a steam bath called a *temazcal;* in Mexican package holidays, a spell in a temazcal is often included. They were used for ritual purification ceremonies, healing, revitalization, cleansing, and general meetings. It is known today that they are very beneficial to the health. They flush toxic metals from the system a hundred times faster than the kidneys; they open clogged pores, removing excess salts; they eliminate uric and lactic acid; they increase blood flow, unclog the respiratory tract, and increase negative ions.

Although today's temazcals are aboveground, they, and the pibnaahs at Chichén Itzá were usually dug five feet into the ground and used a direct fire rather than hot rocks, similar to the method used by Native Americans in California. The design and alignment was similar to that of a Hopi *kiva*, or underground ceremonial room. Though today's kivas are often aboveground and square, the ancient Anasazi (ancestors of the Hopi) examples are round and mostly below ground. According to Frank Waters's *Book of the Hopi,* many Hopis regard Aztecs and Maya as renegade Hopi clans that did not finish their migrations, so we may have here an insight into the pibnaah.

Native American sweat lodges, as well as kivas, are seen as symbolic wombs of Mother Earth, and not only do the Hopi conduct creation myth reenactment ceremonies in kivas, but some tribes design sweat lodges to reflect creation myths. Not only are temazcals used for pregnancy and birth, but those who have used them ritually describe feeling their spirit bodies acknowledging the four elements and experiencing the rebirth and death of parts of the ego that no longer serve growth.

Amazingly, there is an association between kivas and the number nine—perhaps a remnant of the Bolon-Yokte connection, upon which we are seeking to throw light. Every year, there are nine major ceremonies traditionally performed in the kiva. They correspond to the nine universes of the Hopi creation myth. There is one universe for the Creator, Taiowa, one for his nephew, Sótuknang, and seven for created life. The Hopi say there are a total of seven worlds, or eras, and that each one is governed by a psychic center—the same as the top five chakras of the Hindu system. We are in the fourth world, known as World Complete. Our consciousness descended from the crown chakra in the first era down as far as the solar plexus in the current era—each era becoming more materialistic than the last—but at the next world era transition, it will start to reverse direction. Each transition is called an emergence and is symbolized by a labyrinth symbol—identical the Cretan labyrinth symbol. It is also known as the Mother Earth symbol, or mother and child, and the process is seen as a kind of birth process.

There are also said to be nine prophecies that will be fulfilled before the day of purification, which precedes the emergence. These are the coming of the white man, covered wagons, longhorn cattle, railroad tracks, power lines and telephone lines, concrete roads, oil spills, hippies, and, finally, the blue star kachina. Only the last of these nine remains to be fulfilled. When a blue star is seen in the sky, and the blue star kachina dancer removes his mask in the plaza, then the Hopi ceremonies will cease. Though some have said this was Comet Holmes, the fact is that the Hopi ceremonies were still continuing after Comet Holmes came and went (according to an eyewitness report of a personal friend).

Figure 17.2. This mother and child symbol is identical to the Cretan labyrinth symbol and symbolizes a spiritual rebirth from one world to the next. There is also a square version.

Nine Generation Rites

The first of the nine ceremonies is called Wúwuchim, which represents birth. This ceremony is a reenactment of the Hopi emergence—their ascent from the third world, represented by the inside of the kiva, to the current fourth world, into which they emerge at the height of the ceremony, naked and wet like newborns coming out of the womb. They then have their hair washed in nine bowls of yucca suds. This ceremony reaches its height when the Pleiades are overhead at midnight, at which point the newborns get the signal to emerge. From John Major Jenkins's discoveries, we know that the Toltec method of tracking precession also involved watching for the Pleiades overhead at midnight. In this way, they could calculate how close they would be to the zenith sun exactly six months later. According to Jenkins, this was encoded into the pyramid of Kukulcan at Chichén Itzá, which encodes this 360-year-long sun-Pleiades conjunction, which starts with a solar eclipse conjunct the Pleiades in the zenith on May 20, 2012.

The second of the nine ceremonies is called Soyál and concerns seed germination. The seeds of their sacred crop, corn (maize), plus other crops such as beans and squash, are taken into the kiva and germinated, with the help of the kachinas or nature spirits, who are manifested in the form of dancers. This is followed by Powamu, which is a ceremony based around planting and sprouting. The first of the next group of three ceremonies is Niman Kachina, which concerns growth and maturing. Then comes the Flute Ceremony, about irrigation and more planting, followed by the Snake-Antelope Ceremony, which governs fruition. The last three are Lakón, about fertility and planting and harvesting; then Márawu, which concerns flirtation and food gifts; and finally, Owaqlt, which governs conception and gifts. In each group, there is one ceremony that includes an Emergence Ceremony. The ceremonies actually work on three levels: plant, human, and species. They not only help seed germination via crop fertility rituals, they also affect human fertility and involve birth rituals; but on a species level, via the

Emergence rituals, they perform a rerun and purification—a preparation for the Emergence or birth into the next world, the Fifth.

A further insight is allowed by Dave Stuart's second and more complete translation[7] of the final section of Monument 6:

> 7 days, 7 Uinals, 0 Tuns and 8 Katuns previously it happened, on the day 8 Chuen, the 9th of Mak, the Becoming-Ripe-House was constructed [?]. It was the underground house [or shrine] of [the god?] Ahkal K'uk'. It was two and nine-score days, three years, eight-score years and 3 x 400 years [before] the Thriteenth Pik will end on Four Ajaw, the third of Uniiw, when. . . [?] . . . will happen, the descent . . . [?] . . . of B'olon Yookte' to the [?].

So here, Stuart is providing more information about the pib-naah: it is an underground house or shrine and also a Becoming-Ripe House. At Palenque, which is not far from Tortuguero, the three shrines known as the Temple of the Cross, the Temple of the Foliated Cross, and the Temple of the Sun are fairly intact, and in their inscriptions, they are called pibnaahs and associated with Bolon-Yokte.[8] Each shrine at the top of a pyramid represents a cave in a mountain—an entrance to Xibalba, the Mayan underworld—each a path to be taken by the king, Kihnich Kan B'ahlam II (son of Lord Pacal). The Temple of the Sun is the shrine to the Jaguar God (remember Jaguar is a pun for nine), and rites of passage are described, in which the king at the age of six and again a month before his eighth birthday participated in a preadolescent rite called Okte' (literally wood column): at the age of six years, two months, and eighteen days he was, according to the inscription, "Okte'd," and on the half-katun date of 9.10.10.0.0, he "descended into Okte'ship." The Temple of the Cross is the shrine to the maize god and depicts the king undergoing a rite of passage at the age of thirteen, in which he was "tied into Okte'-ship" and received Bolon Okte'. He is shown as a boy wearing a nine-knotted costume. God L, the cigar-smoking lord of the underworld is also shown. At eighteen, there was another rite of passage, in which the king received the K'awill sceptre. The Temple of the Foliated Cross shows the world tree as a maize plant, with corncobs as human heads. The shrine is dedicated to the God Kawil, also known as Bolon Tzacab, the God of Nine Generations, and records the accession to the throne of the king, at the age of forty-eight.

So we have seen that the pibnaah, as well as a steam bath, was a shrine associated with Bolon-Yokte, plus the jaguar god and K'awill, both of which also have associations with the number nine. We have also seen that the rituals performed inside were rites of passage including trips to the underworld and the symbolism of maize. The "becoming-ripe" house was actually a shrine for personal evolutionary development, which has parallels to the kiva with its ceremonies of plant development, human development, and species evolution at the transition between eras. This may throw some light on the connection between Monument 6 and the pibnaah at Tortuguero.

According to Frank Waters in *The Book of the Hopi* (1963), the Hopi saw corn as "a living entity with a body similar to man's in many respects." Mother Earth also had an aspect as Corn Mother. When a child was born, he or she was kept in the dark for thirty days with the child's Corn Mother (represented as an ear of perfect corn whose tip ends in four kernels) beside him or her; also, various rituals were performed involving cornmeal. In a similar way, in the Mayan myth, "*The Popol Vuh*," a series of creations are described in which humans evolve. In the first creation, humankind starts out as mud people, then becomes wooden doll people, who are replaced by monkey people. At the start of the current creation, which is seen as the fourth or fifth by different commentators, Quetzal Snake and companions grind and mold the maize and form the next race of people—the maize people—who are the ancestors of the Quiche Maya. This includes the ninefold blessing of Xmucane, goddess of midwives. According to Martin Prechtel, in the still-surviving mythology of the Tz'utujil Maya, who live in villages surrounding Lake Atitlán in Guatemala, we are in the fifth creation, which is called Earth Fruit World. As we go through the five stages of life, we assimilate the lessons of the five creations, and then at death, we go to the sixth creation.

This relationship between humanity and maize is reflected in the sacred Tzolkin calendar. The anthropological evidence provided by Barbara Tedlock in *Time and the Highland Maya* (1982) indicates that the Tzolkin's 260 days are based on the period of human gestation. When a woman misses her period, there are 260 days until the birth is due. But a 260-day cycle could also be seen as a gestation period of the maize plant. In the highlands of Guatemala, there are 260 days between planting and harvesting of maize.

There may be a connection with the results found by John Burke in his study of ancient sites, *Seed of Knowledge, Stone of Plenty* (2005), particularly Neolithic dolmens, Silbury Hill and Avebury, plus vision-quest sites and stone chambers in North America, and the pyramids at Tikal. Burke and his coauthor, Kaj Halberg, found that in all these cases (at Tikal, it was just at the summit of Lost World Pyramid, and not the later Temples I and II), the sites are positioned on a "conductivity discontinuity" that amplifies Earth currents, and the structure amplifies them even more, particularly just before dawn. The result is a two- to-threefold (even more at the Lost World Pyramid) increase in seed germination that can result after just twenty minutes exposure. These same electromagnetic fluctuations can affect human consciousness, and the sacred sites, the authors conclude, thus had a secondary use—the alteration of consciousness.

New Developments

There have been some important developments in Mayan studies in the past three years that have great significance for the interpretation of Tortuguero Monument 6 and the 2012 creation point. The first of these is Michael Grofe's 2007 dissertation, *The Serpent Series: Precession in the Maya Dresden Codex*.[9] Grofe found a 15,000-year-plus interval depicted in the Serpent Series of the Dresden Codex that is an almost

Figure 17.3. The Serpent Series in the Dresden Codex that show a multiple of the sidereal year, according to Grofe. The dates are read vertically between the coils of the snakes.

exact multiple of the sidereal year. This is strong evidence that the Maya were measuring and recording the cycle we know as the precession of the equinoxes.

In the following year, 2008, Barb MacLeod announced the discovery of the 3-11-pik formula.[10] In analyzing the glyphs on a bone from Tikal, she found three intervals of 8,660 days that add to 1 degree of precession, accompanied by a mirrored period of three times eleven baktuns, which is half a precessional period.

In 2009, on *Tribe 2012,* one of the web's most popular 2012 discussion groups, I started a thread about a forthcoming Mayan conference on 2012,[11] and in the ensuing discussion, while researching a response, I stumbled across Sven Gronemeyer's 2004 thesis on Tortuguero—a document that I had previously thought was only available in an elusive hardcopy version. I made the links available in one of my posts, and John Major Jenkins then downloaded the thesis and enlisted the help of Michael Grofe and MacLeod in translating the Monument 6 text directly from the Mayan glyphs into English.

This has led to some important new discoveries, as Jenkins has just revealed in his *The 2012 Story,* which is hot off the press.[12] Grofe discovered that on Bahlam Ajaw's birth date, the sun was in the exact same position that it will be at the end of the thirteenth baktun on December 21, 2012 (except that, in 2012, precession will have moved the sun/galactic equator conjunction to the day of the winter solstice). Grofe thinks Bahlam Ajaw was claiming a special relationship with the end of the current thirteenth baktun cycle and with Bolon-Yokte, the deity who is connected to that event. Jenkins has also suggested the possibility that Lord Pacal of Palenque did something similar, possibly inspired by Baham Ajaw, and tried to upstage him by having his coronation day on the same day in the solar year as the last day in the next higher cycle in the long count—the twenty-baktun cycle, or Pictun—thus becoming a kind of higher-ranking time lord. Jenkins has suggested in his excellent new book, that the king of Copan, 18 Rabbit, also connected himself to a future baktun ending, as well as the katun ending 9.14.0.0.0, when the sun was again in the dark rift. This is also the last date recorded at Tortuguero before 13.0.0.0.0, when Bolon-Yokte descends.

Grofe has also discovered that Tortuguero Monument 6 shows evidence that the Maya were measuring precession by recording a lunar eclipse that occurred in the dark rift, when the glare of the moon would have been negated by Earth's shadow cast on it, allowing the Milky Way shape to be discerned. They were thus able to calculate the date six months later, when the sun would be in the dark rift. This collaboration between Jenkins, Grofe, and MacLeod is continuing to provide more evidence that Jenkins's galactic alignment theory is based in fact.

Jenkins's theory, as many readers will know, suggests that the Maya deliberately targeted the end date of their thirteen-baktun cycle on the winter solstice of 2012, since they viewed it as the point when the solar god One Hunahpu will be reborn in the mouth of the caiman, or sometimes, the jaguar-toad or a snake, represented astronomically by the winter solstice sun appearing to be in the dark rift in the central bulge of the Milky Way. The convergence of the winter solstice sun with the dark rift is governed by what we call the precession of the equinoxes, caused by the slow wobble of Earth's tilt over approximately 26,000 years. The Maya were measuring this movement by the sun's winter solstice position, rather than the spring equinox. Jenkins found constant references to this as a birth event, where the sun is reborn from the birth canal of the Great Mother, and we have seen that the sweat lodges and kivas were symbolic wombs of the Earth mother, and the kivas were used for symbolic rebirth rituals that see the forthcoming Emergence as a birth.

In 2009, Michael Grofe published an essay called "The Name of God L: B'olon Yokte' K'uh?"[13] in which he pointed out that the right sanctuary panel from the Temple of the Cross at Palenque (one of the pibnaahs) shows an image of God L, the cigar-smoking lord of the underworld, in which he carries the "skeletal centipede," and that on it are clearly shown nine footprints. He concludes that God L and Bolon-Yokte (the God of Nine Steps) could be the same deity, and that Bolon-Yokte could be a group of deities that together, are the lords of the Underworld.

Grofe says that God L rules the dark half of the year, but the maize god resurrects in spring and defeats God L. One Hunahpu, the solar deity that will be reborn in 2012, is a form of the maize god, so Grofe concludes that Bolon-Yokte's "descent" as described on Tortuguero Monument 6, may actually be his "falling to a black place," as the maize god's new era begins. He shows a connection with Maximon, the contemporary equivalent of God L, who, in postclassic Yucatan, was represented by a wooden idol that was ritually fed during the Uayeb days, the five fearful days just before the New Year, at the end of which, he was ritually killed and dismembered. This cigarette-smoking god is nowadays killed by hanging at Easter, due to Christian influences.

Following my reading of Grofe's assertion that Bolon-Yokte could be the same as the nine lords of the Underworld, also known as the Nine Night Lords, or the Bolon Ti Ku, I was amazed to discover an essay by Sven Gronemeyer, published in 2006, in which he shows that the nine night lord glyphs were actually glyphs representing the nine growth stages of the maize plant.[14] This is clearly evident in the glyph for Night Lord Nine, who represents the final completion of the process, and on his head, the ripe ears of corn are easily identified. Gronemeyer shows that the development proceeds in three main phases, and each phase is split into three more. He says that there is a Mixtec Codex—the Fejérváry-Mayer—that shows the threefold development, and that this relates to rites of passage: the transition from a youth to an adult.

Figure 17.4. The three ceremonies

The three stages mirror the three groups of three ceremonies performed annually in a kiva. This seems to confirm the conclusions we reached earlier—that the pibnaah was used for rites of passage and that these rituals, like the annual defeat of the darkness by the light (God L by the maize god), will be played out on a macroscopic scale in 2012, when the maize god, One Hunahpu, will be reborn in the dark rift. The winter solstice (December 21, 2012) is ruled by the Ninth Lord of the Night, who shows the completed germination process via the ears of corn on his head. In other words, the pibnaah at Tortuguero that was connected with 2012 via its commemorative monument was used for the ripening of seeds and humans—an individual version of the mass rebirth and species ripening that will happen at the next creation in

Figure 17.5. The Night Lord Nine, showing the ripe ears of corn on the head

2012—and in preparation for which the pibnaah, like the kiva, also probably held species rites of passage.

Who Are the Nine Gods?

When the Spanish arrived, the Maya had forgotten the 13-baktun cycle, and were using a calendar that was twenty times shorter—a 13-katun cycle, that we call the short count. Each katun consisted of 20 tuns or 360-day years, so a katun was just under 20 years, and the 13-katun cycle consisted of 260 tuns. This means a complete 13-katun cycle lasted about 256 solar years. The Spanish burned all the codices, or bark books, they could find, as they were thought to be devil inspired. There are only four of these codices that have survived—the Dresden, Madrid, Paris, and Grolier codices. During the colonial period, various towns in the Yucatan possessed copies of a book named after the last great prophet, the Chilam Balam, or jaguar priest. The books were written in the European script, but in the Yucatec Mayan language, and each town's copy had unique variations.

The Chilam Balam books contain accounts of historical events and prophecies. The prophecies are mainly day prophecies and katun prophecies, so commentators have, over the years, presumed these prophecies to be about events that are over and done with. Some have admitted that, due to the Mayan conception of time as cyclical, these prophecies can repeat when the cycles repeat, though with variations. One translator, however, has found compelling evidence that some of the prophecies were originally prophecies concerning the end of the thirteenth baktun.

Dr. Maud Makemson, a linguist and astronomer, translated the Chilam Balam of Tizimin and found the following prophecy:

> [I]n the final days of misfortune, in the final days of tying up the bundle of the thirteen katuns on 4 Ahau, then the end of the world shall come. . . . I recount to you the words of the true gods, when they shall come.[15]

In the 13-katun cycle, each katun was named after the final day of the katun in the Tzolkin (260-day) calendar. The cycle started on katun 11 ahau and ended on katun 13 ahau (see figure 17.6). Makemson realized that this statement didn't fit with the facts, since it says the bundle of 13 katuns was tied up—meaning the cycle ended—on 4 ahau. However, she knew that the 13-baktun cycle ended on katun 4 ahau (the final day is a 4 ahau day). Although Makemson had developed her own correlation, which has since been discounted, this observation remains valid, so the prophecy was originally about the end of the 13th baktun in 2012. It seems that when the 13-baktun cycle fell out of use in the early tenth century, some of the prophecies were retained and reapplied to the 13-katun cycle.

| 3111 BC | 2717 BC | 2323 BC | 1929 BC | 1535 BC | 1141 BC | 747 BC | 353 BC | 41 AD | 435 AD | 827 AD | 1224 AD | 1618 AD | Katun start dates in the |
0	1	2	3	4	5	6	7	8	9	10	11	12	current Baktun
	1	13	12	11	10	9	8	7	6	5	4	3	1618 AD
13	12	11	10	9	8	7	6	5	4	3	2	1	1637 AD
11	10	9	8	7	6	5	4	3	2	1	13	12	1657 AD
9	8	7	6	5	4	3	2	1	13	12	11	10	1677 AD
7	6	5	4	3	2	1	13	12	11	10	9	8	1696 AD
5	4	3	2	1	13	12	11	10	9	8	7	6	1716 AD
3	2	1	13	12	11	10	9	8	7	6	5	4	1736 AD
1	13	12	11	10	9	8	7	6	5	4	3	2	1755 AD
12	11	10	9	8	7	6	5	4	3	2	1	13	1794 AD
10	9	8	7	6	5	4	3	2	1	13	12	11	1814 AD
8	7	6	5	4	3	2	1	13	12	11	10	9	1834 AD
6	5	4	3	2	1	13	12	11	10	9	8	7	1854 AD
4	3	2	1	13	12	11	10	9	8	7	6	5	1874 AD
2	1	13	12	11	10	9	8	7	6	5	4	3	1893 AD
13	12	11	10	9	8	7	6	5	4	3	2	1	1913 AD
11	10	9	8	7	6	5	4	3	2	1	13	12	1933 AD
9	8	7	6	5	4	3	2	1	13	12	11	10	1952 AD
7	6	5	4	3	2	1	13	12	11	10	9	8	1972 AD
5	4	3	2	1	13	12	11	10	9	8	7	6	1992 AD
3	2	1	13	12	11	10	9	8	7	6	5	4	2012 AD
													End of the Baktun Cycle on December 21 2012

Figure 17.6. The 13-katun cycles mapped onto the 13-baktun cycle. Each square is a katun; each column is a baktun. Note the 13-katun cycles (that start with an 11 ahau katu) end on a 13 ahau katun, while the final katun of the 13-baktun cycle is a 4 ahau katun.

Just before the prophecy mentioned above, we find this:

The Nine shall arise in sorrow, alas . . . And when over the dark sea I shall be lifted up in a chalice of fire, to that generation there will come the day of withered fruit. There will be rain. The face of the sun shall be extinguished because of the great tempest. . . . Presently Baktun 13 shall come sailing, . . . Then the god will come to visit his little ones. Perhaps "After Death" will be the subject of his discourse.[16]

Here, Makemson has rendered katun 13 as baktun 13, for the reasons just explained. As you can see, these prophecies predict climate change, UFO appearances, crop failure, darkness, and a return of the gods—nine gods—for the end of the current era in 2012. They also support the Tortuguero prophecy, which predicted darkness and a return of the nine gods. However, it isn't all bad news, since the prophecy concludes with: "Then finally the ornaments will descend in heaps. There will be good gifts for one and all, as well as lands, from the Great Spirit, wherever they shall settle down."

As for the phrase *"After Death' will be the subject of his discourse,"* I have explained elsewhere that the possibility that a significant excursion of the geomagnetic field in response to an influx of solar and interstellar plasma could trigger the pineal magnetite to cause an internal secretion of pineal hallucinogens (at least five—three beta-carboline molecules and two methylated trypatamines, including DMT—are manufactured in the pineal gland). In other words, since Rick Strassman's study has shown that internal DMT is produced at birth, death, and during mystical experiences, it seems possible that one interpretation of this phrase is a mass near-death experience for humanity.

The Nine Night Lords

At Tikal is the nine-leveled Pyramid of the Giant Jaguar, and according to Bob Makransky, Tikal was the "home of the Bolontiku" where they have their own temple (in Complex Q), with nine altars in front of it.[17]

At Palenque, in the base of the nine-leveled Pyramid of Inscriptions, is the tomb of Lord Pacal, and the walls show nine deities that are thought to be the Bolon Ti Ku or Nine Night Lords. This suggests that the nine levels represent the nine levels of Xibalba. The Nine Night Lords were, like God L and Bolon-Yokte, present at the last creation and are associated with the underworld—Xibalba. In the Chilam Balam books, it is stated that the Bolon Ti Ku defeated the Thirteen Heaven Gods. To understand the meaning of this, we can take a trip round the world to find a common thread throughout ancient mythology, but first we can take a clue from the Popol Vuh myth.

The Popol Vuh says that two gods, Hun Hunahpú (an alias of the maize god and solar deity) and Vucub Hunahpú, are summoned to the underworld to play a ball game with the Lords of Death (there are seven of them). They are killed, and Hun Hunahpú's head is hung in a tree. Later, Hun Hunahpú's sons—Hunahpu and Xbalanque—descend to Xibalba and are tested in six zones of fear: the bat house, the razor house, the dark house, the jaguar house, the fire house, and the cold house. They outwit the Lords of Death and become immortal, ascending to the sky as constellations. In summary, they descended to the underworld, conquered their fears, and metamorphosed to an immortal state.

In Greek myth, Dionysus descended into Hades to rescue his mother, whom he placed in the stars. In Christianity, Jesus descended into hell and resurrected after three days, then ascended into heaven. In Mithraism, Mithras dies at the winter solstice and is reborn after three days (solar standstill); he waits in heaven for the end of time, when he will return to Earth to awaken the dead and pass judgment.

Yggdrasil and Ragnarok

In Norse mythology, the creator, Gothar, gave birth to nine gods, and their diagram of the cosmos is called Yggdrasil, which is a version of the world tree—an interpretation of reality that is common to shamanic cultures all over the world. These trees usually comprise three realms:

an overworld, an underworld, with an everyday world in the center. Yggdrasil is a giant tree that is surrounded by nine worlds. The lowest of these is Helheim, the domain of the dead, ruled by Hel. Midgard is the middle-earth realm of humankind, and just above it is Asgard, the realm of the Aesir, or principal gods, led by Odin. Odin is said to have sacrificed himself by hanging upside down on the world tree for nine days and nights in order to obtain eighteen runes (two times nine) from the well of wyrd. The other realms are Niflheim, the frosty realm of ice; Jotunheim, the land of giants; Nidavellir, the land of dwarfs; Svartalfheim, the domain of the dark elves; Alfheim, the land of the light elves; and Vanaheim, the world of the Vanir, or fertility gods. Valhalla, the paradise for heroic warriors is part of Asgard, and the nine Valkyries are goddesses who lead the brave heroes there.

Norse mythology also has its end of time—Ragnarok, or the twilight of the gods. Heimdal, born of nine sister-mothers, will blow the Gjallarhorn and the world will be engulfed in flame; the giant wolf gods, Fenris and Loki, will break free, devour the sun, and kill Odin; and Thor will kill the world serpent but will die from its poison. There will be some survivors, including nine of the gods.

This Norse mythology was, of course, the basis for Tolkien's *Lord of the Rings* (as Vincent Bridges has pointed out), which was set at the end of the third age. The nine ringwraiths, or Nazgûl, were nine kings who were corrupted by the nine rings of power and were immortal in the "realm of shadows." The fourth age began with the passing of the one ring that binds the nine, following a battle between good and evil, and this was the start of the age of men. A similar battle will occur at each junction of the ages, and we are now approaching the end of the fourth age. Another fictional manifestation of the underworld and the nine was a film called *The Ninth Gate,* starring Johnny Depp, in which he has to locate all three copies of a seventeenth-century book called *The Nine Gates to the Kingdom of Shadows.* The book contains nine engravings that are parts of a ritual to raise the devil, but only three engravings from each book are the genuine ones, and these are all signed by Lucifer.

Figure 17.7. Yggdrasil and the nine realms

In Siberian shamanism, there is an overworld, middleworld, and underworld that are all explored by the shamans. It is said that the overworld has nine *coats* or levels, that they call God's bodies.[18] During the first days of February, the Clear Tent ritual was held, which lasted for nine days. Ivan Gornok, one of the two last shamans of Taimir nganasans, described the experience to A. A. Popov, a Soviet ethnographer. During the ritual, the shaman travels through all three worlds and, in the underworld, visits the Lake of the Nine Grandads, in which are nine hills with "horns." These are the bellies of nine brothers who are sleeping. The shaman has to travel down one of the horns (penises), thus emerging in the next coat of the lower world, where he finds nine tents where nine women sit. One of these is the "belly tent" and when inside, they find the woman has nine daughters, who feed the visitors. This fractal repetition is reminiscent of a Russian nested doll.

In the Sierra Nevada, in Columbia, the Kogi people have survived isolated from the rest of the world for many generations. Their creation myth says that Aluna, the mother, created a cosmos or womb with nine levels, which are the *nine daughters*. Eight of the nine worlds were infertile; Earth was the only fertile world. Daughter Earth was fertilized by Serankua, one of nine sons. The communal sanctuary is a hut called the Kankurua, which has a nine-level roof structure, in which they can access the nine worlds and the nine states of consciousness. The shamans of the Kogi are called Mamas, and they are chosen at birth and spend their first nine years in total darkness, learning to travel in Aluna, which is comparable to the astral realm of Western esoteric systems.

Shambhala and the Kalachakra Prophecy

In Tibetan Buddhism, there are traditionally said to be six *bardos,* or transitional states, that are experienced between death and rebirth. However, they can apply to any transitional experience in life. These six states of consciousness are birth, dreams, meditation, death, clear-light experience, and transmigration. The bardo clear-light experience starts with profound peace and awareness, but can include karmically created terrifying hallucinations including meetings with forty-two peaceful and fifty-eight wrathful deities. Those who are not spiritually prepared (by meditation and reading the Bardo Thodol or the Tibetan Book of the Dead, with its exercises) could end up transmigrating into a less than desirable incarnation. In the Dzogchen teaching of the Nyingma school of Vajrayana Buddhism, it is said that there are nine bardos: the three extra ones are vision, movement, and instantaneous ordinariness. The nine bardos are connected with the nine *yanas,* or paths of Buddhism, and are symbolized by the nine-pronged *dorje* and *drilbu,* ceremonial tools representing compassion and wisdom. Remember that when Bolon-Yokte returns at the end of the thirteenth baktun, the Chilam Balam indicated, "'After Death' will be the subject of his discourse."

There is a mythological hidden kingdom in Tibet called Shambhala.

Many have searched in vain for this land of paradise. Edwin Bernbaum's book, *The Way to Shambhala,* is probably the best overall guide, and he says that there were two dynasties of kings of Shambhala. The eighth king of the first dynasty founded a new dynasty of which he was the first of twenty-five kings who would each rule for 100 years. The Kalachakra prophecy says there would be a total of thirty-two kings between the time of Buddha's death and the coming of the golden age, which will last at least 1,000 years, when there will be no more toil or conflict and the human lifespan will expand to 1,800 years. Some lamas say that this king, Rudra Cakrin (the Hindu name is Kalki), is now ruling, since there are disputes over the date of Buddha's death.

Figure 17.8. A map of the kingdom of Shambhala, with the eight outer regions and the ninth inner region separated by mountain ranges

Shambhala is shaped like an eight-petaled lotus flower. There are eight regions surrounding a ninth. Each of the eight regions has twelve principalities, but in the center of the heart of the lotus is the central palace, which has nine levels. This is also referred to as Mount Meru, the axis mundi. Shambhala is said to be the heart chakra of the world. The heart chakra, or *anahata,* is usually depicted as a twelve-petaled flower, but sometimes it has eight (there is an extra chakra in Tibetan tantra called the *hrit* chakra, which is just below the anahata and has eight petals). There are several guidebooks for finding Shambhala, but Bernbaum says these have a symbolic meaning:

> In other words, we can read the guidebooks to Shambhala as instructions to taking an inner journey from the familiar world of the surface consciousness through the wilds of the subconscious to the superconsciousness. From this point of view, the deities, demons, mountains, rivers and deserts described by the texts, symbolise the various contents of the unconscious that we have to face and master—or make use of—on the way to awakening the innermost mind. These contents include a number of inner obstacles or psychological blocks of two general kinds. Some come from repressed parts of the surface consciousness: They include hidden fears, desires, illusions, and habits that keep us confined to our usual state of limited awareness. Others have their source in elements of the deeper levels of the mind that act as barriers to keep the superconscious from being overrun by the impure and chaotic contents of the subconscious.[19]

According to Victoria LePage, the eight outer regions of the kingdom of Shambhala represent eight states of consciousness, accompanied by pain and conflict that lead to the ninth, the "radiant mind of enlightenment."[20] In kundalini yoga, it is said that when *kundalini* (the evolutionary serpentlike energy that is dormant in the base chakra of unawakened people) ascends the subtle channel of the spine (the *sushumna*) and reaches the anahata chakra, then the soul awakens. Now recall that the Hopis say at the next emergence, consciousness will reverse its direction, back from solar plexus to heart.

Rudra Cakrin will ride out and "kill the barbarians," ending the age of discord, and inaugurating the golden age, when Shambhala will become visible. Bernbaum says that the killing of barbarians refers to "a decisive inner conflict that results in the emergence or awakening of the innermost mind." So, the Kalachakra prophecy seems to be saying that we are on the verge of a golden age, and just before it emerges, people will confront their own inner demons and shadow material, clearing out the closets as a necessary preparation for life in an idealized world. There is also inference that realms that were previously invisible will become accessible to our senses.

The Shambhala concept is rooted in the pre-Buddhist shamanic tradition of Tibet, known as Bon. The Bon equivalent of Shambala was called Olmolungring and was also a completely pure and spiritual land (usually depicted as a square with many rectangular regions, but in the center are eight regions surrounding a central square region). At the center was a nine-leveled mountain called Yungdrung Gutsek, and each level symbolized the nine stages of Bon that lead to enlightenment. Olmolungring was not a physical place and could not be reached before enlightenment was achieved. However, some scholars have identified the Mount Kailash area as Olmolungring: it has an obvious layered look, due to the weathering of the geological strata.

Heaven, Hell, and Purgatory

In Christian tradition, there are nine choirs of angels around the throne of God: seraphim, cherubim, dominions, thrones, principles, potentates, virtues, archangels, and angels. Twenty-four centuries ago, Plato conceived of nine spheres around Earth that were the "ethereal spheres" of the moon, the sun, Mercury, Venus, Mars, Jupiter, and Saturn, then the sphere of the fixed stars, then the sphere of the zodiac. In the second century CE, Ptolemy used the same scheme, but with the sun's sphere moved to a place between Venus and Mars. The kabbalistic tree of life showed nine sephiroth or spheres above Earth, or Malkuth. The spheres are connected by 22 paths that are related to the 22 letters of the Hebrew alphabet, the 22 trumps of the tarot deck, and the 22 chapters of the Book of Revelation. The trumps refer to the trumpets of Revelation that announce the arrival of judgment day, depicted on trump number 22.

In the thirteen hundreds, Dante wrote his divine comedy, describing the pilgrimage of the soul up though nine circles of hell via the

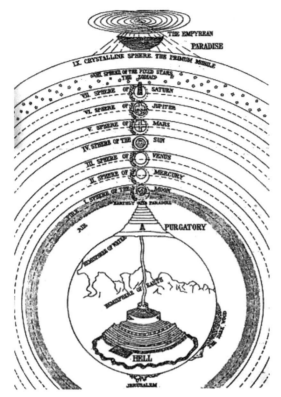

Figure 17.9. The nine spheres of Ptolemy and Plato compared with Dante's nine spheres, sevenfold (really ninefold)

seven terraces of Mount Purgatory and the nine spheres of the planets, stars, and Primum Mobile, all of which are mobilized by the angels, to paradise. There were later medieval variations on this theme by Lull, Fludd, Cusanus, Kircher, and other philosophers. Each of the nine circles of hell hold those unrepentant sinners who are punished for their various crimes, including the seven deadly sins.

Figure 17.10. Purgatory and the nine circles of hell. This drawing by Cactani was not done until 1855, over five hundred years later. Hell has too many circles.

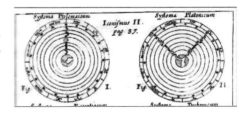

Mount Purgatory is for those who are repentant but need to be purged (cleansed)—hence purgatory. The mountain has seven levels that relate to the seven deadly sins, but there are two extra layers that exist at the base of the mountain, making nine layers altogether—these are the late repentants and the excommunicates. On the first level, which deals with pride, souls carry a heavy burden on their backs, symbolizing the burden of pride. On the second level, the eyes of the envious are sewn shut and they wear clothes that render them virtually invisible. On the third level, anger is corrected by acrid smoke, showing how anger clouds judgment. On the fourth level, sloth or spiritual apathy is dealt with by running continually. On the fifth level, greed is dealt with by lying facedown on the ground, immobile, so that external desire turns inward. On the sixth level, gluttony is treated by abstention from food and drink, and on the seventh level, lust is corrected by a wall of flame that burns away carnal desires. At the top of the mountain is the Garden of Eden, where the souls return to original innocence. Then the climb through the nine heavenly spheres starts, with each level peopled by souls with different virtues, until Dante sees God as a point of light surrounded by nine rings of angels. Dante then goes beyond to a zone called the Empyrean, where the souls of believers form the petals of a rose. There are strange echoes here, of the Shambhala myth.

Nine Vaults of Enoch

The 13th degree of the Scottish Rite of Freemasonry is called the Royal Arch of Enoch.[21,22] Enoch was the great-grandfather of Noah, who is said in the Book of Genesis to have lived to the age of 365 years. The rite records that Enoch built a column of granite and a column of brass, engraved with knowledge of the arts and sciences, intended to survive a coming flood (the flood of Noah, Enoch's grandson). He dug nine vaults in a vertical sequence, one above the other, each roofed with an arch, and the lowest was hewn from solid rock. The crown of each arch had an aperture sealed with a square stone and iron lifting ring, and over the top was built a roofless temple of unhewn stones, with granite paving concealing the top entrance stone. In the lowest vault, he placed a cube of agate in which was embedded a triangular plate of gold, studded with precious gems and engraved with "the ineffable name of God." Many years later, after the flood, when Solomon built his temple, he also built nine vaults, the ninth of which was under the Holy of Holies and which was linked to his palace by a tunnel. Workmen building a Temple of Justice on the site of Enoch's temple discovered the vaults and delivered the agate cube with its triangular golden plate to Solomon, who put it into his own ninth vault below his temple. Like a Mount Purgatory going downward, one has to descend to the ninth and deepest level to achieve the prize.

In 1119, the nine original Knights Templar went to Jerusalem, set up their headquarters in the Al Aqsa mosque on Temple Mount, and spent nine years digging under the site of Solomon's Temple. It is widely thought that they found scrolls and treasure, which ended up in their Paris Temple, before being taken to Rosslyn chapel in Scotland. Rosslyn is a replica of Solomon's Temple and is known to have at least one secret vault and a tunnel.

Several esoteric societies have a nine-level hierarchy of grades. This includes the Rosicrucians, the Theosophists, the Ordo Templi Orientis (before Aleister Crowley added more grades), and the nine initiations of the Ismaelis and the Assassins. It also includes the nine grades of the Priory of Sion (but the Nautonnier, Pierre Plantard, admitted in 1993 that the society was a hoax). The nine-level hierarchy represents increasing levels of spiritual development.

The underworld theme continues in the concept of the labyrinth. In the Cretan myth, the labyrinth was built by Daedalus to house the Minotaur, a monster that was half man and half bull. Every nine years, King Minos sacrificed seven young Athenian men and seven young Athenian women to the Minotaur. When the Greek hero Theseus volunteered as one of the seven male victims, Ariadne, the daughter of Minos, fell in love with him and gave him a ball of thread with which he could find his way out of the labyrinth, provided he would marry her afterward. Theseus killed the Minotaur, rescuing Athens from its fate. Mythology commentators tell us that the labyrinth represents the underworld, to which the hero must descend, with the help of the maiden. Replica labyrinths usually have seven, nine, or eleven rings, representing the levels of the underworld, and the story symbolizes the killing off of our beast within—repressed violence, anger, and sexual obsessions—before we can be ready to integrate with our higher selves (the overself). Note also that the Cretan labyrinth symbol represents the rebirth or emergence into the fifth world of the Hopi.

Precession and the Nine Doors of Louhi

In *Hamlet's Mill,* de Santillana and Von Dechend tell how the Danish myth of Amleth or Amlodhi concerns a mill that was turned by nine maids on an island off Norway, until the mill was stolen and the ship sank, causing a permanent whirlpool. In another version, the mill belongs to King Frodhi, an alias of Freyr, who is one of the Vanir who live in Vanaheim, which is one of the nine realms of Yggdrasil. The huge mill was worked by two giant maidens and ground out gold, peace, and happiness, making a golden age, but it eventually broke and ground out only salt. The Kalavala epic of Finland tells a similar story about a smith called Ilmarinen, who is tricked by Vainamionen, the minstrel, into going to the frozen land of the North, where he has to forge the Sampo, a magic triangular mill that grinds out flour, salt, and money, in exchange for the daughter of Louhi, the wicked queen of the frozen land. When it is finished, Louhi entombs it in a cave in the Copper Mountain, behind nine doors of granite, each sealed by nine locks. The Sampo is called the treasure. Ilmarinen does not win the maiden, however. Eventually, the minstrel and smith go back to the frozen North, open the nine doors by magic, and steal the Sampo; Louhi chases them across the sea, but the mill eventually breaks and falls into the sea.

The mill tree was also the world axis, and the golden age comes and goes according to the shifting of it, which is the precession of the equinoxes. Nine is connected to the precession cycle, since the precessional numbers 72, 108, 216, 432, and 25,920 are all divisable by 9.

In the Hindu Mahabharata and Ramayana texts, the churning of the cosmic ocean (the Milky Way) represents precession, according to de Santillana and Von Dechend, and is caused by a tug of war between two dynasties of gods, who are turning the pole by pulling on a snake that is wrapped around it. The snake usually has seven or nine heads—both forms are depicted at the Angkor Wat temple complex in Cambodia.

Figure 17.11. The churning of the milky ocean from the Mahabharata, using the seven- or nine-headed snake, encodes precession

The stone circles and other megalithic sites found across Britain are known to have functioned as Neolithic calendars. Many have alignments to equinoxes and solstices, or lunar standstills. From some of these observatories, the change in the rise and set positions of stars caused by precession would have been observable. At Avebury, for example, Robin Heath has shown that the line of hills to the east provided a horizon on which precession of half a degree would be clearly evident after thirty-six years observation, as rising stars moved between trees on the skyline. Many stone circles are named after nine maidens; in fact, all the stone circles in Cornwall are locally referred to as the nine maidens, regardless of the number of stones or other names for the sites. There are also the Nine Ladies circle on Stanton Moor and Nine Stones Close, both in Derbyshire, and there are several Wells of Nine Maidens in Scotland.

So the number nine is universally associated not only with the underworld, the overworld, and altered states of consciousness, but also with precession, ancient calendars, and maidens; in fact, nine is the number of the Great Goddess according to mythologist Joseph Campbell.[23]

Nine Goddesses

The Great Goddess has a triple aspect: maid, mother, and crone. These relate to the waxing moon, full moon, and waning moon. The threefold aspect multiplies to a ninefold aspect that relates to the nine months of gestation. One of the best-known groups of nine goddesses is the nine muses, who were Greek goddesses that provided inspiration in the arts and sciences and are said to have inspired Pythagoras, who conceived of the tetractys—a triangular arrangement of nine points around the *bindu,* or seed, as well as a diagram that relates to octaves and other ratios in music. The muses were associated with the oracle at Delphi.

In Arthurian legend, Arthur was taken to the Isle of Avalon (the otherworld) to have his wound healed by nine sisters, one of whom was Morgan le Fay. A Roman historian records a similar island called Sein (breast) off Brittany, that was occupied by nine priestesses, who were healers, could predict the future, control winds and waves, and change into animal shapes. Another island called Annwn (the underworld) is described in a Welsh epic on which is Cerridwen's cauldron, tended by nine virgins who "boiled the cauldron with their breath." The cauldron had a ring of pearls round its rim; it produced an elixir that conferred inspiration, and oracular speech came out of it. King Arthur entered the underworld (Annwn) to steal the cauldron.

The archaeologist Bligh Bond was appointed by the Church of England as director of excavations at Glastonbury Abbey in Glastonbury, the earthly counterpart of Avalon. Bond enlisted the help of a psychic who brought forth the spirits of nine dead monks who called themselves the company of nine, or the nine elect. They told him where to find the grave of Arthur and the lost Edgar chapel, and a grave and chapel were duly dug up just where the nine indicated. When the church authorities found out, Bond lost his job at the abbey, but the episode reinforces the connection between the underworld (Avalon and the world of the dead) and the number nine.

The harmonic vision of Martianus Capella, a fifth-century neo-Pythagorean, assigned the nine spheres around Earth to the nine muses, with a three-headed snake connecting heaven to Earth, as illustrated in Kircher's diagram (see figure 17.12). The mythologist Joseph Campbell says the snake correlates to kundalini, the Hindu fire snake that lies dormant in the base chakra. Campbell says Earth represents the base chakra, so Earth and the next two spheres are equivalent to the bottom three chakras; the next three muses or spheres represent the heart chakra and the top three muses or spheres (excluding heaven) represent the top three chakras. Kundalini's full title is Kundalini Shakti, the Earth goddess who comes up from the ground and, when awakened, rises up the spine, energizing the chakras until she meets Shiva, her male consort, who descends from above, and they meet in the crown chakra, annihilating the ego in a trance called *samadhi*. At the Navatri Festival in India, nine forms of the goddess Shakti are worshipped for nine days. The first three days are a purge, and the first goddess encountered is Durga, who destroys our impurities and defects. The

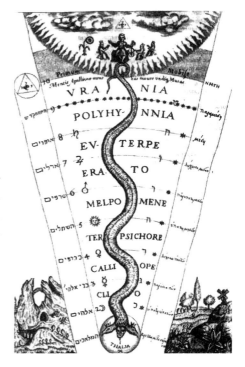

Figure 17.12. Anastasius Kircher's drawing (Ars magna lucis, Rome, 1665), connecting the nine muses to the nine heavenly spheres, relate to the chakras connected by kundalini

second group of three days centers around wealth, and the last three on success.

It is now known, due to John Major Jenkins's discoveries, revealed in his book *Pyramid of Fire*,[24] that the Toltecs, who worshipped Questzalcoatl, the feathered serpent god (Kukulcan to the Maya) regarded Quetzalcoatl in a similar way to kundalini—a serpentine evolutionary energy that climbs up the spine. There is a prophecy from the Chilam Balam of Chumayel that says Kukulcan will return in katun 4 ahau, and the current katun is katun 4 ahau, from 1993 to 2012, so this suggests the descent of Bolon-Yokte could be associated with a mass kundalini awakening.

The Enneads of Heliopolis

Egypt had several *enneads,* or *pesedjets* (nine-god groups), to use the original Egyptian term, rather than the Greek. The most important was the ennead of Heliopolis (or pesedjet of Annu or On), which consisted of Ra-Atum, the creator, who self-begat Shu and Tefnut, the air and moisture gods, respectively. Shu and Tefnut were the parents of Geb and Nut, the earth and sky. Geb and Nut were (like the Maori sky and earth gods Rangi and Papa) in a close embrace and produced children before separating. The offspring were Osiris, Isis, Set, and Nephthys. All these gods are associated with the underworld, or the Duat, which is really the region between the earthly and spiritual worlds, according to Jeremy Naydler. Atum-Ra traveled each night through the Duat. Shu was the division between the living world and underworld, and he protected Ra on his journey through the Duat by using magic spells to ward off Ra's enemy, the snake-demon Apep. The Pyramid Texts suggest that Tefnut was the atmosphere of the Duat. Geb was sometimes seen as god of the underworld and protector of the dead; Nut contains the Duat as part of her body. Osiris was the god of the dead, resurrection, and judgment, and Isis as his wife, was thus queen of the Duat. Set protected Ra on his nightly journey through the Duat, and Nephthys, the helper of the dead, also accompanied Ra and Set on the boat.

In the Book of Coming Forth by Day (known as the Egyptian Book of the Dead), nine human components are described. They are the *khat,* or physical body; the *ka,* or double, which is equivalent to the etheric body; the *ba,* or heart-soul, equivalent to the astral body and symbolized by a bird with a human head; the *akh* or *khu,* or spirit-soul, which is a divinized ba; the *sahu,* or spiritual body, which carries the akh; the *khaibit,* or shadow; the *sekhem,* or vital power; the *ren,* or name; and the *ab,* or heart.

Jeremy Naydler has done a great job of decoding this Egyptian soul science (psyche-ology).[25] The Osirian initiation was centerd on achieving the experience of the ba, where consciousness is externalized into the astral body and the physical body can be observed from another viewpoint. However, the next stage in the process was to neutralize the *khaibit,* symbolized by a dark human silhouette, since it represents "all the untransformed earthly appetites and obsessions that fetter the ba to the physical realm and prevent it from moving on." The divinization of the ba creates the akh or khu (shining one or illuminated one), symbolized by another bird, the crested ibis. It is also called the imperishable one, which returns to its source beyond the Duat. In order for the akh to be released from the body, a new spiritual body had to be germinated from the physical body as a vehicle for the akh. This spiritual body is the *sahu.* This sounds like the immortal man in Taoist yoga that is gestated in the abdomen and expelled through a psychic opening in the top of the head to appear as a person sitting on a lotus within a golden sphere.

When Robert Monroe found himself floating outside his body in the 1950s, he thought he was going mad, until his doctor told him that the experience was not uncommon, but people just didn't like talking about it. Monroe had been listening to subliminal learning tapes while he was asleep at the time he had the experience, so he tried to replicate it by experimenting with sound. He discovered that the brain could be entrained into producing theta waves while awake using binaural beats, where the difference between frequencies heard in each ear is the required frequency—in this case, around 4Hz. He set up the Monroe Institute, a charitable binaural research and education facility in Virginia, to explore the phenomenon.

In *Far Journeys,* Monroe describes the results of thirty years of exploration of the astral realms. The first realm experienced by those leaving their bodies is the physical world, identical to everyday life but with extra inhabitants—the souls of the recently dead and those who are unaware that they have passed on, plus the dreaming bodies of those who are asleep and dreaming. Next is the innermost ring; then the waiting ring; then the major ring, which is split into four quarters— the inner, lower, upper, and outer; then the outermost ring; and beyond that graduation. This adds up to nine astral realms. Personal development allows the soul to climb the rings until it makes it to graduation, after which no more earthy incarnations are necessary.

Nine Steps to Transformation

In *Mercurius,* Patrick Harpur says that the aim of the alchemists was to restore man's unity with nature and to heal the rift between heaven and Earth that had been caused by the fall.[26] They tried to reinstate the golden age by reproducing the operations taught to humanity by Hermes Trismegistus. He explains that in tribal societies "when people are profoundly subject to physiological processes," such as puberty or pregnancy, they have to be "cooked" in an oven. This symbolic cooking is a rite of passage, and "some Amerindian tribes place pubescent girls and women who have just given birth into 'ovens' hollowed out of the ground." The Hermetic vessel, he says, is "analogous to the ritual tomb, or womb, or oven in which rites of passage take place," and the physical changes inside it "are symbolically correlated with the spiritual changes of the alchemist." The magnum opus, or great work, of the alchemists incorporates all the rites of passage, according to Harpur:

> Solution = the birth of Sol; Separation = his initiation at the hands of hitherto unconscious desires and effects such as occur at puberty;

Conjunction = marriage (and death in the forbidden union between Sol and his mother/sister/daughter Luna); Putrefaction = burial (a mixture of cremation and burial, perhaps cooked: rotting: cremation: burial); Congelation = rebirth (the same configuration as solution/birth but transformed to a new spiritual status); Sublimation (Rubedo) = ? Some state for which nature supplies no equivalent. The Opus re-enacts one's whole life in a short (or shorter) space of time in order to raise it up into consciousness and recreate it.[27]

There are usually said to be seven stages of alchemy. Harpur gives eight; Michael Maier, a sixteenth-century Rosicrucian alchemist, described nine stages of "involutive-evolutive transmutation of the threefold body of the human being, the threefold soul, and the threefold spirit."

At the end of the thirteen-baktun cycle, the sun will be reborn as One Hunahpu according to Mayan mythology. Perhaps this could be a macroscopic alchemical initiation for Earth: the rebirth of sol. Could this be a possible rite of passage for sublimation? In chemistry, sublimation is "the transition from a solid to a gas, with no intermediate liquid stage." Here we may have a clue.

In the spiritual alchemical process of Taoist yoga, there are nine impediments to the vital breath, which allows restoration and circulation of the generative force. These are called the nine unsettled breaths, and they are "caused by anger which lifts and fear which lowers the breath; by joy which slows it down; by grief which disperses it; by terror which throws it out of gear; by thinking which ties it up; by toil which wastes it; by cold which collects and heat which scatters it." The generative force is collected in the *lower tan t'ien* center (just below the navel), where it is purified. Then it is raised to the *middle tan t'ien* at the solar plexus, where it is transmuted into vitality. After this it is sent to the *upper tan t'ien* (pineal area), where vitality is transmuted into spirit. Each of these centers is called a *cauldron,* but when the upper tan t'ien takes over, it is called the *precious cauldron.*[28]

Charles Musés has described a nine-step ritual movement called the

Pace of Yu, which relates to the nine components of hexagram 63 of the I Ching (three yang lines and six yin semi-lines).[29] Hexagram 63 is, surprisingly, the climax of the series, rather than hexagram 64. It means climax and the equilibrium achieved afterward. It is an encoded form of transmitting knowledge of the nine cauldrons of transformation, in which are brewed nine ingredients for the elixir of immortality. These are called the nine numinous jewels. The cauldrons are also called the nine cranial palaces, which resonate to the seven (plus two hidden) stars of Ursa Major. Musés says the process is governed by the Great Goddess, so again, we have nine, the Goddess, and the cauldron as a key to transformation to a higher state. The process describes a sacred pregnancy—the germination and nurture of an embryonic immortalized self.

Figure 17.13. Hexagram 63 of the I Ching and its nine
parts that correlate to the Pace of Yu

Musés says hexagram 63 means "journeying across the great stream of time and death into a region of harmony." This reminds us of what the Bolon-Yokte have in store for us upon their "descent" in 2012— their discourse will be on the after-death state. Since, like the Taoists, the Egyptians also had a soul-craft technology, this idea complex may be associated with the Eye of Horus, as the various components of it were hieroglyphs for measuring volume and time. They add to 63/64,

Figure 17.14. The Eye of Horus with its fracional
components that give 63/64

and there is one myth in which Horus gave his eye to Osiris to help him rule in the netherworld.

Alberto Villoldo has recently announced that he is giving a series of nine Peruvian initiations or rites called the Munay Ki.[30] They are "nine healing gates" that allow a conquering of fear and a "clearing of psychic sludge left by past traumas" in order to transform the energy field and communicate with luminous beings and to allow aspirants to start the process of change toward becoming *Homo luminous*. The rites are said to be in preparation for 2012, when the Andean priests, or Paqos, of the Qero people—direct descendants of the Incas—say that Taripay Pacha will start the Age of Meeting Ourselves Again, according to Juan Nunez del Prado, and when the three worlds *hanaq pacha, kay pacha,* and *ukhu pacha* (overworld, middleworld, and underworld) will converge. Villoldo is the only source on the Munay Ki, so I don't know how genuine it is. However, it does seem a very good fit for the pattern that we have revealed here.

Healing and Revealing the God Self

The Mayan myths tell of a descent of heroes to an underworld of six houses to conquer the lords of death and to conquer their own fears, but other Mayan myths mention an underworld of nine levels, that relate to the Nine Lords of the Night. The latest studies by Mayan epigraphers indicate that these night lords are the same as the God of Nine Steps (Bolon-Yokte) who is set to descend at the next creation in 2012, and that these nine gods relate to the germination phases of maize, human individuals, and the human species evolutionary quantum leap. We have seen that all across the world, the number nine is associated with the underworld, trips into the underworld to confront what turn out to be our own demons, and then trips upward to heaven in a pilgrimage of the soul toward an enlightened state.

The various myths around the number nine seem to boil down to three main themes:

1. Healing the wounded king: A descent to the underworld of nine levels; a confrontation with inner violence, rage, and fear; at the deepest level, a divine connection is regained, leading to healing and rejuvenation.

2. Ascent to the ninth heaven: Consciousness rises through nine spheres; Shiva and Shakti unite; the Goddess returns leading to a whole-mind integration of right and left brains.

3. Cyclic return of the gods: A golden age will return, governed by precession; circa 2012, our inner cauldrons will be activated along with the germination process of a subtle body that can survive in a postmortem state.

In other words, to put it in a nutshell, in 2012, or thereabouts, according to the evidence presented here, something will trigger a confrontation with our shadow selves at a time of social and environmental upheaval; the kundalini evolutionary energy will be awakened; there will be an integration of subpersonalities as we enter an enlightened state, accompanied by expanded perceptions, the generation of a plasma body, and contact beyond the physical spectrum. Then the golden age will begin.

Notes

1. Dave Stuart, quick translation of Tortuguero Monument 6, http://groups .google.com/group/utmesoamerica/browse_thread/thread/2ad64b039cb60983 /0396cfd4957fd61e#0396cfd4957fd61e (accessed July 9, 2012).

2. Sven Gronemeyer, "Tortuguero, Tabasco, Mexiko: Geschichte einer klassischen Maya-Stadt, dargestellt an inhren Inschriften; Band 1: Textband and Studie," www.wayeb.org/download/theses/gronemeyer_2004_1.pdf (accessed July 9, 2012).

3. Sven Gronemeyer, "Tortuguero, Tabasco, Mexiko: Geschichte einer klassischen Maya-Stadt, dargestellt an inhren Inschriften; Band 2: Katalogband und Analyse," www.wayeb.org/download/theses/gronemeyer_2004_2.pdf (accessed July 9, 2012).

4. Sven Gronemeyer, "The Maya Site of Tortuguero, Tabasco, Mexico: Its History and Inscriptions," in *Acta Mesoamericana,* vol. 17 (Markt Schwaben, Germany: Verlag Anton Saurwein, 2006).

5. John Major Jenkins, "Comments on the 2012 text on Tortuguero Monument 6 and Bolon Yokte K'u," May 2006, http://alignment2012.com/bolon-yokte .html (accessed July 9, 2012).

6. Markus Eberland and Christian Prager, "B'olon Yokte' K'uh. Maya Conceptions of War, Conflict, and the Underworld," in *Wars and Conflicts in Prehispanic Mesoamerica and the Andes: Selected Proceedings of the Conference Organized by the Société des Américanistes de Belgique with the Collaboration of Wayeb (European Association of Mayanists), Brussels, 16–17 November 2002.* British Archaeological Reports International Series, no. 1385, edited by Peter Eeckhout and Geneviève Le Fort (Oxford, U.K.: John and Erika Hedges Ltd., 2005), 28–36.

7. Dave Stuart's more complete Monument 6 translation, http://books.google .com/books?id=PqYrYwtVCqQC&pg=PA133&dq=Dave+Stuart,+Monument +6+translation&hl=en&sa=X&ei=uCLOT5zzEMiY6AGjoL21DA&ved=0C EUQ6AEwAg#v=onepage&q=Dave%20Stuart%2C%20Monument%206%20 translation&f=false (accessed July 9, 2012).

8. Robert Wald and Michael D. Carrasco, "Temple XIV," adapted from "Rabbits, Gods, and Kings: The Interplay of Myth and History on the Regal Rabbit Vase," a paper presented at the Maya Meetings at the University of Texas at Austin, March 11–21,http://learningobjects.wesleyan.edu/palenque/structures/ temple_xiv (accessed July 9, 2012).

9. Michael Grofe, "Precession in the Dresden Codex,"http://proquest.umi.com/pqdli nk?did=1407490561&Fmt=2&VType=PQD&VInst=PROD&RQT=309&VNa me=PQD&TS=1201138293&clientId=79356&cfc=1 (accessed July 9, 2012).

10. Barb MacLeod, "The 3-11-Pik Formula," http://alignment2012.com/3-11Pik- Formula.html (accessed July 9, 2012).

11. Mayanists 2012 symposium Feb. 6–8 at Tulane University, http://2012.tribe .net/thread/b932bc9b-4c58-4233-8e61-331b1d52b943 (accessed July 9, 2012).

12. John Major Jenkins, *The 2012 Story: The Myths, Fallacies and Truth Behind the Most Intriguing Date in History* (New York: Jeremy P. Tarcher/Penguin, 2009) 263–77.

13. Michael Grofe, "The Name of God L: *B'olon Yokte' K'uh?*" *Wayeb Notes,* no. 30 (2009), www.wayeb.org/notes/wayeb_notes0030.pdf (accessed July 9, 2012).

14. Sven Gronemeyer, "Glyphs G and F: Identified as Aspects of the Maize God," *Wayeb Notes*, no. 22 (2006), www.wayeb.org/notes/wayeb_notes0022.pdf (accessed July 9, 2012).

15. Maud Worcester Makemson, *The Book of the Jaguar Priest: A Translation of*

the Book of Chilam Balam of Tizimin, with Commentary (New York: Henry Schuman, 1951), 16.

16. Ibid., 15–16.

17. Bob Makransky, "Tikal and the Nine Mayan Gods,"www.dearbrutus.com/ tikal_and_the_nine_mayan_gods.html (accessed July 9, 2012).

18. Evgueny Faydysh, "Cartography of Subtle Reality," chap. 6 in The Mystic Cosmos, www.shalagram.ru/knowledge/mysticcosmos/mystic_cosmos_chapter6.htm (accessed July 9, 2012).

19. Edwin Bernbaum, The Way to Shambhala: A Search for the Mythical Kingdom Beyond the Himalayas (Boston: Shambhala Publications, 2001), 207, 245.

20. Victoria LePage, Shambhala: The Fascinating Truth behind the Myth of Shangri-la (Quest Books, 1996), 33.

21. "Royal Arch of Enoch or Master of the Ninth Arch: The Thirteenth Grade of the Ancient and Accepted Scottish Rite, and the Tenth Degree of the Ineffable Series," The Web of Hiram, www.brad.ac.uk/webofhiram/?section=ancient_ accepted&page=ArchofEnoch.html (accessed July 9, 2012).

22. "Grand, Elect, Perfect and Sublime Mason: The Fourteenth Degree of the Ancient and Accepted Scottish Rite, and the Eleventh Degree of the Ineffable Series," The Web of Hiram,www.brad.ac.uk/webofhiram/?section=ancient_ accepted&page=14Grandelectmason.html (accessed July 9, 2012).

23. Joseph Campbell, "The Mystery Number of the Goddess," in In All Her Names: Explorations of the Feminine in Divinity, edited by Joseph Campbell and Charles Musès (San Francisco, New York: Harper, 1991).

24. John Major Jenkins, Pyramid of Fire: The Lost Aztec Codex: Spiritual Ascent at the End of Time (Rochester, Vt.: Bear & Co., 2004).

25. Jeremy Naydler, The Temple of the Cosmos (Rochester, Vt.: Inner Traditions, 1996), 9, 193–212.

26. Patrick Harpur, Mercurius: The Marriage of Heaven and Earth (Victoria, Australia: Blue Angel Gallery, 2007).

27. Ibid., 247–48.

28. Charles Luk, Taoist Yoga: Alchemy & Immortality (London: Rider & Co., 1970), 218.

29. Charles Musès, "The Ageless Way of Goddess," in In All Her Names, edited by Joseph Campbell (San Francisco: Harper San Francisco, 1991).

30. See "Munay-Ki, the Next Step in Evolution," www.munay-ki.org (accessed July 9, 2012).

Contributors

Omar W. Rosales, J.D., is an American writer, anthropologist, expedition leader, and filmmaker best known for his book *Elemental Shaman.* Rosales travels the world to profile spiritual masters and transmit their messages for humanity. Famous interviewees include the Manchen Lopon of Bhutan, His Holiness, the seventeenth Karmapa, and His Holiness, the fourteenth Dalai Lama. A student of noted Mayanists William R. Fowler, Arthur Demarest, and Edward Fischer, Rosales graduated with an honors degree in anthropology and economics from Vanderbilt University in the late 1990s. After college, he served as a captain in the United States Marine Corps. His assignments included two overseas tours in Japan. Rosales subsequently graduated from the University of Texas School of Law in 2005. An experienced hiker and expedition leader, Rosales currently lives in the Pacific Northwest.

Joseph Selbie studied ancient Western cultures at the University of Colorado and ancient Eastern cultures at UC Berkeley. He has had a keen interest in ancient history since grade school. He has taught and lectured on the principles of Eastern philosophy for over thirty years. Selbie lives with his wife at Ananda Village, a spiritual community in Northern California.

David Steinmetz's background includes forty years of scientific work, including astronomy at the University of Arizona and optics at Xerox Palo Alto Research Center. Currently, he teaches about the yugas, ancient world cultures, astronomy, and physics at the Ananda College of Living Wisdom. He has been writing and lecturing on the topic of the yugas for more than a decade. Steinmetz lives with his wife at Ananda Village, a spiritual community in Northern California.

Dr. Manjir Samanta-Laughton is an award-winning international speaker and author with two bestselling books translated into several languages. She is a former medical general practitioner, bioenergy therapist, and holistic doctor at the Bristol Cancer Help Centre and has now become a leading light in the field of linking cutting-edge science and spirituality. She has over ten years experience as a speaker around the world in Ireland, the United States, Italy, and Japan, including keynote speeches at several universities. Samanta-Laughton has also been extensively interviewed by the media, including the BBC, Channel 4, Edge Media TV, *The Guardian,* the *Sunday Express,* and many more. In 2008, in recognition of her work, she joined a prestigious group of scientists and philosophers for a meeting in Japan examining the underlying assumptions behind science, which has become the influential Science Evolve group. Her books are *Punk Science: Inside the Mind of God,* published by O books, and *The Genius Groove,* published by Paradigm Revolution Publishing. She lives in Derbyshire, United Kingdom, with her partner, James.

Lucy Wyatt, after studying international relations and Italian at university, went on to work for the National Economic Development Office, then in commercial design and marketing within Sir Terence Conran's empire, and then edited a business magazine for a City of London stockbroker firm. Wyatt comes from an illustrious family of mathematicians, architects, and writers and herself has a lifelong fascination for the ancient past and the political and economic realities of the bigger picture. She lives with her family on an ecofarm in Suffolk, where she puts much of what she has learned from her research into practice. *Approaching Chaos* is her first book.

Joscelyn Godwin is professor of music at Colgate University in Hamilton, New York. He was born in England and came to the United States in 1966 to study musicology at Cornell University. Since then, he has written, edited, or translated over thirty books on aspects of music and the Western esoteric tradition. Titles that have remained in print for many years include *Robert Fludd: Hermetic Philosopher and Surveyor of Two Worlds* (1979), *Harmonies of Heaven and Earth* (1987), *Arktos: The Polar Myth in Science, Symbolism, and Nazi Survival* (1993), and *The Theosophical Enlightenment* (1994). In 1999, Godwin published the first complete English translation of *Hypnerotomachia Poliphili,* Francesco Colonna's erotic-architectural fantasy novel of 1499. He has also collaborated with his son,

Ariel, on the translation of modern Pythagorean and Hermetic masterworks by Hans Kayser, Petrus Talemarianus, and Saint-Yves d'Alveydre. His most recent books are *The Golden Thread: The Ageless Wisdom of the Western Mystery Traditions* (2007), *Athanasius Kircher's Theatre of the World* (2009), and *Atlantis and the Cycles of Time* (2010). For biographical information on Godwin, see *Who's Who in America, Baker's Biographical Dictionary of Musicians,* and *Gale's Contemporary Authors.* A complete list of his writings is available at his website: https://sites.google.com/a/colgate.edu/jgodwin.

Gregory Sams's first book *Uncommon Sense: The State Is Out of Date,* took chaos theory into a sociopolitical context. His new book *Sun of gOd: Discovering the Self-Organizing Consciousness That Underlies Everything,* is the culmination of seven years of focus on the subject of solar sentience and its relevance to humanity and everything in creation. www.gregorysams.com or www.sunofgod.net.

Christopher Knight is known and respected worldwide for his seminal investigations into ritual and belief systems. His first book, *The Hiram Key,* published in 1996, became an immediate bestseller, selling over a million copies and is now published in thirty-seven different languages. Knight followed this book with a string of bestsellers chronicling his further investigations

Alan Butler's professional background is in engineering, though he has been a professional writer/researcher for over two decades. His lifelong historical studies extend to an in-depth research into the Cistercian monastic movement and the Order of the Knights Templar, about which he has written extensively. As a professional writer who has always possessed an absolute fascination for history, Butler set out on a two-decade search that led to the decoding of some of the most important details regarding prehistoric knowledge and achievement in Europe. Butler is a recognized expert in ancient cosmology.

Harry Sivertsen's and **Stephen Redman's** qualifications for this investigative work are quite broad in that between them they hold degrees in electrical engineering, information technology (IT), archaeology, history, and religion. Sivertsen, the primary researcher and analyst of this unusual duo, is a retired carpenter with a long-standing interest in the histories of building development, measures origination, religion, myth, history, and early astronomy. His BA degree studies as a mature student related to history and religion. Sivertsen, assisted by his architectural-technician wife Gillian, commenced this investigation over twenty-five years ago, and since 2000, he has had the assistance of IT engineer Redman in the presentation and background historical research of both *Deluge* and *Measurements of the Gods*. Redman is a former telecommunications systems engineer and published author, who also holds a second degree in his lifelong interest, prehistoric archaeology.

Jonathan Talat Phillips is cofounder of Reality Sandwich, a web magazine for transformational culture, and the social network Evolver.net, coordinating over forty Evolver regional chapters. He is creator of "The Ayahuasca Monologues," founder of the NYC Gnostics, and has a bioenergetic healing practice in New York City.

Flavio Barbiero is a retired admiral in the Italian Navy who last served with NATO. He is the author of several books, including *The Bible without Secrets* and *The Secret Society of Moses,* and is an archaeological researcher in Israel. He lives in Italy.

Gary A. David has been intrigued by the Four Corners region of the United States for nearly twenty-five years. In 1994, he moved to Arizona and began an intensive study of the ancestral Pueblo People and their descendants the Hopi. In late 2006, after more than a decade of independent research and investigation of archaeological ruins and rock art, his book *The Orion Zone: Ancient Star Cities of the American Southwest* was published by Adventures Unlimited Press. The 2008 sequel is titled *Eye of the Phoenix: Mysterious Visions and Secrets of the American Southwest.* The third book in the series, *The Kivas of Heaven: Ancient Hopi Starlore,* was published in late 2010. These books are available from www.adventuresunlimitedpress.com or by calling toll-free 1-815-253-6390. Autographed copies of the books can be obtained from www.theorionzone.com. David's articles have appeared in *Fate, World Explorer, UFO, Atlantis Rising,* and *Ancient American* magazines, and in Graham Hancock's anthology *Lost Knowledge of the Ancients.* Translations of David's work have appeared in Erich von Däniken's magazine *Zagenhafte Zeiten* and on the website www.antiguosastronautas.com. His writing was also featured on recent History Channel episodes of *Decoded* and *Ancient Aliens*. David continues to give lectures and international radio interviews.

Antoine Gigal is a French writer, researcher and explorer, and founder of Giza for Humanity Organization as well as the International Women Explorer NGO. For the last twenty years, she has lived mainly in Egypt and has explored all of the most remote archaeological areas, especially those not yet open to the general public. With the eye of a scrupulous researcher, Gigal brings us unprecedented access to new and firsthand information about the understanding of very ancient Egypt and ancient civilizations. She is the author of *The Secret Chronicles of Giza* (in French) and of numerous groundbreaking articles, which have appeared in various magazines in English, French, Italian, and Dutch, mainly about aspects of Egyptian and megalithic civilizations never before revealed. She has lectured extensively (in English, French, and Italian) since 2002 across the world (South Africa, France, United Kingdom, and Italy) and has appeared in History Channel TV series 2011 (*Ancient Builders, Lost Worlds, Ancient Aliens, Secret Code*), and radio shows, among them *VoiceAmerica, Goldring, Hillary Raimo Show, Sovereignmind, Red Ice Creations,* and *Other World Radio*. Gigal organized several Giza for Humanity conferences in Paris, France, with international speakers: "Some Ancient Mysteries in 2009", "Ancient Technology and Pyramids in 2010", and "The Physics of Ancient Egypt in 2011." She discovered twenty-three pyramids in Sicily not yet listed and the complex surrounding the pyramids of Mauritius.

Anthony Peake lives near Liverpool in England. As well as writing two books, he has also written many articles for magazines and journals in the United States, Canada, Australia, South Africa, and the United Kingdom. He is also regularly in demand as a lecturer and public speaker.

Daniel Pinchbeck is the author of *2012: The Return of Quetzalcoatl* and *Breaking Open the Head: A Psychedelic Journey into the Heart of Contemporary Shamanism*. He is the editorial director of Reality Sandwich and Evolver.net.

Geoff Stray has been studying the meaning of the year 2012 for over twenty-five years. In 2000, he summarized his findings on his website, Diagnosis 2012, attracting international input. It still remains the largest data base on 2012. Stray is the author of *Beyond 2012: Catastrophe or Ecstasy,* published in the United Kingdom in 2005 (later published in the United States, in 2009, as *Beyond 2012: Catastrophe or Awakening*). The book is an overview of visions, calendars, prophecies, and theories about 2012 and has been called the encyclopedia of 2012. He is also the author of *The Mayan and Other Ancient Calendars* (2007) and *2012 in Your Pocket* (2009) and has written articles for various magazines including *HERA, Salvia Divinorum, Caduceus,* and *New Dawn.* Stray has contributed an essay to the bestselling book *The Mystery of 2012.* He has given talks in the United Kingdom, Europe, North and South America, and Scandinavia and has appeared in documentaries such as *2012: The Odyssey, Timewave 2013, 2012: An Awakening,* and *2012: Mayan Prophesy and the Shift of the Ages.* He lives in Glastonbury, United Kingdom, where he also makes handmade footwear.

Index

Page numbers in *italics* refer to illustrations.